THE ORDEAL OF THE JUNGLE

THE ORDEAL
OF THE JUNGLE

RACE AND THE CHICAGO
FEDERATION OF LABOR,
1903–1922

DAVID BATES

Southern Illinois University Press
Carbondale

Southern Illinois University Press
www.siupress.com

22 21 20 19   4 3 2 1

Cover illustration: crowd of strikebreakers; photo, tinted and cropped,
   from *The World's Work*.

Library of Congress Cataloging-in-Publication Data
Names: Bates, David, [date] author.
Title: The ordeal of the jungle race and the Chicago Federation of Labor,
   1903–1922 / David Bates.
Description: Carbondale, IL : Southern Illinois University Press, [2019] |
   Includes bibliographical references and index.
Identifiers: LCCN 2018050718 | ISBN 9780809337446 (pbk. : alk.
   paper) | ISBN 9780809337453 (e-book)
Subjects: LCSH: Chicago Federation of Labor and Industrial Union
   Council--History--20th century. | African Americans--Employment-
   -Illinois--Chicago--History--20th century. | Chicago--Race relations-
   -20th century. | Chicago Race Riot, Chicago, Ill., 1919. | Working
   class--Illinois--Chicago--Social conditions--20th century. | Labor
   movement--Illinois--Chicago--History--20th century.
Classification: LCC HD6519.C442 B38 2019 | DDC
   331.8809773/1109041--dc23 LC record available at
   https://lccn.loc.gov/2018050718

Printed on recycled paper ♻

For Chris Pappas, who's still teaching me things I didn't know

CONTENTS

ILLUSTRATIONS

ACKNOWLEDGMENTS

Some clichés are clichés because they've been proven true; perhaps none more than the truism that writing a book is a social act. With that in mind, I must first offer thanks to James Barrett, Clarence Lang, Sundiata Cha-Jua, and David Roediger for their perceptive critiques of early versions of this manuscript. I also received tremendous support from colleagues (and friends) Ashley Howard, Alonzo Ward, Kerry Pimblott, and Stephanie Seawell. Each proofread multiple drafts of this book, and each provided a unique critical perspective on everything from theoretical orientation to structure and organization to word choice. Guidance through the publishing process was provided by James Wolfinger and Roxanne Owens of DePaul University and David Settje of Concordia University Chicago.

This book would not have been possible without generous financial assistance provided by a publication grant from the Textbook and Academic Authors Association, and by the College of Arts and Sciences at Concordia University Chicago. Special thanks are due to O. John Zillman and Rachel Eells at Concordia for their assistance in this process.

The images that appear on this book's cover, and in four of its six chapters, were surprisingly difficult to locate and obtain, and I could not have done so without the patient assistance of Leslie Martin and Angela Hoover of the Chicago History Museum and Val Harris of the Special Collections department of Daley Library at the University of Illinois at Chicago. Jason Davis of Chicago Scanning also deserves thanks for his expert assistance in digitizing selected images.

I owe an enormous debt of gratitude to the staff of Southern Illinois University Press. During my eighteen months preparing the initial manuscript—a daunting prospect for a first-time author—Sylvia Frank Rodrigue patiently fielded my questions, assuaged my anxieties, and guided me through the process of being a first-time author. It is not an overstatement to say that without her hard work, her generosity, and her encouragement, this book would not exist. As I completed final editing of the manuscript, the patience and expertise of copyeditor Lisa Marty, indexer Sherry Smith, and, in particular, project editor Wayne Larsen all proved invaluable as well.

My deepest thanks go to my partner, Meg. Her eyes were the first to proofread every draft, and her questions, comments, and critiques were vital. More importantly, she imparted an invaluable sense of calm, even when I was at my most exhausted and frustrated. Her loving support was my greatest inspiration in finishing this long, difficult, and ultimately rewarding process.

THE ORDEAL OF THE JUNGLE

INTRODUCTION: RACE AND
AMERICAN LABOR HISTORY

———

I n the summer of 1919, Chicago exploded into a weeklong paroxysm of
racial violence that left thirty-eight people dead, more than five hundred
injured, and more than a thousand homeless.[1] Pitting white and black
Chicagoans against one another in pitched gun battles, the Chicago race
riot of 1919 "furnished an excuse for every element of Gangland to ... test
their prowess by the most ancient ordeals of the jungle," as Carl Sandburg
vividly recounted.[2] Those ordeals were the bloody climax of months of
bitter racial clashes between white Chicagoans and the black migrants
who flooded into the city as part of the Great Migration—clashes that
were born of "gut-level animosities ... nurtured ... at the common de-
nominators at which races coexisted—at the shop level in industry, at
the block level, at the neighborhood recreational level," in the words of
William M. Tuttle Jr.[3]

But the Chicago race riot was also the climax of another, longer story:
the efforts of the city's labor leaders to organize an interracial union. By
the time of the riot, the Chicago Federation of Labor (CFL) had been
working for more than two years to organize the city's stockyards without regard to race, ethnicity, gender, or skill level. Initially at least, these
efforts were enormously successful. At various points, it was estimated
that in many departments, white and black participation in the Stock
Yards Labor Council (SLC), as the organizing body was called, exceeded
90 percent. But by the time of the riot, the SLC's position in the black
community had become tenuous at best; the violence of the riot and the
recriminations of its aftermath would make their presence positively toxic.
Within months, the SLC would be disbanded entirely. By early 1922,
after abortive last-ditch strikes in steel and meatpacking, the CFL would
recede into obscurity for more than a decade. Reflecting on these failures,
a black trucker later explained that he had "got along fine" during a stint
as a union butcher. But that stint had been brief, and left him suspicious
toward unionism. "Strikes are too hard on the man that ain't in the union,"

———

he said. Unions, he concluded, "are all right if you are on the inside, but mighty hard if you ain't."[4] The anonymous worker's wariness was born of hard experience. By the early 1920s, African Americans felt forcibly estranged from Chicago's labor movement.

This book traces the long and complex history of that estrangement, and of the complex interplay of forces—organizational missteps, shop-floor confrontations, and employer predation—that produced it. Labor unions had built a long and infamous history of racial exclusion by the time of the CFL campaign. Most unions were craft oriented and thus shunned unskilled workers, immigrants, and African Americans. Though the CFL's leaders earnestly sought to transcend such bigotry, their view of racial inclusion was limited and the structure of their campaign produced a de facto segregated union that proved repellent to black workers. White union members took this intransigence as substantiation of longstanding suspicions that African Americans were a "scab race." Employers targeted the union mercilessly, using strategic hiring and firing practices to en-flame racial tensions, divide their workforce, and defeat the campaign. As a result, both black and white workers entered the 1920s as easy prey for the whims of bosses.

Previous historians have examined this phenomenon in a variety of ways. Practitioners of the so-called "old labor history," distinguished by its focus on the structure of union institutions and campaigns, analyzed the chasm between the stated commitment of the American Federation of Labor (AFL) to colorblind organizing and the frequently (and often openly) racist nature of its unions. These historians largely concluded that racial conflicts within the working class were produced by racist union structures and the divide-and-conquer tactics of employers. Philip Foner raged against the AFL's accommodation of whitewashed trade unions, while Sterling Spero and Abram Harris argued that unions largely viewed African Americans as "member[s] of a race which must not be permitted to rise to the white man's level."[5] Much of this analysis concerns Chicago and the meatpacking industry in particular. Alma Herbst's masterful study of black Chicagoans in the slaughtering industry argued that racial tension was largely the result of considered attempts by employers to divide the races. Whereas immigrant workers, even those introduced as strikebreakers, quickly achieved promotions and were assimilated into native white working-class culture, black workers saw few gains at the workplace. Relegated to the lowest-paying and most unpleasant jobs, African Americans remained outside the traditional scope of unions, allowing employers to capitalize on a divided workplace and reserve black workers as a captive "strike insurance" force for packing bosses.[6] Walter Fogel reached a similar conclusion, maintaining that the CFL's efforts "probably appeared more calculating than altruistic to black workers" who were largely aware of the AFL's problematic racial history and influenced by the paternalism of employers.[7]

The so-called "new labor history" inverted this approach; rather than examining large-scale structures of union organization, new labor historians focused their energies on local studies of workers' attitudes and culture. As a result, many scholars have focused their attention more on moments of contact and even cooperation between white and black workers.[8] This scholarly turn resulted in a major reassessment of the Chicago labor movement during World War I, and particularly the racial conflicts that arose within it. Recent scholars have focused their attention on the ways in which conflicts between rank-and-file workers contributed to racial division. Many of these historians relocated the center of conflict from the union hall to the shop floor and even the community. James Barrett, for example, attributed the federation's failure to organize an interracial union to a combination of community divisions and interference by packing bosses.[9] In his classic account of the Chicago race riot of 1919, William Tuttle similarly entreated historians to stop "wast[ing] . . . energy debating the AFL's attitudes toward black workers . . . when the truly bitter, and functional, racial animosities were not at the national but at the shop level."[10] James Grossman, in his history of black migration to Chicago, argued that the burgeoning culture of African Americans, particularly migrants from the South, led blacks to reject "white institutions" like unions in favor of organizations shaped around the black experience.[11] Still others, such as Paul Street, place responsibility for the racial enmity of packinghouse shop floors at the feet of packing bosses, arguing that "certainly no group has exercised a more potent influence on modern American labor history" and noting that "their racially divisive intent" devastated the SLC's efforts. Rick Halpern has offered a more hopeful take, arguing that the struggles of the 1910s and 1920s served as a prelude to the interracial triumphs of the Packinghouse Workers Organizing Committee (PWOC) in the 1930s.[12]

Chicago's labor movement in the early twentieth century, in short, is well-trod scholarly ground. This book is distinguished from these earlier approaches in two major ways. The first is its methodological orientation. Rather than viewing union structures and shop floor and community relations as being distinct, this book weaves them together into a cohesive narrative that demonstrates the ways in which they worked in tandem to reinforce stereotypes, distrust, and resentment among white and black workers. This approach, promulgated and debated by a number of historians, has variously been dubbed the "new new labor history" by Joseph McCartin and the "new old labor history" by Howard Kimeldorf, and combines the strengths of both methods.[13]

This syncretic method is particularly important in the context of Chicago's early twentieth-century labor movement. While it is true that the face-to-face interactions of workers on the shop floor were the wellspring of violence throughout the CFL campaign and beyond, it is also true, as McCartin has argued, that "human agency is no mystical, transhistorical force," but is, instead, "rooted in and constrained by historical structures."[14] Any labor history must, then, begin with an examination of union structures, because unions are in many cases a central organizing force within workers' lives. An analysis of working-class race relations exclusively centered on cultural attitudes or neighborhood conflicts, without an equally critical understanding of how unions are implicated in those relations, lacks full explanatory power.

In the case of Chicago's labor movement in the first decades of the twentieth century, an understanding of the structure of the CFL campaign—of the ways in which both black and white workers' attitudes and choices were shaped and bound by their implication in a major labor-organizing campaign—is vital for understanding how and why that campaign failed. The structure of the CFL campaign, and black and white workers' response to it, were based on the material conditions in which workers and union leaders lived, be they economic, political, or social, and the appeal (or lack thereof) of union membership as opposed to other forms of social and cultural organization. Only by examining workers' position within these literal and metaphorical structures can one disentangle the ways in which the union's campaign, despite its legitimately progressive aims, replicated the racially exclusive policies it sought to surmount; the complex and even contradictory responses of black workers to the CFL's appeal; and the resentment of white workers against those who would not lend their full-throated support to the campaign. To that end, this book makes extensive use of sources such as the CFL's meeting minutes; official reports of city, state, and federal agencies; and memoirs of union leaders to reconstruct the large-scale processes by which the CFL's drive was made and unmade.

With that said, an examination of rank-and-file workers—their behavior, their communities, their attitudes—is equally crucial to understanding the failure of the CFL's efforts. This is particularly true in the case of race. Structural conditions like union organizing are insufficient to explain the racial enmity that stalled the CFL's drive, boiled over into violence on the shop floor, and finally erupted into the Chicago race riot of 1919. Resentments between white and black workers also had deep roots in cultural values and practices, personal experience, and, perhaps above all else, historical memory. Examining these phenomena reveals the complex ways in which workers' class and racial identity formed along parallel, and, at times, intersecting, paths. As white workers embraced the union as the representative of their class interests, black workers increasingly rejected unions in favor of race-based organizations. This analysis avoids labor history's great pitfalls, pointedly examined by Herbert Hill: that the ideals of interracial solidarity are imputed by benevolent unions or the flames of racial resentment are fanned by unscrupulous employers. Examining worker attitudes does more than avoid this determinism, however. Such an analysis also acknowledges "the primacy of race in the development of the social order," in Hill's words.[15] In so doing, this book illuminates the complexity of oversimplifying race relations into a simple black/white binary. Neither race was a single undifferentiated bloc; white workers were divided along lines of ethnicity, while a stark contrast existed between black workers who were native-born Chicagoans and those who had migrated to the city from the South. Workers of both races were, of course, also differentiated by a variety of other factors—age and experience, skill level, religion, politics, and values. By delving into the testimony of workers, as well as a variety of newspapers (both white and black), this book traces the ways in which these various identities helped shape racial attitudes, and explains how those attitudes curdled from suspicion to hatred to violence. Relatedly, and most critically, incorporating the experiences and attitudes of workers reveals the dizzyingly protean forms that those experiences and attitudes could take, from camaraderie to paternalism to frustration to resentment to hatred, and the ways in which such attitudes were constantly shaped and reshaped by contemporary conditions, such as the Great Migration, the East St. Louis race riot of 1917, the Alschuler award of 1918, and the economic depression of 1921.

In sum, examining the CFL drive using this combined approach clarifies the ways in which the material conditions and lived experiences of class and race shaped workers' attitudes and behaviors in this period.

Because the CFL's progressive goals were not matched by its antiquated structure, it created an environment that marginalized and disempowered black workers, causing a tragic cycle in which black workers rejected the union, faced the recrimination of whites, and were thus further repelled. But the attitudes that underlay black workers' suspicion of unionism, and white workers' distrust of black workers, have deep historical roots and must be examined through the everyday words and deeds of the rank and file. Ultimately, this combined approach explains how the CFL— among the most independent and militant unions in the nation during this period, and one legitimately dedicated to interracial solidarity— ultimately catalyzed racial resentment and violence.

A second major innovation of this book is its periodization. To understand the CFL's organizing drive, one must understand the roots of racial enmity in Chicago's unions, as well as the ways that enmity exploded into violence in the late 1910s and early 1920s. To that end, this book begins in the early twentieth century, exploring strikes in the city's restaurant, meatpacking, and trucking industries and the bitter racial legacies they left. But this book also recasts events contemporaneous to the CFL's push for an interracial union. Most critically, it examines the Chicago race riot of 1919 as a central event in the defeat of the CFL. Where other scholars have argued that the race riot fomented a general sense of racial discord throughout the city, this book traces the particular ways in which the CFL's response to the riot typified its inability to unite white and black workers. Similarly, the book's final chapter examines defeats in steel (1919) and meatpacking (1922) strikes—defeats that were occasioned not merely by the predation of employers, as scholars have long held, but by the continued weakness of the CFL's organizing program.

Other scholars, including William Tuttle, James Barrett, and Rick Halpern, have examined Chicago's labor movement in a roughly similar chronology. Each of these historians, however, viewed the city's unions through a specific lens. Tuttle illuminated the ways in which labor conflict helped spark the race riot of 1919. Barrett examined the processes of ethnic and class formation among working-class immigrants. Halpern examined the period as part of a larger five-decade narrative tracing race relations in meatpacking.[16] My periodization, on the other hand, focuses specifically on the city's labor movement—in particular, the CFL's organizing drive and its impacts on rank-and-file workers—from 1903 to 1922. This chronology clarifies the ways in which the CFL's efforts, in their goals and values, represented a major break from the American labor movement, even as their methods remained consistent with other unions of the period. This unique combination allows this narrative to examine, as Hill says, "episodic occurrences of interracial solidarity" without "ignoring the overall historical pattern" of working-class racism.[17]

Together, this method and periodization delineate both the possibilities and limits of interracial unionism. The CFL presents a unique case: its ends were legitimately progressive, but constrained by its paternalistic methods and antiquated structure. In this way, it provides an alternative to narratives regarding AFL unions, which had neither the inclination nor the structure to organize black workers on an egalitarian basis, as well as narratives celebrating radical unions such as the Industrial Workers of the World (IWW), which had both. Excavating the CFL's structure, and the decisions leading to it, provides a clearer picture of how even the most progressive of intentions can be ground to a halt. That the union's calls for solidarity curdled into animosity, estrangement, and violence was by no means inevitable (the triumph of interracial industrial unionism in the 1930s, in Chicago and elsewhere, is evidence of this fact), but rather the product of considered choices by a variety of people. By exploring the interactions of these people—union leaders; black and white workers and their families; employers; community leaders; activists; politicians; and city, state, and federal officials—*The Ordeal of the Jungle* not only avoids, but actively challenges, what historian Daniel Letwin has called the "ahistorical dichotomies" of solidarity and hatred that often dominate discussions of race and unionism.[18] Examining all of these factors in concert reconstructs a crucial period in the history of race and labor in America and provides a critical new conceptual perspective on the possibilities and limits of interracial unionism.

The Ordeal of the Jungle is roughly divided into four main sections. The first, comprising chapter 1, deals with the antecedents of the CFL campaign. Chicago has a long and bloody history of labor conflict, and the CFL's efforts to build a new form of racially progressive unionism had their roots in the brutal strikes of the early twentieth century. Three of these conflicts—the waiters' strike of 1903, the meatpacking strike of 1904, and the teamsters' strike of 1905—are particularly instructive. In 1903, Chicago's waiters, organized into interracial unions, walked off the job to protect the closed shop. Black workers were ultimately sold out by their white comrades, leaving the city's African Americans deeply skeptical of unionism. In both the 1904 meatpacking strike and the 1905 teamsters strike, employers deployed black strikebreakers, resulting in the harassment, beating, and even murder of black workers. All three of these defeats reinscribed unions as white spaces, leaving a legacy of mutual distrust on the part of black and white workers alike.

The second section, comprising chapter 2, examines the CFL's attempts to transcend racial divisions and build a new interracial unionism. Specifically, it examines CFL president John Fitzpatrick and his campaign of so-called "progressive unionism," an ideology under which the federation would organize all workers, regardless of race and skill, into so-called neighborhood locals based in local communities. Recognizing that the thousands of black workers flowing into Chicago during World War I represented the balance of power between labor and capital, Fitzpatrick began a campaign to organize the city's unskilled workers, particularly African Americans. In 1917, the union took its case to a federal arbitrator and won almost all of its demands—seemingly portending a new day in the Chicago labor movement.

Unfortunately, that new day did not arrive. The third major section, comprising chapters 3 and 4, discusses the internal flaws that damaged the CFL campaign. Chapter 3 focuses on the structural issues that hampered interracial organizing. The CFL's chosen mode of organizing, though well intentioned, created a de facto segregated structure that tended to reinforce, rather than break down, existing patterns of racial exclusion. African American members thus viewed the CFL's campaign with distrust, limiting the federation's ability to build a truly interracial union movement. Chapter 4 outlines the CFL campaign's other major issue— namely, ongoing clashes between white and black rank-and-file workers. Many white workers harbored racist attitudes toward African Americans, rooted in the bloody labor conflicts of the late nineteenth and early twentieth centuries and in long-standing racist ideologies. The influx of African American migrants from the South only deepened these tensions, as employers flooded the city's slaughterhouses with nonunion black employees and engaged in practices of racial paternalism in an effort to provoke racial strife and undermine the union. A series of violent shop-floor confrontations between white and black workers proved that the packers' strategies were successful.

The fourth and final section, comprising chapters 5 and 6, explores the decline and demise of the CFL's vision of progressive unionism. Chapter 5 reconstructs the Chicago race riot of 1919 from the perspective of labor, and explicates the ways in which it decimated the CFL campaign. The conflict's unique violence—which included pitched street battles between white and black Chicagoans—created an atmosphere of mutual racial distrust that was difficult to overcome. Even more important was the riot's aftermath, largely overlooked by historians, in which a series of racially motivated wildcat strikes left the union more divided and powerless than ever. Chapter 6 details the three final blows to Fitzpatrick's vision of progressive unionism: a bitter internal struggle for control of the stockyards union that ended in accusations of graft and murder, and the failure of national strikes in steel (1919) and meatpacking (1921). By the early 1920s, beset by infighting and utterly unable to appeal to black workers, the CFL had been driven out of both meatpacking and steel, and Fitzpatrick's vision of progressive unionism was dead.

The collapse of progressive unionism cannot, then, be attributed to white racism, or black resistance, or employer predation. Rather, it must be understood within the context of a complex interplay of workers, both black and white, and their employers. Union structures, rank-and-file conflicts, and employer resistance combined to doom the campaign to failure. A true understanding of the CFL's efforts must account for all of these factors. With this goal in mind, we turn first to a discussion of the Chicago labor movement and its racially charged struggles in the late nineteenth and early twentieth century—struggles whose bitter legacy would define the CFL's campaign, and help doom it to failure.

1.
"A DEEP, DARK PLOT": RACE IN THE
CHICAGO LABOR MOVEMENT, 1894–1905

I n the summer of 1903, at the height of a hotly contested strike by Chicago's waiters and hotel workers, the *Chicago Tribune* printed an editorial excoriating black workers for taking part in the work stoppage. Entitled "Foolish Colored Men," the editorial acknowledged that African Americans faced "outrageous" levels of racial enmity within the city, but maintained that the best way to transcend such feelings was to return to work. White workers had "set the colored man a bad example" through their aggressive union organizing, the paper argued, "but if [black workers] were sensible they would refuse to imitate the whites in these particulars."[1]

For black workers, the reality was not nearly so simple as choosing obedience or militancy. As workers, they were implicated in the labor conflicts that embroiled Chicago in the early twentieth century; as African Americans, they were subject to exploitation by bosses and prejudice by unions. The seeds of racial discord that poisoned the Chicago Federation of Labor's organizing drive of 1916 to 1922 were sown in the early years of the twentieth century, as a series of labor struggles fostered suspicion, disunity, and hatred among the city's workers. This chapter examines three such antecedent events: the waiters' strike of 1903, the stockyards strike of 1904, and the teamsters' strike of 1905. More specifically, it interrogates the process by which each strike was transformed from a labor conflict into a racial one. Most of this racial animus was directed against strikebreakers. But in each strike, white workers faced at least one moment of potential interracial solidarity. In each strike, this moment was lost in a flood of recrimination and violence. White workers, in short, so ferociously guarded their racial privilege that they sought to reinscribe Chicago's restaurants, packinghouses, and streets as white spaces. Each of these three strikes ended in defeat for its respective union, and together they consigned the CFL to obscurity for close to a decade. But it was racial hatred that would ultimately form the most bitter and lasting legacy of each strike, and that would most significantly impact the course of the CFL's organizing campaign more than a decade later.

The violence of the 1903 to 1905 period can best be understood in the unique context of Chicago unionism. The CFL was officially chartered in late 1896 by the American Federation of Labor (AFL) and grew at a dizzying pace, increasing its membership from thirty-four local unions at its founding to more than two hundred by 1906. Despite these impressive numbers, the CFL itself was essentially a loose confederation of autonomous local unions, and thus its powers—maintaining strike funds, providing unemployment assistance, mediating interunion disputes, coordinating publicity and political pressure—were exercised on an almost entirely voluntary basis. More importantly, because the constitutional authority of the Federation was vested wholly in the local unions, there was no mechanism by which locals could be compelled to change their behavior or repudiate their policies, even if such behavior or policies might damage the Federation as a whole.[2] Nowhere was this fact more unfortunately demonstrated than in the question of black union membership.

The CFL constitution, like that of the AFL, specifically forbade exclusion on the basis of "race, color, or creed," but the reality was more complicated.[3] The dearth of black union membership in the CFL's early years was partially a function of external factors. For one thing, Chicago's black population was minute; in 1910, on the eve of the Great Migration, African Americans represented only 2 percent of the city's population.[4] Moreover, policies of segregation enforced by employers were often reflected in the composition of unions. Industrial jobs—many of which remained skilled positions—were not considered "Negro jobs," making black union membership a moot question. Service industries such as hotels and restaurants employed larger numbers of African Americans, but these workplaces were segregated, and so black workers were organized into segregated locals, if they were organized at all.[5]

It was also true, however, that white workers feared competition with black labor. Thanks to exclusionary practices by tradesmen, precious few black workers were skilled in a trade; many changed jobs and even industries frequently, seeking better pay and treatment.[6] This transitory labor force, possessing little skill and demanding little pay, was a nightmare for white union members, who recognized that it could easily be deployed to undermine a strike. The irony of this fear, of course, was the complicity of unions themselves: by barring black workers from their ranks, Chicago's unions were largely responsible for the creation and maintenance of this low-paid, unskilled, and fluid cadre. Moreover, despite white fears that African Americans represented a "scab race," many black workers evinced a high degree of class consciousness and solidarity. As we will see, many black strikebreakers were recruited by employers under false pretenses and were disgusted when they learned they were being used to break a strike. Some black strikebreakers went so far as to walk off the job. But ultimately, African Americans' exclusion from union membership replaced the potentiality for class unity with the reality of racial animus.[7]

It is with this context in mind that we now turn to the waiters' strike of 1903, the stockyards strike of 1904, and the teamsters' strike of 1905. In each of the three cases, African American workers were violently expelled from the labor movement and the workplace. In each case, white workers rallied around one another, through their unions—and, in the latter two cases, their communities—further closing ranks against black labor. In each case, black workers displayed a high degree of class militancy, and in each case, it was ignored, as class anger turned to race anger and black workers were forced to defend themselves from whites. Most significantly, each conflict bequeathed to Chicago's labor movement a legacy of racial hatred and helped inexorably connect Chicago's labor movement to its racial dynamics.

Chicago's restaurants and hotels represented a rare industry: one whose workforce was both racially diverse and heavily unionized. Because black and white waiters served different clienteles, they were organized into segregated locals. If the actions of the most powerful black local, Colored Waiters 509, are any indication, black workers took tremendous pride in the organization and maintenance of their membership. Local 509's business agent, Ben Ricketts, was a regular correspondent to *Mixer and Server,* the official journal of the cumbersomely titled Hotel and Restaurant Employes' [sic] International Alliance and Bartenders' International League of America. Ricketts swelled with obvious pride in his local, boasting of the local's hall as bustling with waiters "chat[ting] about the bright future the great International will create for them." The excitement of the black waiters was nearly palpable: "There is unionism on every lip, unionism in the very air we breathe . . . every one [sic] is impressed with the magnitude of this gigantic undertaking."[8] The waiters union was thus a rarity: not only were black workers organized, they represented a proudly militant faction of the union.

Given this sense of pride, it is not surprising that black waiters were at the vanguard of the waiters' strike of 1903. The conflict began in the spring, when the restaurants of H. H. Kohlsaat and Co. summarily fired their black employees and replaced them with white waitresses. Infuriated, the black waiters alerted their comrades. By that afternoon, more than five hundred employees, white and black, had walked off the job at various downtown restaurants.[9] Sensing an opportunity, union leadership demanded a wage increase and a reduction in hours—many waiters worked twelve hours a day, seven days a week—and refused to call off the strike until all the strikers, white and black, were reinstated. Though some CFL leaders expressed anxiety about potential public backlash against a strike in the hospitality industry, the Federation pledged its financial and moral support to the waiters.[10]

The waiters employed a variety of creative protest tactics to pressure the employers. Supplies were cut off, as union teamsters refused to cross the waiters' picket lines to deliver ice and other essentials. A group of the union's business agents entered a struck shop, ordered coffee, and surreptitiously urged the strikebreaking waitresses to join the strike. Within a few minutes, the waitresses walked out. In another case, forty-three black strikers marched into a Kohlsaat restaurant, sat at the counter, ordered coffee and lunch—and remained there, eating as slowly as possible, for more than two hours. The restaurant was forced to turn away dozens of patrons for want of seating.[11] With the strike quickly growing, the Chicago Restaurant Keepers' Association offered an ultimatum: agree to arbitration of the strike dispute, or be locked out.[12] Enraged, the union expanded the strike to the city's hotels. Maids, bellhops, elevator operators, cooks, and waiters all abandoned their posts, some in the middle of their shifts. Local newspapers related tales of well-to-do hotel guests who donned aprons and performed their own cooking and serving.[13]

Despite the strikers' creativity and militancy, the CFL's fears of public backlash were quickly substantiated. Even the generally prolabor *Chicago Daily News* excoriated the strikers for "putting themselves, the employers and the public to the loss and annoyance of a strike."[14] The *New York Times* lamented that "it is at the expense of the City of Chicago that all these furious and vindictive proceedings are taking place" and concluded that "the organization of labor seems to be too complete for its own good."[15] A strike of restaurants and hotels was viewed in some quarters as a threat to the city's public interest and even its safety. The *Tribune* argued that "the trade of the city will be injured" by the shuttered hotel; in an unhinged editorial, the *Times* warned that the strike could lead to an increase in homelessness and starvation.[16] Meanwhile, concerned consumers began a counterprotest under the aegis of the so-called Anti-Tipping League, which urged the public to refrain from giving gratuities to service employees. "Unionism is to be met with unionism," its advocates claimed, arguing that the waiters' union should be able to protect its members "without levying tribute on the public."[17]

Such pressure took its toll; significantly, the first cracks within the ranks of the strikers followed racial lines. In mid-June, vice president J. T. Brewington of Colored Local 509 resigned his post, claiming that the union's refusal to arbitrate was "a form of highway robbery" that pitted the union against "the press, the pulpit, the bench, the bar, and the sensible labor leaders."[18] Brewington was not alone in his apprehension. Many of the black strikers were growing concerned that they might never be reinstated. Compared to white waiters, the black workers were lower paid and worked under worse conditions in segregated facilities. More importantly, the restaurant owners had openly targeted black waiters already, and would almost certainly do so again. A cadre of black waiters spoke in support of Brewington's appeal, and pledged to follow his example if the union did not change its course.[19]

With dissension growing, the strikers agreed in mid-June to arbitrate. AFL president Samuel Gompers arrived in Chicago in June to personally broker the peace.[20] On June 20, Gompers negotiated an end to the strike that capitulated to most of the Restaurant Keepers' demands. Most onerously, employers only had to rehire 85 percent of striking workers; those who were rehired were required to work in "peace and harmony," i.e., to refrain from any workplace discussion of the strike.[21] The workers were disgusted. Many felt that the union could have extracted more concessions from the employers, particularly in the way of reinstatement, without the interference of Gompers. Their anger grew as they dutifully flowed back into work, only to find many of their places filled. Crowds of infuriated workers pressed into the city's restaurants and lunch counters, denouncing the arbitrated contract and demanding to be given their jobs back. When their efforts proved fruitless, their anger turned toward the union. Dozens of men and women filled the union hall until a mass meeting was finally called, at which union leadership reassured members that most would be reinstated within ten days.[22]

Black workers were particularly dissatisfied. The arbitrated contract provided a 10 percent wage increase for white waiters and waitresses, and a 12 percent increase for miscellaneous white workers. Raises for black workers, on the other hand, were more vaguely scaled to salaries at "the big hotels, with the Palmer house as a standard." The arbitration also gave the employers greater power over certain workers, such as bartenders and cooks, who quickly found common cause with the black waiters. Ben Ricketts, the formerly idealistic business agent of Local 509, glumly summed up the feeling of the black waiters: "Our cause has been belittled, our principles trampled upon, the trust that we placed in a so-called arbitration or conciliation body has been betrayed."[23]

The crisis deepened in July, when five hundred black waiters walked out of downtown restaurants in protest of the arbitrated contract's meager wage increase. Repeating their earlier tactics, the black waiters informally occupied the restaurants, "gathering on sidewalks [and] taunt[ing] all those who entered."[24] Robert Callahan, the international president of the waiters' union, cited the arbitrated contract as sacrosanct, declared the strike illegal, and ordered the black waiters back to work. When they refused, Callahan traveled to Chicago and met with the Restaurant Keepers' Association to "arrange for what he considered . . . improved wages and conditions." Callahan negotiated what he assumed would be a satisfactory compromise, but in a stunning show of solidarity, the waiters' union's Local Joint Board unanimously rejected this new agreement and ordered a general strike.[25]

Despite the admirable display of interracial unity displayed by the Local Joint Board, the union's white membership was largely unwilling to risk their jobs to protect their black comrades. White waiters in five of the city's largest restaurants declared that the arbitrated contract was perfectly satisfactory, and refused to heed the strike call.[26] Abandoned by the waiters in Chicago's largest shops, the black workers quickly became isolated and marginalized. In its "Foolish Colored Men" editorial, the Chicago Tribune argued that if black workers insisted on repudiating their labor agreement, "nobody will sympathize with them—not even the labor men."[27] Public opinion, now tinged with racial undertones, swelled against a renewed strike. A restaurant patron was heard to remark that the striking waiters "ought to be shipped down south where they lynch them for less than this."[28]

The situation quickly escalated, as the issue of race took center stage for employers and employees alike. Buoyed by the public's fury at the black waiters and sensing a split in the union's ranks, the employers moved to consummate their original plan. In late August, black waiters looked on helplessly as Kohlsaat's hiring agents recruited white women from Milwaukee, St. Louis, Indianapolis, and other Midwestern cities to take their places. The words of Kohlsaat's president, F. R. Barnheisel, were authoritative: "The day of the negro waiter in the downtown district is over."[29] Other members of the Restaurant Keepers' Association soon announced plans to follow Kohlsaat's example. Although the Local Joint Board attempted to negotiate with the restaurants, the combination of a fractured union and a determined employer offensive was simply too much to overcome. With nonunion waiters arriving in the city daily and their former positions being "filled at will," it was clear that the black waiters had suffered a tragic defeat.[30]

The black waiters felt "indignant at their leaders," with most agreeing that their participation in the strike—a strike that they initiated and helped lead—had cost them their jobs.[31] Unfortunately for the black waiters, their ordeal was only beginning. Callahan returned to the union's international headquarters and immediately called a meeting of the executive board, at which he demanded the revocation of Colored Local 509's charter—ostensibly for failure to pay their per capita dues, but almost certainly also as punishment for their wildcat strike.[32] Without a charter, the local was no longer entitled to financial support from the national union. Much of that money was used to pay for the room and board of members who lived above local restaurants and had been evicted for their participation in the strike. Lacking the support of both the white Chicago locals and the international union, many black waiters were left destitute. A member of Local 509 claimed that some of the men had fallen into "the clutches of poverty," with close to a dozen families left homeless.[33] The international union had done nothing when local employers targeted black employees for the second time, allowing restaurant owners to purge their businesses of black waiters. Now, the international union demanded that Local 509—most of its members out of work, many homeless, and some starving—pay up.[34] One final humiliation remained. Fully two years after the revocation of Local 509's charter, its members applied to be reseated in the CFL, a crucial first step toward rebuilding their shattered organization. The federation, though sympathetic to the local's plight, was forced to deny the application under pressure from Callahan and the international—an act of staggering heartlessness that only furthers the idea that they were more concerned with a racial coup than financial restitution.[35]

The waiters' strike is in many ways a moment out of step with its time. A group of black workers stood at the vanguard of an interracial union and, for a time, found themselves enjoying a tremendous degree of solidarity with their fellow workers. Unfortunately, the legacy of the strike lies not in such moments of solidarity, but in the betrayal that resulted in the expulsion of black waiters from their union and from Chicago's hospitality industry as a whole. Black waiters served their union with distinction and pride, leading a militant walkout against an open attack on their rights as workers. The strike they initiated was ended with a negotiated settlement that placed their wages below those of white workers. When they protested, they were summarily abandoned by their fellow unionists, targeted by racist employers looking to "clean up" their workplaces, and ultimately expelled from the union.

The legacy of the waiters' strike would prove a long and bitter one. For black waiters, class solidarity seemed a losing proposition. If black workers who held significant leadership roles in interracial unions could be offered as a sacrifice on the altar of employer avarice, then union membership was a sham. A year after the strike, the black newspaper the *Broad Ax* would chide the unwillingness of white workers to stand with their black brethren, remarking that strikebreakers "are to be pitied more than sensured [sic] for their lack of self-esteem and manly principles."[36] For most African Americans, however, the waiters' strike proved that unions were white organizations. In its 1922 report, the Chicago Commission on Race Relations relayed a widespread conviction, still bitterly held nearly two decades later: "There is a widespread belief among Negro workers that the colored waiters were 'double-crossed' by white unions in this strike."[37] For many black workers, the preeminence of white privilege, the willingness of white workers to discard class solidarity for racial advancement, and the betrayal of union leadership were the bleak legacies of the 1903 waiters' strike.

Like the waiters' strike of 1903, the stockyards strike of 1904 began with an encouraging moment of solidarity. By 1900, Chicago's meatpacking industry employed more than twenty-five thousand workers.[38] Two-thirds of these workers were unskilled, with many being foreign born as well. Through extreme division of labor, employers were able to break the hold of the skilled "butcher aristocrats" who had long dominated the industry and control the wages of skilled and unskilled workers alike.[39] The last bulwark of the skilled butchers' power was the Amalgamated Meat Cutters and Butcher Workmen (AMCBW), a powerful national union that comprised twenty-two locals representing thousands of members in Chicago alone. Though the AMCBW organized some small locals for the unskilled workers, the packers refused to negotiate with them, subjecting the unskilled workers to low wages and irregular employment. Feeling their livelihood threatened by the presence of the unskilled workers, in 1904 the AMCBW made common cause with the unskilled workers, demanding a wage scale with tiers for both skilled and unskilled employees. Though the packers offered a modest pay increase, they refused to guarantee wages for the unskilled workers. The AMCBW voted almost unanimously for a strike. On July 12, 1904, the stockyards strike of 1904 began.[40]

The results were immediate and staggering: five thousand men walked out of Armour, more than four thousand at Swift, three thousand at Morris—a total of more than twenty thousand in Chicago alone.[41] Significantly, however, most of these strikers were white. At the time of the walkout, black workers were an insignificant portion of the total stockyards workforce; by 1904, African Americans—almost exclusively unskilled—represented only about 5 percent of the total workforce in Chicago's meatpacking industry.[42] That number increased almost immediately. The packers sought to break the strike by placing foremen at the stockyards' gates, authorizing them to hire as many people as possible to come inside and work.[43] More galling to the strikers, the packers sent labor agents, paid on commission, to scour the nation for replacements. Thousands of men were hauled in by train from areas as close as Joliet and Evanston and as far as Missouri and Cincinnati, with many simply "picked up at various towns along the way."[44] This strategy paid immediate dividends: at eleven thirty on the first night of the strike, a pair of electric cars bearing fifty black strikebreakers pulled into the yards under the escort of a dozen police.[45]

The 1904 stockyards strike became defined, almost immediately, by racial enmity. Although the vast majority of the strikebreakers deployed in the stockyards—some observers estimated as many as 85 percent— were white, it was the black strikebreakers who faced the most violent reprisals. Sympathetic railroad workers alerted the strikers to the arrival of trains loaded with strikebreakers, which the strikers bombarded with rocks and bricks. The strikebreakers were no safer within the city; just two weeks after the beginning of the strike, a mob attacked a group of two hundred black workers leaving the yards.[46]

Racial resentment was further enflamed by the housing of the black strikebreakers. For reasons of both safety and practicality, asking new migrants to find housing on their own was impossible. As a result, carpenters

Men working with cattle carcasses hanging in a slaughterhouse in the stockyards. For many black workers, the 1904 strike was their first opportunity to enter the city's meatpacking industry, but they quickly became the victims of violence at the hands of white strikers. DN-0000985, Chicago Daily News negatives collection, Chicago History Museum.

began constructing bunks within the stockyards warehouses the moment the strike began. On the first night of the strike, a group of black strikebreakers was marched into the beef house at Morris, which would become their home for the duration of the strike. Throughout the strike, new arrivals, hefting mattresses, blankets, and sacks of clothes, were shepherded through the stockyards gates under police guard. Bunks were built in four tiers, and the rooms were packed with close to a thousand men.[47] Conditions were horrific. As one might expect in rooms so densely populated during a Chicago summer, safety and sanitation were sorely lacking. The rooms had no windows, and men slept on bare cots in the stifling heat. One investigator claimed that conditions in the barracks had "no advantages over sleeping in the cattle pens"; indeed, at least one of the dormitories was a converted hog house. An outbreak of smallpox swept through the bunks. Rumors circulated that the packers had obtained reams of blank death certificates and were smuggling corpses out of the yards under cover of darkness.[48]

The "scab hatcheries," as they became known, were by no means exclusively reserved for black strikebreakers. The *Chicago Tribune* made note of the bunks' "cosmopolitan mixture" of "negroes, Italians, [and] Scandinavians."[49] But the boarding of strikebreakers became inexorably tied to race in the public imagination. For the union men, the filth of the conditions reflected African Americans' status as a "scab race" unfit for meatpacking work. A white striker referred to the strikebreakers as "men in whom the savagery of Africa has been intensified by generations of the [worst] savagery of wage- and chattel-servitude, accompanied by a final education in the slums."[50] Indeed, conditions within the yards only strengthened long-standing public perceptions of African Americans as purveyors and consumers of vice. The strikebreakers were kept under guard and not permitted to leave, save for company-approved excursions.[51] But while in the yards, the packers placed no restrictions on the behavior of the strikebreakers. On weeknights, they entertained themselves with games of poker and craps or impromptu boxing matches, using gloves and a ring provided by the packers; on weekends, musicians were brought in and dances were held.[52] As a result, white Chicagoans' view of the strikebreakers became tied to sensational tales of immorality, which inevitably carried racial undertones. Increasingly hysterical reports charged that two hundred cases of syphilis were being treated each week and that the yards had devolved into "a saturnalia."[53] When asked about conditions in the yards, a police captain responded simply, "It's hell down there." A striker feared that "every woman now working in the Yards is the free prey of whatsoever brutalized negro may care to use her for his purposes."[54] These rumors of degeneracy infuriated white workers and strengthened their resolve to chase black workers from the stockyards entirely.

The tragic irony of the attacks on black strikebreakers is that the replacement workers had significant grievances against the packers as well. Many of the men who had been "imported" from Missouri and central Illinois were not aware until their arrival that their newfound jobs were coming at the expense of striking workers. Labor agents often recruited African Americans to work in furniture factories, then brought them into the stockyards once they reached Chicago.[55] This resentment led to unexpected moments of solidarity. Just two weeks after the opening of the strike, a group of black strikebreakers at the Hammond meat plant went on strike themselves, demanding an increase in their daily wage from three dollars to five.[56] At the end of July, a group of strikebreakers from the Armour and Morris plants—between three hundred and five hundred men—gathered to discuss poor treatment, specifically their inability to cash their paychecks (there was no bank within the stockyards, and the union-friendly banks and saloons of the surrounding neighborhoods refused to honor the pay stubs of strikebreakers). After a lengthy conversation, the men walked out. In August, a thousand more black strikebreakers abandoned their posts amid a massive parade of the strikers; at least a dozen of the strikebreakers joined the parade and received union buttons.[57]

These scenes were truly surreal: the black strikebreakers-turned-strikers filed out of the yards escorted by a group of white union workers who guaranteed their safety. Union families lined the streets to cheer on the erstwhile strikebreakers, who eventually reached the Loop and departed the convoy with thanks and handshakes for the union men. In August, a thousand more black strikebreakers abandoned their posts amid a massive parade of the strikers; at least a dozen of the strikebreakers joined the parade, and the union.[58] The strikebreakers' anger at the stockyards bosses reveals that the violence to come was not inevitable. Though most had never been part of a union, the brutality of stockyards employment made possible class-based alliances between white and black workers.

Ultimately, however, racial divisions proved unbridgeable. Assisted by a CFL strike fund of more than four thousand dollars a week, the white community rallied to support one another. One *Tribune* estimate held that of the twenty thousand strikers, more than fifteen thousand were of foreign birth, many of whom lived alongside one another in the tenements "back of the yards."[59] The close contact between coworkers on killing floors (as opposed to the tending of vast, dehumanizing machinery in mills and factories), as well as the growth of ethnic neighborhoods near the stockyards, created a sense of common cause between various white ethnicities. As a result, ethnic whites—even those who worked as strikebreakers— maintained mutually reinforcing ties between their community and their work. If anything, white strikebreakers were frequently rewarded for scabbing. Strikebreaking gave them a foothold in the meatpacking industry (most white strikebreakers were kept on after the 1904 strike) and generally cost them little social capital within their ethnic communities. Indeed, many meatpacking workers who began their careers as strikebreakers, particularly those from eastern Europe, would form a key component of the CFL's attempts to organize the stockyards in the 1910s.[60]

Black workers had no such advantages. Because the number of black workers in the pre-1904 stockyards was so low, and because the AMCBW was a skilled craft union that was largely closed to them, the workers had had little opportunity to engage with fellow employees on the shop floor before the strike. Indeed, for many African Americans, strikebreaking represented their first opportunity to join the industry. But black workers were also barred from common cause with the unskilled white strikers, as they lacked the community contacts that helped forge solidarity among the immigrant whites. The so-called Black Belt neighborhood was physically distant from the stockyards and the surrounding white ethnic communities, making solidarity almost impossible.[61] Campaigns by packing bosses only deepened whites' impression of African Americans as a "scab race." The packers paid strikebreakers $2.15 per day—well above the normal daily unskilled rate of $1.85, though still below the union's demand of $2.85.[62] The packers also took special care in singling out black workers for propaganda campaigns that portrayed meat companies as benevolent parents and unions as deceitful hucksters. Company managers often welcomed newly arrived strikebreakers with a lavish Sunday dinner and beds made with fresh linens, even as white strikers struggled to provide for their families.[63] As a result, where white strikebreakers could overcome their class betrayal through ethnic ties, black strikebreakers—inescapably marked by racial difference and resented as "imported"—were dismissed by the white union workers as "debased, bestialized," and "wholly without [a] sense of class solidarity."[64]

Black workers lacked both protection from the union and the binding of community ties, and were subject to the persistent myth—augmented and exploited by the packers—that they were members of a "scab race." As a result, race quickly supplanted class as the strike's central issue, and black strikebreakers—and African Americans in general—became the central targets of the strikers. One black worker leaving the Armour plant boarded a streetcar with his son. Spotting him, a crowd of two hundred strikers assembled and chased the car down, pelting it with bricks and stones. The two were badly injured and were forced to take refuge in the home of a packinghouse boss, an act that only further infuriated the crowd.[65]

Deepening the tension was black strikebreakers' use of armed self-defense against the strikers' attacks. In one case, a strikebreaker riding a streetcar was threatened by a mob; he calmly pulled a revolver and gunned down the mob's leader.[66] Black strikebreakers who were not housed in the yards began to arm themselves as a matter of course. Many carried revolvers and did not hesitate to fire into the mobs that regularly menaced them coming to and from work. In fact, black strikebreakers armed themselves in such numbers that police began frisking the men as they boarded streetcars or entered the yards.[67] Some strikebreakers initiated the violence themselves. On at least one occasion, a group of white strikers was set upon by a gang of black strikebreakers, who stabbed two of the white strikers and left them for dead.[68] Such open warfare between white strikers and black strikebreakers only exacerbated racial conflicts and reinforced white workers' desire to cleanse the stockyards of black workers entirely.

Black workers were by no means the only victims of violence. Strikers stoned a white sixteen-year-old girl, beat a pair of white students attending the Armour Institute (a technical college funded by the eponymous meat magnate), and regularly engaged in brawls with police.[69] But a virulent racism increasingly defined the strikers' actions, as evidenced by the repeated persecution of black workers who were *not* involved with the strike. The streetcar attacks were often initiated from the streets by strikers loitering in front of saloons. Rather than identifying specific strikebreakers, they often spied black faces on the cars and immediately assembled a mob. After the aforementioned streetcar shooting incident, the crowd—disappointed at being thwarted—turned its anger on a black barber's porter, dragging him out of his shop and beating him, despite his having no connection to the strike or even the stockyards.[70] In another case, a black man identified in police reports as E. Raglan was walking along Forty-Third Street when a man standing on a curb yelled "There goes a strikebreaker!" Raglan was not a strikebreaker. He had traveled to Chicago from Kansas City of his own accord and was planning on looking for work outside the stockyards. The crowd was not appeased. They threw sticks and rocks at Raglan. Soon neighborhood children began sounding the alarm, and hundreds of men emerged from saloons and tenements to join the chase. Raglan managed to escape by climbing atop a building, where he was eventually rescued by police.[71] As the racial spirit of the strike spread, black Chicagoans were persecuted in nonviolent ways as well. In the restaurants surrounding the stockyards, a group of waitresses walked off the job to protest the presence of black cooks.[72] Indiscriminate attacks on black Chicagoans who were not involved with the strike reflect the increasingly racial nature of the stockyards conflict, as black people, not just black strikebreakers, were increasingly demonized by the strikers.

Despite the violent attacks against them, the black strikebreakers served their purpose: by late summer, the strike was quickly losing ground. In early August, the packers declared victory, claiming that they had added more than one thousand new men, with more than five hundred union strikers returning to work as well. Packinghouse output confirmed their triumph. In the first week of August, the struck houses were producing 30 percent of their prestrike output; that number would rise to 50 percent by mid-August and 70 percent by the beginning of September. With the strike slipping away, the AMCBW attempted unsuccessfully to declare a national butchers' strike and meat boycott on September 3. A series of negotiations between the packers and union took place throughout the next week, until finally the AMCBW put the strike to a vote. The strikers' votes did not match their actions—though they voted to continue the strike, more were flowing back into the yards every day. With their numbers dwindling and their coffers exhausted, the AMCBW officially ended the strike on September 8.[73]

It was a total defeat. The union had not secured a wage increase for the skilled men, nor a wage scale for the unskilled. As a final insult, the packers refused to reinstate the union men as a group, claiming they would rehire them only on an individual basis.[74] Before the strike, the AMCBW had organized thousands of Chicago butchers into numerous locals. After the strike, a mere one hundred union butchers in a single local represented the entirety of the ACMBW's presence in the city until the CFL organizing drive more than a decade later. Even that solitary local met in secret, fearing company reprisal—a far cry from the union's aggressive prestrike posture. The union's officers and many of the strikers were blacklisted from the industry.[75] For the better part of the next decade, the AMCBW effectively ceased to exist in Chicago.

White union workers did achieve one goal, however: black workers were almost completely eliminated from Chicago's meatpacking industry. Though most of the white strikebreakers were kept on, almost all of the black strikebreakers were immediately fired. The few who attempted to remain in the yards and hold onto their positions were chased away under threat of death.[76] By 1910, out of more than ten thousand unskilled and semiskilled workers employed in the yards, only sixty-seven were African American.[77] Despite their disappearance from the industry, black workers were almost universally blamed for the failure of the strike. Though whites had firmly established their dominance in the city's meatpacking industry, they feared the strike's defeat set a grim precedent for the future. These fears were not unfounded. The packers, recognizing that the maintenance of a small black workforce could be used to manipulate wages and worker attitudes, would later use race to divide workers during the

CFL campaign. In the meantime, the black worker, in the eyes of white unionists, had become tied immutably to strikebreaking, becoming, in the words of Alma Herbst, "a hated and foreign creature."[78]

The stockyards strike had a grim coda: in mid-September, almost a week after the strike had ended, a group of black men were dragged from a streetcar by a gang of white butchers and beaten. None of the black men were stockyards workers. In the investigation of the beating, the police uncovered what they termed "a 'deep, dark plot' to drive negro workers from the packing houses."[79] A year later, a white butcher at the Chelsea market was attacked at Sixty-Seventh Street and Kimbark Avenue and severely beaten. During the assault, his attackers spat out the following motive: "You taught the niggers how to kill cattle when the strike was on at the stockyards last summer, didn't you?"[80] It seems fitting that the violence of the 1904 strike extended beyond the strike itself. The ultimate legacy of the strike was not merely the destruction of the AMCBW, but a furious racial hatred and a widespread conviction that African Americans were a "scab race."

But the race-baiting of the waiters' strike and the bloodiness of the stockyards strike were mere preludes to the paroxysms of violence that would grip Chicago during the summer of 1905. In April of that year, the city's teamsters declared a strike against downtown retailers in sympathy with the United Garment Workers. The strike quickly reached a fever pitch of bloodletting, as strikebreakers, police, and even shoppers suffered the fury of the teamsters. Although the union contained both black and white members, the strike would quickly develop a viciously racial character. Black strikebreakers, black police officers, black citizens unaffiliated with the strike, and even some black union teamsters were brutally attacked. For a period, the strike devolved into race warfare, with the teamsters arraying themselves against the retailers, the police, and black Chicagoans. The wanton brutality and naked racism of the strikers helped destroy any remaining semblance of class unity between the races. The open wounds of the 1905 teamsters' strike would have critical effects on the CFL's organizing campaign of 1916 to 1922.

In its broad contours, the teamsters' strike proceeded in much the same fashion as the stockyards strike the year before: beginning with a militant display of union solidarity, the strike quickly devolved into disproportionate fury at a small number of black strikebreakers and collapsed amid an orgy of violence. In April 1905, the Brotherhood of Teamsters demanded that Montgomery Ward rehire striking members of the

United Garment Workers, who had been fired for their participation in a strike months before.[81] When Montgomery Ward refused, the teamsters vowed to honor the strike's original picket line. On April 4, union teamsters stopped all deliveries to and from Montgomery Ward. Within a few weeks, the strike had grown from less than a hundred participants to more than eight hundred, as other large retailers—Marshall Field; Pirie, Scott; and John V. Farwell among them—were struck. By the end of April the union spirit had spread to an estimated three thousand workers.[82]

At least at first, the strike was in many ways an acid test for a new, aggressive unionism. The CFL united militant unions like the Teamsters and Teachers Federation under the banner of an aggressive campaign that enthusiastically engaged in boycotts and sympathy strikes. As a result, the CFL held numerous meetings at which teamster head Cornelius P. Shea called on federation unions to strike in sympathy with the garment workers and teamsters. The CFL also allocated significant funds to the strikers, evincing a high level of unity between the federation's various locals. Perhaps most strikingly of all, particularly given the bloodshed to follow, the Teamsters were an avowedly interracial organization. In fact, black Chicago teamster T. A. Stowers proudly addressed the Teamsters international convention in 1903 and spoke on the ways in which unionism could ameliorate racial conflict. [83]

This sense of interracial unity was immediately tested with the introduction of black strikebreakers. As with the stockyards strike, the enmity directed at black strikebreakers was far disproportionate to their actual numbers. Of the roughly fifty-eight hundred strikebreakers employed, it is estimated that no more than a thousand were black; some estimates place the number at less than three hundred.[84] Despite exhortations from the union's international headquarters not to "consider the colored strike breaker [as] any worse . . . [than] the white man who deliberately takes another workman's place when he is on strike," strikers quickly seized on race as the central issue of the strike.[85] In a public letter that echoed the language describing the "scab hatcheries" of the stockyards, the teamsters claimed that black strikebreakers had come north only because they had "outraged every law of decency in their Southern homes." The *Chicago Socialist* referred to the black strikebreakers as "social outcasts" who represented "the class of negroes" frequently lynched in the South "for an unmentionable crime."[86]

The presence of black strikebreakers seemed to confirm longstanding white suspicions that African Americans were somehow uniquely suited for the moral degeneracy of strikebreaking. A month into the strike, the teamsters attempted to appeal directly to the public by circulating thirty thousand leaflets to patrons of State Street department stores. The circulars carried a pointed attack against the employers "filling our places with colored men from Southern cities," whom they derided as a "class of men who are continuously loafing." No mention of white strikebreakers was made.[87] In a similar vein, Teamsters president Cornelius Shea laid out the union's demands as follows: that the Employers' Association reinstate all fired strikers, arbitrate the Garment Workers' strike, and "get rid of the colored strikebreakers." It is significant that in the same speech, Shea claimed that "white strike breakers had become sick of their jobs."[88] In other words, white strikebreakers would, of their own volition, eventually tire of doing the employers' bidding; black strikebreakers would have to be forcibly removed from their places in the industry. Such rhetoric reflected the workers' deep-seated desire to chase African Americans from the city's driving business entirely.

Because employers were determined not only to win the strike but to destroy the union, they augmented those feelings whenever possible. The Employers' Association of Chicago, a collective of downtown merchants targeted by the strike, circulated a pamphlet in black neighborhoods that claimed that through strikebreaking, "the colored laborer will assume a responsible place in society . . . upon equal terms with the whites."[89] Raising the specter of social equality not only enflamed the racial animus of white strikers, but also implied that black strikebreakers had entered into a conspiracy with employers. Such fears were reinforced by the Employers' Association's provision of lodging for the newly arrived black strikebreakers. As during the stockyards strike, the public was scandalized by reports of gambling, heavy drinking, and prize fights at 405 South State Street, where more than two hundred of the men were housed. For white Chicagoans, black strikebreaking increasingly came to be seen as uniquely degenerate. As one report put it, the African American workers, "many of them turbulent, some of them criminals," were "all . . . provocative in the manner of their employment," a statement that reflects the connection between strikebreaking, blackness, and immorality in the white imagination.[90]

The Employers' Association also incited violence by the strikers, hoping that such attacks would induce crackdowns by police. It was widely speculated that the Employers' Association actively sought to provoke a race riot so that federal troops could be deployed to crush the strike. As one business-friendly observer noted, "Nothing hurts the cause of the striker with the public more than violence." To that end, the Employers' Association "gave the strikers every opportunity to injure themselves."[91] These opportunities took several forms. For one, employers ordered freight to be moved only in long trains, claiming that these were easier to protect than single wagons; of course, this formation was also "the most conspicuous and the most likely to cause blockades," inviting violence from strikers and, subsequently, reprisals from police.[92] Unlike the meat packers, who brought in their strikebreakers by train under cover of darkness into the gated safety of the stockyards, the Employers' Association moved strikebreakers through the streets in broad daylight, and even ordered other strikebreakers, armed with clubs, to march alongside the wagons as an escort. All the while, one newspaper account put it, these guards were "taunting and threatening, waving their weapons—doing everything in their power to provoke a fight."[93] Employers also periodically sent empty wagons careening through the streets in an attempt to redirect the mobs from attacking full wagons, or possibly to entice them into attacking property that was of little value (but that would nonetheless subject the attackers to arrest).[94] Even more revealingly, a Wells Fargo executive was reportedly heard to remark, "There must be a certain number of people killed before this thing ends, and the sooner they are killed the better."[95]

Despite the violence directed at them, the black workers—as in previous struggles—often made common cause with the strikers. Part of this was due to purposeful deception on the part of the Employers' Association. Many of the strikebreakers, brought in from St. Louis, Kansas City, Detroit, Minneapolis, and Milwaukee, were told that the strike was over; some were not told a strike had ever occurred. At one point, the union took the Employers' Association to court to protest the "importation" of strikebreakers. During the trial, several of the black strikebreakers pleaded their own ignorance and condemned the disingenuousness of the employers.[96] Other strikebreakers directly militated against the Employers' Association. A month into the strike, a group of black strikebreakers walked off the job due to a concern with basic self-preservation. Claiming that the sticks issued by employers were insufficient, the men demanded revolvers, and struck when they were rebuffed. Word of the strike's violence also spread beyond Chicago. A group of one hundred prospective strikebreakers jumped a train from St. Louis when they heard rumors "of the violence to which they would be subjected."[97]

Strikebreakers guarded by police during the 1905 teamsters' strike. Though the presence of black strikebreakers was itself provocative, the Employers Association actively sought to inflame tensions by parading the strikebreakers through the streets with a full police guard. "Sometimes It Took Many Police to Protect A Few Wagons," in Stanley Powers, "Chicago's Strike Ordeal," *World's Work* 10, no. 3 (July 1905): 6381.

But as with the stockyards strike, these examples of solidarity were insufficient to stay the wrath of the union. By the middle of May, the strike had transmogrified into a race war. Increasingly, as a reporter observed, "the real issue between capital and labor is to be dodged and the fight made along lines of color."[98] Strikers stationed themselves on rooftops and hurled bricks and even bottles of acid onto strikebreakers and police below. Strikebreakers were dragged from their wagons and beaten while mobs looted or destroyed their contents and set the wagons ablaze. In one case, a black strikebreaker was attacked by a mob and held down as a union teamster hacked at him with an axe, gashing open his head and severing three fingers. Miraculously, he survived.[99] A group of strikers created an impromptu garrison at Twenty-Seventh and Wentworth Streets. A group of white strikers patrolled this border, carrying signs bearing the message "Negroes not allowed to cross this Dead Line" and beat anyone who dared defy the order.[100] Such tactics served to pacify resistance within the union as well as without. When asked by a reporter why he wouldn't go back to work, one white striker responded simply, "Because I don't want to be killed."[101]

As with the stockyards strike, white ethnic communities closed ranks against employers and strikebreakers alike. One striker recalled how the mothers, sisters, and wives of strikers armed themselves with clubs and attacked strikebreakers. "In all the riotous scenes attending the strike," he remembered, "nothing ... approach[ed] the fierceness of the attacks by these women." The children of striking teamsters—angered by deliveries of coal by nonunion drivers to their schools—went on strike. At Carter H. Harrison School, for example, fifteen hundred of the school's seventeen hundred students struck. The youngsters organized school-by-school "locals," maintained pickets, and even elected business agents. The entire enterprise might be considered endearing were it not shot through with the same racial enmity that increasingly animated the "grown-up" strike. The young picketers smashed open the gates of wagons, spilled their contents onto the ground, distributed them among the community, and stoned the nonunion men. The children's actions carried an unsettling combination of childish playfulness and adult brutality. After one black strikebreaker was beaten unconscious, "a crowd of boys played football with the victim's blood-stained hat."[102] For their part, the strikers seemed to take a perverse pride in the actions of their sons and daughters. When the students were arrested and they (and their parents) were brought before a judge, the CFL decried, in a statement laden with unmistakable racial overtones, "an illegal crusade to discipline, denounce, and disgrace little children in our public schools who have dared to protest against hired thugs and scabs imported from the slums of Southern cities" and resolved to "most heartily indorse and commend the boldness, spirit and humanity of the striking children and extend to them our hearty thanks."[103] Significantly, no coded references to white strikebreakers were made.

Marginalized, physically menaced, and seeing no refuge save itself, the black community, too, banded together. After a particularly brutal attack during which a black strikebreaker was killed, a mob of black citizens armed themselves with stones and clubs and took to the streets; police dispersed the throng and arrested its leaders before they could enter white neighborhoods. Nonetheless, it was reported, "every white man that entered the 'black belt' was assaulted or chased away by armed negroes, who paraded the streets, crying for 'justice' and 'down with the white trash.'"[104] In May, CFL leadership invited the pastors of the city's six largest black churches to a conference, at which they were "urged to antagonize efforts of the employers to import any more colored strike breakers." No such conference was planned with white clergy to attempt to curb white strikebreaking.[105] In response, a mass meeting of more than one thousand African Americans was convened at Bethel African Methodist Church on the South Side. Black community leader Dr. George C. Hall galvanized the crowd by raging, "We are not going to ask the people to stop this, we are going to stop it ourselves!" The group voted in support of a series of resolutions condemning the teamsters' racist propaganda, commending black strikebreakers for "risking their lives to obtain work" and demanding increased police protection for the strikebreakers.[106]

Once again, black nonunion men took to arming themselves with knives and revolvers and using them when necessary. In one case, a "quarrel concerning the strike" erupted between a white striker and black strikebreaker on a streetcar; it ended with the black worker pulling a straight razor and slashing the striker's face six times.[107] The violence committed by strikebreakers could be as ugly as that of the strikers, as the conflict came to resemble race warfare. In one infamous case, a group of boys led by eight-year-old Enoch Carlson shouted derisively at a pair of black men walking through their neighborhood. One of the men, who "appeared intoxicated," lashed out at the boys. When they continued jeering, he pulled a revolver and fired at them, killing Carlson. His death infuriated the white community, who had to be calmed by police to prevent a lynching.[108]

But black strikebreakers' own use of violence was not chaotic, nor merely a response to white hatred. Increasingly, black Chicagoans began to evince a sense of racial pride in resisting the strikers' attacks. In the wake of the death of Enoch Carlson, the boy's mother and her white neighbors reported receiving "several anonymous letters containing threats and warnings to beware of the consequences of race persecution." The *Broad Ax,* a local black newspaper, lamented that because the strikers "trample[d] the laws of this city under their feet, and . . . place[d] no valuation on human life," the black strikebreakers were compelled to do likewise—"hence the killing of . . . Enoch Carlson." Such threats extended even to government officials. During a street scuffle, United States appraiser J. G. Blair cracked a joke about one of the black strikebreakers, who immediately leapt from his wagon and thrust a revolver in Blair's face. Blair apologized profusely and the strikebreaker returned to his wagon, but not before saying, "You're just white trash and I ought to shoot you anyhow."[109]

Just as significant was the growing presence of African Americans among the city's police force. At the beginning of the strike, the Chicago Police Department consisted of roughly twenty-three hundred officers. Within a month, more than half had been assigned to strike duty, and hundreds of other city employees, from clerks to dog catchers, had been deputized, armed, and charged with keeping order—a task that generally consisted of protecting strikebreakers, making police among the strikers' most despised enemies.[110] Mayor Edward Dunne also used the strike as occasion for an aggressive recruiting campaign that brought in more than two hundred new officers by the end of May. Among the hundreds of police quickly sworn in during the mayor's recruitment drive, a significant number—as many as 40 percent—were black. These men held perhaps the most unenviable positions in the city. Many of them only took the policeman's oath because the city's toxic racial atmosphere had forced them from other means of employment. One newly deputized officer previously owned a restaurant on Western Avenue, but white customers, inflamed by the strike, refused to patronize his business, and he was forced to close.[111]

Black police were constant targets of white mob violence; at least one nonunion wagon driver claimed that "the presence of negro police as their guards would invite more trouble than no protection at all." In one case, a black police officer was pelted with rocks and bricks and chased for blocks before he managed to seek shelter inside a patrol box. When the box was battered with stones, the officer threatened to kill the next man who approached him. When fifteen-year-old Michael Nejedly hit him with a stone, the officer fired his revolver, killing the boy instantly and provoking threats of lynching from the white community.[112]

Worse, black officers had few allies even within their own department. In the midst of the police department's massive recruiting drive, at least three men refused duty; one of them explained his decision by saying, "You won't get me to protect any of those negroes" and claiming it was "against [his] creed" to "fight for a lot of negro strike breakers."[113] The mayor's office was flooded with complaints that white officers were ignoring the appeals of their black coworkers for assistance. Many black police were actively undermined on the job by their white colleagues; a number of newly deputized police were white union "sluggers" who took the policeman's oath so as to commit their mayhem behind the protection of a badge.[114]

Unfortunately for Chicago's African Americans, their use of armed self-defense only further enraged the white community. Black strikebreakers who fought back were frequently arrested and their weapons confiscated. Certain judges, such as the one who presided over the Harrison Street police court, were known to levy large fines against African Americans who were cited for carrying revolvers, while letting whites arrested for the same crime go free. African Americans' use of violence also further marginalized them from white unionists. The executive board of the CFL condemned the violence of strikebreakers while maintaining, absurdly, that the white strikers had been perfectly peaceful: "There was no violence committed by union men," the board claimed, "but it was shown conclusively that the violence was committed by thugs brought here for that express purpose by the Employers Association."[115]

As in the stockyards strike, the strikers' attacks were not limited to black strikebreakers. Pickets cordoned off portions of State Street and Wabash Avenue and intimidated shoppers who patronized the downtown stores. Strikers tracked the movements of a Montgomery Ward floor manager for a week before attacking and bludgeoning him. In April, a mob raided the stables of the employers, beat seven guards, smashed fifteen wagons, and stampeded thirty horses through the streets. Police even uncovered a plot to dynamite a major warehouse of Montgomery Ward; the scheme was only foiled thanks to heavy rains that soaked the bomb and rendered it inert.[116] Yet, as the strike wore on, African Americans—highly visible thanks to employer tactics, unable to draw on white immigrants' ethnic connections, and increasingly associated with the greed of bosses and the degeneracy of strikebreaking—bore the brunt of the strikers' wrath.

Indeed, as rage at black strikebreakers became generalized into a fury at the black community, the strikers expanded their attacks to include African Americans who had no connection to the strike, or the trucking industry more generally. Correspondents from the *New York Times* were shocked to report several instances of white mobs boarding streetcars and randomly attacking passengers, "giving as a reason later that they were strike breakers, when, in fact, they had nothing to do with the strike."[117] In one such case, a black porter named James Robinson was chased down Wells Street by a mob that mistook him for a strikebreaker. Robinson eventually found refuge in a saloon, but was arrested after he was found to be carrying a revolver. The mob that chased him, the *Tribune* wryly noted, "was not fined."[118]

Even African Americans unaffiliated with the strike were murdered. Another black porter, Edward Jasper, was returning from work late one night, when a crowd at Sixteenth and State Streets called him "a nonunion teamster of the Employers' Teaming company" and gave chase. The mob overtook Jasper, beat him with rocks and bricks, and left him unconscious on the sidewalk; he suffered a fractured skull and later died. In a similar case, a black man named Charles Tull, who had recently arrived in the city from Iowa, was mistaken for a strikebreaker and attacked. The crowd had already sent for a rope to lynch Tull when police arrived and rescued him.[119] These attacks were not merely cases of mistaken identity; they were targeted assaults that carried the full weight of the strike's racialized character. The attacks began to resemble a form of race warfare or racial cleansing. As early as May, strikers dragged a group of fifteen black riders from a streetcar and ordered them to leave the city "under penalty of a severe beating."[120]

Perhaps the most tragic evidence of the strike's overwhelmingly racialized nature can be found in attacks on black *union* teamsters. Like the waiters, the teamsters were an interracial organization, with a number of black members. As the strike dragged on, however, whites began to abandon all pretense of class unity and engaged in several vicious attacks on black union teamsters. The black unionists "were more or less in peril of their lives," even if they were union teamsters in good standing and conspicuously displayed union buttons.[121] In one case, a white teamster pelted a black man with rocks until the latter was left with no choice but to draw a revolver and shoot him dead. As it happened, the black teamster "was a union man himself, employed by a company which is not involved in the strike." Nevertheless, "his color was black and displeasing to the strike sympathizer," provoking the attack.[122] In a similar case, a black teamster named William O'Day—also a union member, and also working for a nonstruck shop—was assaulted by a striker named Albert Enders. Despite O'Day's protestations that he belonged to the union, "Enders said that, being a 'nigger,' he deserved a beating anyway and continued throwing missiles."[123]

By late summer, the strike was losing momentum. As early as May, Mayor Dunne appointed a committee to investigate both the strike's high degree of violence and the rumors of corruption that swirled around it. The teamsters were charged with graft, blackmail, and willful breaking of contracts, while the employers were accused of "willfully spreading the strike with the intention of precipitating a greater labor crisis" and destroying the union once and for all.[124] Ultimately, the charges against the teamsters proved more damaging. Indictments were handed down against a dozen union leaders, including the president of the CFL, for their role in the "conspiracy" to violate the teamsters' contract. The secretary of a carriage drivers' local confessed that the union had hired thugs to attack strikebreakers. Union head Cornelius Shea, who directed the actions of the hired sluggers from a famed whorehouse known as the Kentucky Home, was accused of taking a payoff to end the strike. Teamster locals grew frustrated with the international union's levying of new duties to support the strike, a process that bankrupted some locals in the city. In July, tiring of the entire debacle, the union purged Shea, who fled to Philadelphia, and attempted to negotiate a settlement of the strike. By August, most of the men were reinstated.[125]

The 1905 teamsters' strike was staggering in its scope: during its 105 days, it involved some 5,000 strikers, caused more than 400 serious injuries, and resulted in the deaths of 21 people.[126] Perhaps appropriately, the violence was not yet finished. As the strikers flowed back into the struck shops, they found occasion to vent their anger one final time. In late July, a mob of strikers a thousand strong attacked a nonunion wagon, beat one of the drivers "into insensibility," destroyed the wagon's contents, and set its horses loose. Union men unable to immediately regain their old jobs attacked five Montgomery Ward strikebreakers and beat them.[127]

The strike's extraordinary level of violence chiseled its legacy into the historical memory of the city in two major ways. First, it seriously diminished the power of labor in the city. The teamsters quickly became viewed as a corrupt, ineffectual organization. Nor was the CFL above reproach, as it had a local reputation for being "honeycombed with dishonesty and graft," in Truman Bigham's evocative phrase.[128] As a result, the federation's vision for a militant, cooperative unionism was crushed and the CFL's power greatly diminished. Though the CFL would clean house beginning with the election of John Fitzpatrick as president in 1906, it would take the better part of a decade for Fitzpatrick to restore the federation to a position of prominence in the city.[129]

Second, and more importantly, the 1905 teamsters' strike ossified the venomous tensions that had come to define relations between white and black workers. For the white strikers, the black presence during the strike reinforced their conceptions of African Americans as a "scab race." Their fury at black strikebreakers and police recruits had become generalized against the city's entire black population. The teamsters' strike had often resembled a race war. Now, with the strike finally settled, it appeared that the conflict's racial battle lines remained indelibly drawn.[130] Just as significantly, the strike caused the black community to reflect on its own role in the city's workplaces. The intense violence of the strike, beginning with attacks on black strikebreakers and later generalized against the entire black community, turned many African Americans against unionism entirely. In the wake of the strike, black Chicago lawyer S. Laing Williams spoke before the National Negro Business League, and again hailed the strikebreakers. He praised the men who "paraded the streets with no weapons, except walking sticks" as "bricks, shoes, stones, and everything possible were hurled at them." But, he explained with an unmistakable note of pride, "They marched with heads erect and firm steps." The strike "demonstrated that the negro who is called to do difficult work under difficult conditions is every inch a man." Williams closed by echoing the sentiments of the Bethel Church meeting. African Americans must be wary of any sort of class solidarity and rather uplift themselves as a race: "the men who must toil with their hands shall not be allowed to drift and become the victims of organized labor's contempt or the easy tool of selfish and soulless capital."[131] Even as white unionists grew more leery of black workers, so too did black workers find themselves distrustful of unionism. This oppositional relationship would come to define the class and racial conflicts of the coming decade.

Despite the differences between the three episodes recounted here—the relatively peaceful struggle of the waiters, the bitter fight of the stockyards workers, and the stunning violence and racial enmity of the teamsters' strike—each helped to create a noxious racial atmosphere in which class conflicts, particularly those centering on unionism and the workplace, became highly racialized. At the center of each was an effort by white workers to cleanse African Americans from their unions and workplaces—through threats and coercion if possible, through violence if necessary. Ultimately, they were successful in all three industries. In the case of the waiters, union leadership sold out their black members, thus leaving them vulnerable to the predation of employers. Stockyards workers viewed black workers as an invading horde stealing the very lifeblood of the white community and chased them from the meatpacking industry. The teamsters carried these resentments to their tragic conclusion, fomenting a race war on the streets of Chicago.

In each case, black workers were expelled from the workplace on account of their race; in each case, racial feeling (and, in the latter two cases, violence) escalated; and in each case, black workers grew more indignant and resentful of white racism. By the end of the teamsters' strike, the black community had grown as skeptical about unionism as the white community had of black "fitness" for union membership. During the next decade, the CFL would rebuild itself with a new vision of inclusive, militant, progressive unionism. To succeed, the federation would be forced to reckon with the brutal lessons of 1903 to 1905.

2.
"EVERY NEGRO CAN MAKE A FIGHT":
RACE AND THE CFL CAMPAIGN, 1916–1921

In February and March 1918, seeking to avert a threatened strike, federal judge Samuel P. Alschuler and the President's Mediation Commission traveled to Chicago to arbitrate disputes in the meatpacking industry. Frank Walsh, the attorney representing the CFL, impressed upon Alschuler the horrors of life in Packingtown. He guided him through the filth and danger of the killing floors and the squalor and open sewers of the Back of the Yards neighborhood. He ruthlessly cross-examined meatpacking bosses until they admitted that their lavish lifestyles were built on brutal conditions and below-subsistence wages. But Walsh also argued vociferously that unionism provided a way out—not only a path to higher wages and safer conditions, but a path to dignity among workers and mutual respect between employer and employee. Perhaps most revealingly, Walsh explained the ways in which the union, and the union alone, was capable of uniting the city's diverse workforce. "The white man's unions," he argued, "are as loyal to the rights of the black man as they are to a white man." If Alschuler and the commission would agree to the union's demands for a living wage, shortened hours, and, in particular, recognition and the right to collective bargaining, it would allow "every negro ... to have a grievance" and ensure that "every negro can make a fight."[1] The CFL, Walsh claimed, was fighting not only for workers' rights, but for interracial peace and cooperation.

Walsh's concern for the rights of African American workers reflected a new direction for the CFL. For nearly a decade after the devastating defeats of 1903–1905, the influence of the CFL remained minimal. Local unions watched helplessly as employers brutalized their workers through processes of consolidation and de-skilling. As the Great Migration brought hundreds of thousands of black workers to the city, CFL head John Fitzpatrick saw the opportunity not only to resurrect the federation, but to reshape it into an independent, activist body that embraced workers of all races and levels of skill. Within two years, the CFL promulgated a new form of militant, community-based unionism that embraced industrial organizing, independent politics, and the aggressive recruitment of both immigrants and African Americans. In the process, the CFL grew to become one of the most powerful central labor bodies in the United States—so powerful, in fact, that a threatened meatpacking strike in late 1917 compelled wide-ranging federal intervention and secured the union's first major victory in the stockyards.

The defeats suffered by the CFL in the early twentieth century were devastating. As employers consolidated their control of the workplace, Chicago's union workers found themselves in full retreat. Reconstituting the city's labor movement was made even more difficult by the staggering diversity of its workforce, which included large numbers of "new immigrants" from southern and eastern Europe. Additionally, hundreds of thousands of African Americans, pushed from southern farms by the brutality of the so-called nadir period, moved north to take advantage of industrial opportunities in factories. Chicago, a major destination for the Great Migration, became more diverse than ever, and presented a unique challenge to labor organizing.

With Chicago's unions largely defeated, employers spent much of the decade of 1905–1915 securing their grasp on the city's workforce. Perhaps no industry better typifies this process than meatpacking. Between 1899 and 1918, Chicago's meatpacking firms grew from thirty-nine plants employing 25,000 workers to forty-six plants staffed by nearly 46,000 employees. In the mid-1910s, a series of mergers gave rise to the famous "Big Five" packers: Swift, Morris, Armour, Cudahy, and Wilson. By 1917, these five firms slaughtered and packed 82.2 percent of the cattle, 76.6 percent of the calves, 76.4 percent of the sheep, and 61.2 percent of the swine that passed through Chicago's stockyards. Such consolidation translated into massive profits, particularly given the nation's mobilization for World War I. In 1915, meatpacking companies earned $17 million more than their annual average for the prewar period. In 1916, that number rose to $36 million; by 1917, it had reached $68 million.[2]

This growth, combined with a massive labor surplus caused by prewar immigration, allowed meatpackers to consolidate control of their workforce. Whenever possible, the packers "de-skilled" the processes of butchering and processing and replaced skilled workers with unskilled ones. These unskilled workers were reminded constantly of the ease with which they could be replaced by the crowds of "desperate job-seekers" who packed the stockyards gates every morning. CFL president John

Fitzpatrick lamented the ability of the packers "to maintain [an] enormous unemployed situation" and use it to their advantage.[3] As for the skilled workers, a labor force increasingly composed of low-paid, easily replaceable workers allowed bosses to break the power of the "butcher aristocracy" whose skill and experience were crucial to the functioning of the yards. By breaking down the process of production into a series of ever-smaller tasks requiring no particular skill, the packers undermined the solidarity and militancy that had led skilled butchers to walk off the job in 1904.[4]

This campaign brutalized the city's meatpacking workers. By 1912, Chicago's slaughterhouses paid 82 percent of their employees less than twenty cents an hour. Thanks to the vagaries of seasonal and shift work, the average workweek for an unskilled operative was only 37.5 hours. Working conditions were atrocious. Not only were workers subjected to the filth, danger, and stomach-churning gore famously portrayed by Upton Sinclair in *The Jungle,* employers brutally expressed their power to their workers. Stories circulated that superintendents had viciously beat a worker for perceived insouciance, that a worker had fallen four stories down an elevator shaft and received no medical attention, that a protesting employee had been hauled away and held in a mental institution against his will.[5] Such tales, apocryphal or not, only reinforced the packers' air of omnipotent control over the yards.

These attacks decimated unionism within the stockyards. Between the defeat of the 1904 strike and the dawn of the CFL's renewed organizing campaign in 1916, only one local of the Amalgamated Meat Cutters and Butcher Workmen continued to function in the yards, with a membership of less than a hundred. Fitzpatrick later recalled, "Each year we went into the district and carried on . . . a campaign of organization," despite the fact that "we knew our efforts were futile and no results would come from them." With the packers on the offensive, the CFL had been entirely driven from the city's largest industry.[6]

The presence of an increasingly diverse workforce also hampered the CFL's attempts to rebuild stockyards unionism. A 1917 survey of workers in one large meatpacking firm revealed that "new immigrant" workers from southern and eastern Europe composed nearly 40 percent of the workforce. Native-born whites, by contrast, made up less than a quarter, with African Americans making up 20 percent. The neighborhoods around the yards underwent a similar transformation, as southern and eastern Europeans increased their share of the population from 19 percent to nearly 50 percent.[7] Such divisions made labor organizing exceedingly difficult. Not only were the packers able to maintain constant control over an interchangeable workforce, their employment of unskilled new immigrants reinforced divisions at the workplace and dampened the potential for unity, as natural divisions between the skilled and unskilled workers became augmented by barriers of language, nationality, and ethnicity.[8]

What little unionism existed was often strained by nativism and xenophobia. The new immigrants were bitterly resented by many native-born workers, who feared that the newcomers' willingness to work for low wages, and their sheer massive numbers, would choke native-born whites out of the job market. As early as 1902, steelworkers in South Chicago filed a formal protest with the federal government against the presence of Hungarian and Croatian workers who, they claimed, were undercutting native wages. CFL leaders noted that immigrants were easily "exploit[ed] for political and economic ends." Discrimination against immigrants' foreign customs was also pervasive. The South Chicago workers' protest made note of the immigrants' "unhealthy and overcrowded living conditions," while the CFL lamented that to his native-born comrades, the immigrant laborer was generally "nothing more than a 'dago' or a 'hunkie.'"[9] Such divisions made organizing extraordinarily difficult. Ethnic and national diversity presented logistical problems as well. Before beginning any campaign to organize the yards, CFL leaders estimated that they would need to hire five full-time foreign language organizers. John Fitzpatrick noted that rebuilding the CFL was seemingly impossible as long as "the doors of the country [were] open to the toilers of the world."[10]

Into this tangle of employer power and workplace division appeared a new presence: the black worker. Though African Americans had found work in the stockyards before the World War I era, most of them were strikebreakers brought in to destroy the 1904 strike and were dismissed soon after. But the brutality of southern racism, coupled with the opportunities offered by wartime mobilization of northern industry, attracted hundreds of thousands of African Americans to the North. Enticed by the promise of industrial work, many of the migrants found their way to Chicago, where they were eagerly employed by the packers. The arrival of massive numbers of black migrants in the city would increase the division of the stockyards workforce—but it also held the key to rebuilding the city's labor movement.

African Americans came north for a variety of reasons. The brutality of life in the South was certainly a major "push" factor. The majority of black southerners lived and worked as rural sharecroppers. Owning no land of their own, sharecroppers were subject to the whims of overseers. As a result, they faced chronic poverty—the average daily pay for black farm workers in the South was around seventy-five cents—and constant racial abuse, including violence. The prevalence of "lynch law" and the discrimination of southern judges made recourse next to impossible. Conditions for farmers were made worse by an infestation of boll weevils in 1915 and 1916, which devastated southern crops; black sharecroppers, subject to the largesse of land bosses, suffered most from this plague.[11] An editorial in the AMCBW's newspaper linked the plight of African Americans to those of industrial workers, claiming that southern farm owners were "the same landlords who exact such enormous fixed charges as rents or interest from industrial enterprises as to leave less than living wages, and who take toll of those scanty wages after they get paid."[12] With life in the rural South wretched and violent, it is no wonder black southerners looked to the North as a "promised land."[13]

But such brutality had been a hallmark of black life in the South since the end of Reconstruction. The sudden migration of African Americans was due also to the emergence of "pull" factors. Chief among these was the northern industrial job market. Though employers had managed to maintain a labor surplus throughout the prewar period, wartime restrictions slowed immigration to a trickle. Arrivals of immigrants dropped from 1.2 million in 1914 to 326,700 in 1915 to less than 300,000 in 1916 and 1917. In 1918, barely 100,000 immigrants entered the United States.[14] In addition, hundreds of thousands of young, able-bodied workers enlisted or were conscripted into the armed services, augmenting the shortage. The rising wages that resulted were a major attraction for black workers—sharecroppers making seventy-five cents per day in Mississippi could make four times that much, or more, in Chicago. African Americans began pouring north at an immense rate. Between 1910 and 1920 alone, more than 400,000 African Americans moved from the South to the North.[15]

Migrants flooded into dozens of northern cities, seeking economic advancement, political and social equality, and freedom from discrimination and violence. But as William Tuttle has argued, "It was Chicago more than any other Northern city that represented 'the top of the world' and 'freedom' to Southern blacks." The city's sheer size—reflected in its diverse manufacturing base, its mail-order houses, and spectacles like the Columbian Exposition of 1893—made Chicago not just a city, but also "a state of mind."[16] Black Chicagoans encouraged these notions. The *Chicago*

Defender (which was banned in most southern states but was smuggled south and circulated widely by black railroad porters), encouraged migration whenever possible, calling itself a "herald of glad tidings" to black southerners and encouraging them to join "The Great Northern Drive."[17] The *Defender* frequently printed letters from prospective migrants, partially in hopes of attracting the attention of employers, but also simply to let migrants know their voices were being heard. Their letters reflect a clear yearning for a better life. One man expressed his desire for "a job in a small town somewhere in the north where I can receive verry [sic] good wages," but emphasized that his highest priority was to live "where I can educate my 3 little girls and demand respect of intelegence [sic]." Another hoped "to leave the South and Go and Place where a man will Be any thing Except a Ker [sic]." He claimed to prefer to go to Chicago or Philadelphia, but would accept life anywhere "so long as I Go where a man is a man."[18] This desire for economic and political opportunity led them inexorably toward Chicago.

As a result of this attraction, Chicago's black population exploded during this period, from 44,103 in 1910 to 109,458 in 1920. African Americans also made up a more significant proportion of the city than ever before. Between 1910 and 1920, the black population in Chicago more than doubled, from 2 percent to 4.1 percent. During that same period, Chicago's black population increased 148 percent, while its white population (including immigration) increased a mere 21 percent.[19] The arrival of hundreds of thousands of African Americans had a profound effect on the city's workforce. Between 1910 and 1920, the number of black industrial workers in Chicago rose from 27,000 to 70,000. By 1920, African Americans were estimated to compose between 16 percent and 21 percent of the city's total industrial workforce. Such numbers were of particular importance to the CFL; an estimated 12,000 African Americans had found employment in the stockyards by 1920.[20]

The arrival of the migrants began a bitter struggle between union and employer for the loyalty of black workers. From the beginning, the packers were at an advantage. Though they no longer had the benefit of a labor surplus, the black migrants represented still another disparate group whose race could be used to divide the workforce. Union leaders accused the packers of sending labor agents into southern states to recruit black labor. Though the packers denied the allegations, such recruiting was widely known to be a common practice. A *Tribune* article from 1917 reported that "labor agencies [and] stockyards interests" were in large

Distribution of Negro Population, 1910. This map, taken from the Chicago Commission on Race Relations 1922 report *The Negro in Chicago*, shows the limits of the city's black population. In 1910, African Americans made up just 2 percent of Chicago's population and were scarcely present in the city's major industries, such as meatpacking. Chicago History Museum, ICHi-173839.

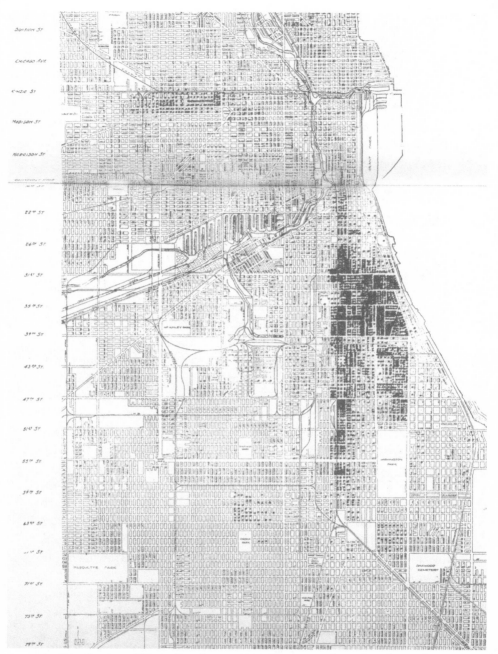

Distribution of Negro Population, 1920. This map, also taken from *The Negro in Chicago*, dramatically illustrates the effect of the Great Migration on Chicago. Between 1910 and 1920, the city's African American population more than doubled. It quickly became clear that black workers would determine the success or failure of the CFL's organizing campaign. Tensions around housing due to the growth of the Black Belt into surrounding neighborhoods would contribute to the Chicago Race Riot in the summer of 1919. Chicago History Museum, ICHi-173840.

part "responsible for the flow of southern colored men to Chicago," and advertised that "stockyards firms are in need of from 10,000 to 14,000 men and they offer . . . to guarantee lodging and food for one week to southern Negroes."[21] The packers' counteroffensive had driven unionism from the stockyards. The power of the packers, combined with a labor surplus and the increasing diversity of the workforce due to the arrival of new immigrants from southern and eastern Europe, created a divided workforce that made organization exceedingly difficult. The arrival of thousands of black migrants from the South appeared to exacerbate this problem, as the stockyards workforce became even more divided. But black workers would prove to be the lynchpin of a revitalized CFL campaign and the center of the federation's efforts to remake itself as a militant, diverse union.

To attract black workers to the CFL, the union's first task was overcoming decades of divisions within the labor movement engendered by the discriminatory policies of its parent organization, the American Federation of Labor (AFL). From its inception, the AFL was a craft federation concerned solely with the organization of skilled tradesmen. But AFL leaders quickly realized the potential threat that unorganized black workers might pose, and, in 1893, the organization's constitution was amended to demand "that the working people . . . unite and organize, irrespective of creed, color, sex, nationality, or politics." Such sentiments were echoed in countless resolutions and public statements; the AFL frequently reassured immigrant and African American workers "that its best efforts have been, and will continue to be, to encourage the organization of those most needing its protection, whether they be in the North or the South, the East or the West, white or black."[22] Samuel Gompers and other AFL leaders never tired of repeating such boilerplate to black and immigrant leaders who complained of the AFL's intransigence in pursuing interracial organization.

In practice, of course, the AFL's racial policies were highly problematic. AFL leaders openly lobbied for the passage, and later the extension, of the Chinese Exclusion Act and supported literacy tests and other barriers to legal immigration. AFL conventions rang with resolutions decrying the "multitudes of peoples from foreign shores" who brought to America "their prejudices, their disposition toward violence, their contempt of law and order."[23] Black workers were subject to similar attacks. Gompers and other leaders often claimed that due to their historical conditions, African Americans were all but unfit for union membership. Being "but a little more than half a century from a condition of slavery," Gompers argued, black workers "could not be expected . . . [to] have the same conception of their rights and duties as other men of labor have in America."[24] Of course, the complaint that black workers were at fault for their low representation in the AFL was laughable. As organizer and CFL leader William Z. Foster wrote in 1919, "For the tense [racial] situation existing the unions are themselves in no small part to blame." The fact that many international unions "sharply draw the color line" only fanned "the flames of race hatred." Indeed, throughout the 1890s, the AFL retained only two black organizers, both of whom were eventually discharged—one for refusing to organize black workers into segregated locals, and one for "agitat[ing] for racial equality."[25]

In short, the AFL's member unions were skill- and craft-oriented, composed almost exclusively of native-born white tradesmen who enjoyed relatively high wages and job security, and thus their primary concerns were the enforcement of job rules and union control on the shop floor. The specter of unskilled workers terrified many skilled workers; such feelings were only augmented by existing racial bigotry. Most AFL unions, therefore, refrained from organizing black workers, and—despite the rhetoric of the AFL constitution—many barred African American membership outright. These policies became self-reinforcing. Craft unions that gained a foothold in an industry barred black workers from membership; in closed shops, where union membership was a condition of employment, black workers were therefore excluded from the industry entirely. Such isolation helped to confirm the superiority of white labor in the minds of union leadership: black workers were disqualified from taking certain jobs, and then blamed for their inability to do so.[26]

The AFL's structure prevented it from resolving such inequities. The fundamental, unifying principle of the AFL was craft autonomy—the right of each international union to organize and police its own trade. As a result, the AFL constitution vested tremendous power in individual unions, and the authority of Gompers and the AFL executive council to govern their membership policies was practically nonexistent. The oft-cited amendment declaring the federation's dedication to organizing all workers "irrespective of creed, color, sex, nationality, or politics," for example, was a statement of purpose, not a mandate. Thus it did not carry the weight of constitutional provisions that enforced, for example, the collection of dues or the election of officers.[27] The entire situation was tragically self-perpetuating. In 1918, a group of African American leaders wrote Gompers, pleading with him to force all of the AFL's unions to open their doors to black members. Gompers's response crystallizes the executive council's powerlessness. "It is difficult," Gompers wrote, "for the national organization to control the actions of local unions ... inasmuch as the National body is made possible by the delegates appointed by the locals."[28] Lacking both the motivation and the power to force international unions to accept black members, Gompers and the AFL executive council were content to issue ineffectual statements that gestured toward interracial unionism rather than attempting to reform the AFL's policies.

At times, member unions attempted reforms on their own, with little success. A resolution at the 1890 AFL convention excoriated the machinists' union, which specifically forbade the membership of African Americans. The resolution noted that the federation "looks with disfavor upon trade unions having provisions which excludes from membership persons on account of race or color," and "most respectfully request[ed]" that the machinists "remove from their constitution such conditions, so that all machinists shall be eligible to membership."[29] The resolution met with sufficient response from the convention that Gompers felt compelled to visit the machinists' 1891 convention. There, according to Gompers, union leaders "declared that in all probability" the call to open membership to African Americans "would be complied with at their next session." What followed was a long and complex affair during which the machinists were split into two unions. The splinter faction "pledged ... that, when the older organization shall eliminate the objectionable clause and be willing to amalgamate, the new one will be pleased to do so on an honorable basis." Gompers, who deplored dual unionism as the lone mortal sin of organized labor, intervened and reunited the two sides. Though the color bar was removed from the machinists' constitution, the act was purely a formality—in practice, the union still refused to organize or accept black members.[30] The machinists' situation shows both the shortcomings of the AFL's structure and the racial ideas held by many of its leaders. Gompers lacked the power to force the machinists to accept black members—but even when presented with an opportunity to influence the union, he chose to accept a purely cosmetic solution.

As a result of these policies, unskilled workers, particularly African Americans, viewed unionism with skepticism at best and hostility at worst. In 1920, a group of sixty black delegates attended the AFL convention in Atlantic City, New Jersey. At least three of the delegates, representing Virginia and Alabama, attempted to propose a resolution condemning lynching and demanding the creation of an organizing committee for black workers. Another noted that it was "impossible for Colored Men to obtain a charter from the Metal Trades Headquarters of any craft," and demanded that the AFL order that "the colored brother [be] entitled to any charter according to his trade." Both proposals were promptly voted down.[31]

The longstanding refusal of the AFL to consider such proposals resulted in a firestorm of criticism from African Americans. Black newspapers regularly railed against the exclusion of black workers from white unions. Particularly galling was the labor movement's condemnation of black strikebreaking, even as most unions denied entry to African Americans. In a letter to the *Defender*, a black undertaker named Daniel Jackson demanded to know "how labor unions ever expect to attain what they strike for if 10,000,000 men in this country are refused trades-union benefits." Jackson wondered at the illogic of the AFL's criticism of strikebreaking, considering that many unions refused membership to black workers: "What a club in the capitalist hands would Negroes be to beat organized labor with!"[32] The most impassioned such critique was written by famed *Chicago Defender* editor Robert Abbott. In a ferocious editorial entitled "Come Now, Lord Gompers!" Abbott referred to Gompers as "the labor tyrant of the United States" and concluded that "whatever progress the Race has made in the world of labor in the free states has been in spite of and not because of the American Federation of Labor."[33]

Despite its claims to interracial unity, such suspicions applied to the CFL as well. Black Chicagoans remembered all too well the "double-crossing" they had suffered during the waiters' strike of 1903, and many regarded the CFL with tremendous suspicion as a result. Chicago Commission on Race Relations' interviews with black workers reveal significant misgivings as to the CFL's claims to interracial equality. A foreman in a box factory claimed "unions ain't no good for a colored man, I've seen too much of what they don't do for him." The man claimed he had worked at the stockyards, where he was recruited by the AMCBW, but said "I wouldn't join for nothing." Another man, who migrated to Chicago in 1894, lamented, "I wish it was so you could join a union regardless of your color." Black workers, he claimed, "need protection on our jobs as well as the white man." Nellie, a young woman who worked as a clerk for a major mail-order company, believed that "unions don't mean anything to colored people," and that unions that admitted black members only did so to prevent African Americans from strikebreaking.[34]

Robert Abbott had a similar problem with Chicago's labor leaders. Abbott was not shy about expressing his criticisms of the CFL. "People who were born and raised in Chicago, who have never visited the intelligent cities of the East, call Chicago a civilized city," he once wrote, arguing, "I don't." Abbott felt that "the weakest point" in the city's "conflict between money men and union laborers in Chicago is that both parties are wrong, ignorant, stubborn and revengeful." Labor in particular acquiesced to the demands of "the money man [who] says for spite that [he] will not employ a Negro." Abbott concluded that if the CFL did not work to create a truly interracial union, "foreigners and Negroes will be obliged to keep from starvation by work of any kind because the white American boy of Chicago puts all his trust in Gompers."[35] The historical discrimination faced by black workers in organized labor made African Americans reticent to embrace the CFL campaign.

Indeed, the result of such history was a widespread suspicion that the CFL's efforts to organize black workers was for the sake of convenience, rather than a genuine spirit of racial cooperation. Black organizer Andrew Holmes would later trace the history of this apparent "un-Belief in the sincerity of the White man's invitation to come into Organized Labor."[36] Articles in the black press frequently expressed this suspicion. The *Defender* worried that the CFL campaign might suffer the same fate as "feeble efforts at organization in the past."[37] Another *Defender* editorial argued that black workers "really do not know what they are to get from organized labor in the face of past injustices," there was no reason for African Americans to believe that the CFL campaign would be different from previous efforts.[38] CFL organizer William Z. Foster lamented such feelings. "We found that we had tremendous opposition to encounter," he later recalled. CFL organizers confronted an "attitude . . . that the colored man would not be allowed to join the unions at all." Despite the best efforts of the union, Foster found that history ensured that such feelings persisted. "The colored man as a blood race has been oppressed for hundreds of years," he said. "The white man has enslaved him," and, as a result, black workers "don't feel confidence in the trade unions."[39]

For the CFL to succeed in uniting these ethnically, racially, and linguistically disparate workers would require a new kind of unionism—one that discarded the AFL's staid hierarchies of race and craft and embraced a large, diverse body of workers. To that end, CFL president John Fitzpatrick and radical organizer William Z. Foster would restructure the federation around the values of what historian John Keiser has called "progressive unionism"—an ideology that embraced both skilled and un-skilled workers across boundaries of race, sex, and ethnicity and challenged the AFL's craft-organizing model and its often reactionary attitudes to-ward women, immigrants, and African Americans.[40] Fitzpatrick and Fos-ter were an odd pair, but one perhaps perfectly suited to the execution of such a transformation. Fitzpatrick emigrated to the United States from Ireland as a child and began working in the stockyards at the age of eleven. Burly, charismatic, and plain-spoken, he was the very picture of a labor leader. Fitzpatrick's rise to leadership of the CFL is in many ways a story of the man's principles. He became president of the federation in 1906, a position he would hold continuously for the next forty years. Fitzpatrick made it his first priority to snuff out the corrupt reign of his predecessor, Martin "Skinny" Madden—which one contemporary observer memo-rably described as "honeycombed with graft"—and made honesty and integrity the cornerstones of his tenure.[41] Fitzpatrick's reputation was burnished by his painstaking adherence to his own scruples. He abstained from swearing and drinking (even refusing to attend union meetings in saloons) and patronized union labels whenever and wherever possible, bragging that "my shoes, my clothes, my hat are all manufactured . . . where union men and women work." Fitzpatrick packed his own lunch each day, refusing to dine at downtown restaurants staffed by nonunion cooks and waiters. Fitzpatrick, in other words, was a union man through and through.[42]

Foster's path to the CFL was more circuitous. A native of New England and Pennsylvania, Foster held a wide array of jobs, including streetcar motorman, railroad builder, and sawmill attendant, before becoming involved with the radical Industrial Workers of the World (IWW). Frus-trated by the IWW's lack of cooperation with other unions, Foster joined the Brotherhood of Railway Carmen and the International Trade Union Educational League, which brought him to Chicago in 1915. Though not as traditional a unionist as Fitzpatrick, Foster had become frustrated with Marxism and anarchism and felt that his dream of syndicalism—control of the means of production by small cadres of workers—could be achieved only by "boring from within" existing AFL structures.[43]

Such a revolution was uniquely possible under the aegis of the CFL, which Foster lauded as "the most progressive central labor union in the United States."[44] That progressivism was no accident, but rather the prod-uct of careful maneuvering by Fitzpatrick. The structure of the AFL, relying as it did on the supreme power of the international unions and their locals, rendered city federations like the CFL relatively powerless to police their members. In a paradoxical way, however, this freed Fitzpatrick to challenge AFL traditions in areas such as organizing and governance. Fitzpatrick could advocate what amounted to heresy—organizing unskilled workers, immigrants, and African Americans, for example—without fear of reprisal, so long as his actions did not violate the autonomy of Chicago's union locals. Progressive unionism, then, would not be instituted from the top, but would be the product of compromise and agreement among the CFL's various locals.[45]

Fitzpatrick and Foster quickly found an ideal place to test the mettle of their ideology. In spring 1916, the AMCBW—attempting to take advantage of the wartime labor shortage—opened an organizing drive in the stockyards of Chicago. The going was tough. As a craft union, the AMCBW had little experience organizing unskilled workers and quickly found itself frustrated by the immensity of its task. For their part, the unskilled workers were largely ignorant of, or outright hostile to, unionism, fearing that signing a union card would cause more trouble than it would save. Most damagingly, the AMCBW was so weakened by years of systematic employer assault that it could make no meaningful offer of protection to the unskilled workers. Though the union made some small gains, it quickly became clear that success could only be achieved with the considerable financial and organizational resources of the CFL.[46]

Clearly, the first step in implementing progressive unionism was a reorganization of the structure of the CFL. Traditional craft unions had proven insufficient to organize the great mass of unskilled workers. The idea of organizing workers into "one big union," in the style of the IWW, was also rejected. The CFL remained a loose federation of individual local unions, each of which fiercely guarded its autonomy. None would have agreed to hand over their jurisdictional powers to the CFL, making the idea a nonstarter. Ultimately, Fitzpatrick and Foster adopted the compromise solution of federated unionism, a form of organizing Foster had learned from his time in the railway crafts. Under a federated structure, all of the local unions of a particular industry (meatpacking, in this case) would join under the stewardship of a central committee. The committee would be responsible for the organizing of all new members, who would then be parceled out into the individual locals claiming jurisdiction.[47]

For nearly a year the AMCBW campaign sputtered as Fitzpatrick and Foster consolidated support within the CFL. In July, Foster made a proposal to the federation, sponsored by Fitzpatrick, to organize the stockyards. Knowing that success would require the cooperation of any number of local unions, Foster attempted to inspire those assembled. He railed against the rising cost of food, claiming that stockyards workers were "near starvation" while the meatpacking plants continued churning out thousands of tons of profit-making meat per year. The duty of the Federation, he argued, was to begin "a joint campaign of organization" with "the co-operation of all trades affected." The key words, of course, were "joint campaign." The executive council agreed, and approved a plan to create a new body responsible for organizing skilled and unskilled meatpacking workers: the Stockyards Labor Council (SLC).[48] Chicago's first iteration of federated unionism, the SLC was a coordinating committee composed of a dozen union locals representing various crafts in the city's meatpacking industry. The crafts themselves ran the gamut of meat processing, and included everything from butchers and blacksmiths to coopers, horse shoers, and egg inspectors. At a series of meetings throughout August 1917, Foster explained to union heads that the packers could only be defeated by a unified campaign directed by a centralized, democratic governing body.[49]

The SLC immediately embarked on a federated organizing campaign. This carried several advantages. First, rather than relying on a patchwork group of local unions to organize workers, the committee was able to bring the full resources of the CFL, including organizers and financial support, to bear on the campaign. Second, the SLC's federated structure allowed the immediate organization of all stockyards workers, regardless of craft, skill level, race, gender, or ethnicity. Once they were members, unskilled workers would be doled out to so-called "neighborhood-based organizations": local unions with ties to the workers' ethnic and ward communities. This not only forged significant ties between union members and their neighborhoods; more importantly, it also allowed the CFL's member unions to present a united front against employer oppression and prevented the division of union workers along the lines of skill or craft—and, by extension, by race or ethnicity. Third, and most critically, the use of a federated structure allowed the campaign to be coordinated and controlled by a single central committee, meaning that membership in one local was as good as membership in the next. The structure of the campaign thus shattered traditional divisions between workers and promoted solidarity within, and across, union locals.[50] With the stockyards being organized along federated lines, the CFL had taken a crucial step forward in its efforts to reshape Chicago's unions.

The CFL also sought to take control of local and national politics. Though Foster had little interest in political involvement—he felt it involved too much compromise—Fitzpatrick believed that both major parties were enemies of the working class, and saw an opportunity for reform. Both parties had appointed antiunion judges, both had called out police and militia against strikers, both had pledged their fealty to corporate interests. Fitzpatrick was of the belief that true democracy was impossible without independent political action.[51] In November 1918, Fitzpatrick and the CFL called one of the largest official gatherings of rank-and-file workers in American history. Nearly a thousand union delegates, representing ninety-three towns in thirty-five states, poured into Chicago to hear the CFL chief speak. At the conference, Fitzpatrick presented a resolution officially calling for the formation of a labor party. The proposal passed nearly unanimously, as did another resolution calling for the establishment of a constitution that vested control of the party in local union bodies. "Labor's Fourteen Points" put forward a plan for political reform centered on public ownership of utilities, public housing and sanitation, and nationwide recognition of unions and the right of collective bargaining. On December 29, 1918, 160 delegates of dozens of local unions chartered the Cook County Labor Party.[52]

With the establishment of the Labor Party, the CFL toppled yet another longstanding pillar of AFL orthodoxy. By 1919, the Illinois Federation of Labor had overwhelmingly approved the creation of a state labor party in direct opposition to the values of the AFL, calling it a "deplorable state of affairs" that Gompers and other AFL officials were "still spending valuable time and our money digging up the lists of old office holders and office seekers for the friends of labor, when no such animal exists in the ranks of the old political parties."[53] Like the SLC, the party—particularly its iteration in Cook County—was intended to function as an independent representative of local rank-and-file workers, beholden neither to the pressures of party politics nor the policies of the AFL. As a result, it focused its energies primarily on local issues of concern to workers. At the convention of the Cook County Labor Party on January 12, 1919, the party named its candidates for public office, including Fitzpatrick for mayor and Polish SLC organizer John Kikulski for city clerk. Much of its platform, too, reflected local concerns. Fitzpatrick spent much of his time slamming the corrupt Republican administration of William Thompson for its "sham love for union labor."[54] The party's posters were emblazoned with promises such as "Municipal Ownership and Operation

... Democracy in the Schools ... Better Labor Conditions ... Protection of Health" and railed against "the money kings of 'kingless' America."[55] Party organizers sought to gain support from famed progressives like settlement worker Mary McDowell, who praised the party as "the party of promise."[56] The formation of a federated structure and a base for independent political action revitalized the CFL and set the stage for a major organizing campaign.

Perhaps the most significant aspect of the CFL's campaign was its focus, from the very outset, on black workers. Fitzpatrick and Foster realized from the outset that the success or failure of their efforts would hinge on their ability to organize across racial lines. Three of Chicago's five largest employers of black labor were meatpackers: Swift (nearly 2,300 black employees), Armour (just over 2,000), and Morris (1,400), with Wilson close behind (more than 800). The only other local companies that employed more than a thousand African Americans were Sears Roebuck and International Harvester.[57] An interracial campaign would not only allow the full organization of the stockyards; just as importantly, it would forestall the possibility of black strikebreaking. As Illinois Federation of Labor president John Walker put it, unions could make the black worker "a source of strength ... rather than a source of weakness and a club in the hands of the grasping employer."[58] The organization of black workers quickly came to define the campaign. Foster regarded the organizing of black workers as "imperative" and vowed "to organize the colored worker if it was humanly possible to do so."[59] Shortly after the first organizing meeting of the Stockyards Labor Council, Foster explained to the Council's members that the campaign would only be successful if it "realized fully the necessity for the organization of the colored worker."[60]

It should be noted that the CFL's concern for black workers was not born of pure pragmatic self-interest. Union officials were legitimately concerned with the suffering of black workers. SLC organizers sympathetically listened as black workers listed their grievances. One was not given the opportunity to work overtime, while less-senior white workers were regularly given this privilege. Another was wrongly blamed for the misconduct of a white worker and summarily fired; when he protested, the company attempted to rehire him as a "new hand," which would have eliminated all of his seniority rights. Still another worker claimed that an assistant foreman "had openly made the statement that he would not work with 'niggers.'" When the Chicago Commission on Race Relations conducted its survey of black packinghouse workers in 1919 and 1920, the most pervasive complaint was "lack of opportunity for advancement or promotion."[61]

With these grievances in mind, the CFL began actively recruiting African Americans from the inception of its campaign. Foster and Fitzpatrick realized that white organizers' life experience and perspective would render them ineffective in appealing to black workers. At the urging of black hog butcher and SLC delegate A. K. Foote, the SLC hired and trained a cadre of black organizers to work within the African American community. The CFL also acquired black organizers from the United Mine Workers of Illinois, the AFL, and the Women's Trade Union League. The organizers held a series of educational meetings within the Black Belt, speaking directly to black workers in meeting halls and on street corners. By October, the SLC had installed a new black local within the stockyards, Local 651. CFL leaders took great relish in publicly refuting the packers' contention that "the American Federation of Labor . . . [did] not recognize the colored workers" and declared that Local 651's charter "made the colored workers an integral part of the labor movement of the United States."[62]

But deploying black organizers was not enough. From the beginning, CFL leaders knew that to "encourage the colored workers to join the labor movement," they would have to prove their ability to "eliminate race prejudice . . . and secure a living wage and decent working conditions" for black workers.[63] As a result, the union attempted special appeals to black workers. Advertisements touting the liberating possibilities of union membership appeared in black newspapers. Mass meetings of African Americans, often led by Foster and/or Fitzpatrick, were regularly held in the Black Belt. CFL officials took care to pursue black grievances as aggressively as possible—particularly those that involved racial discrimination—and even expelled locals that refused to remove the color bar from their constitutions.[64] At every available turn, the CFL reinforced its message of racial equality and interracial solidarity.

Much of the success or failure of that message would depend on the union's ability to promote it among the black community. The CFL sought whenever possible to create the sort of connection between neighborhood and union that was prevalent among the white immigrant residents of Packingtown. In 1919, the all-black Local 651 opened a cooperative store in the heart of the Black Belt, allowing the union to promote its message within the community as well as at the workplace. CFL officials also attempted to obtain the support of black community leaders, particularly black ministers. Though they met with only mixed success, it was not for lack of trying; such conferences were a constant feature of the campaign. CFL officials repeatedly met with the Colored Baptist Minister's Alliance and submitted themselves to questioning before such bodies as the A.M.E. Sunday School Convention in 1920.[65]

Union leaders attempted not only to recruit members and support for organized labor, but also to impress upon black community leaders the corruption of the packers. Packing bosses used donations to black churches and organizations such as the Urban League and Wabash Avenue Y.M.C.A. as a sort of bribe to turn black community leaders against unionism. Thus CFL leaders spent much of their time recounting tales of the packers' coldness to the plight of rank-and-file workers. A favorite was the attempt of one packing concern to sell company bonds to a group of two hundred black women workers; when the women refused to buy, the "good-hearted foreman, through sympathy for them," revoked their lunch break and sent them home without pay. The only defense against such a fate, the CFL argued, was for workers to "mak[e] use of their economic power by joining an organization of Labor, and bargaining collectively in the interest of the working class," regardless of race.[66]

They also appealed to black workers through the press. Black organizer Andrew Holmes wrote a number of pieces for the *Chicago Whip*, detailing the union's dedication to interracial principles. The union's "policy of no racial discrimination," he explained, "is a means to the end of obtaining some of the equal rights in the industrial arena" for "progressive colored people."[67] G. W. Reed, a black woman who worked as an SLC organizer, was even more direct in a guest editorial for the *Butcher Workman*. She declared that the SLC "stand[s] with outstretched waiting hands, inviting you to come and enjoy the democracy that has been built up with walls that can not be pierced with discrimination and race hatred." Reed argued that "there will be no peace until the white man learns that the black man must be considered," a result that could only occur through the union, the instrument "through which discrimination and race hatred may be driven out of this country."[68]

The Labor Party likewise adopted a progressive attitude toward African Americans. Among the founding principles of the Labor Party was a declaration of "the political and industrial equality of races, nationalities and creeds." The opening convention of the party contained one of the most comprehensive antiracism platforms of its time. Claiming that "the present economic and social system keeps the American Negro in a condition of slavery," the party insisted that "the labor movement of America cannot attain the full realization of its industrial and social program without the solid organization and co-operation of the Negro workers" and pledged to "secure for the Negro a citizenship equal in every respect to that of his white brother."[69]

By August 1917, Foster had completed the work of affiliating the SLC locals and felt confident in launching a full union assault on the yards. On the evening of Saturday, September 8, an automobile parade was held in Packingtown, with dozens of workers enthusiastically decking their cars in red, white, and blue bunting and tearing through the streets. Throngs of workers and their families, holding union-issued sparklers, lined the sidewalks to cheer them on. The next evening, the SLC began holding nightly mass meetings that went on for two full weeks, never drawing less than two hundred attendees and occasionally drawing more than twelve hundred.[70] The battle for the stockyards had begun with a roar of support from the workers.

That roar only grew louder in the coming weeks. The nightly meetings spread word-of-mouth excitement throughout the yards. Neighbors huddled on the street corners and stoops of Packingtown to discuss the coming of the union. The energy and dynamism of the SLC campaign clearly outstripped that of any previous organizing effort. For the first

John Fitzpatrick of the Chicago Federation of Labor addressing workers. From the outset, the CFL's campaign was characterized by its recruitment of workers regardless of race, ethnicity, gender, or skill level, as demonstrated in this photo of John Fitzpatrick speaking to a mass rally. Chicago History Museum, ICHi-021355.

time, unskilled workers felt themselves a major priority to organized labor—they were no longer stuffed into cumbersome "common laborer" locals, but organized into a body that represented all meatpacking workers and promised to transform the yards.[71] With the passion of unskilled workers ignited by the excitement of the campaign, the SLC enjoyed a staggering level of success in its organizing. One Columbia Hall meeting was scheduled to be followed by a mass meeting fifteen blocks away, at Thirty-Third and Morgan Streets. Foster, sensing the opportunity for a mass demonstration of the SLC's power, organized a parade of stockyards workers between the two sites. More than five thousand workers took part in the march. Such a display of solidarity would have been unthinkable mere months earlier. Foster took pleasure in noting that the campaign's success occurred "in contrast to the opinion expressed by some when the campaign was begun that there were too many nationalities, etc., and it would be impossible to carry on an organization campaign."[72] Foster boasted that SLC organizers were bringing in three hundred to six hundred new members every day. Packinghouse workers proudly displayed their buttons both on and off the job—a crucial symbol, in Foster's mind, that "they were intensely interested in the outcome of the campaign."[73] That interest was reinforced and stimulated by the CFL's assiduous cultivation of ethnic ties. The union hired John Kikulski, a charismatic local of Polish extraction, to organize among the city's Polish and Lithuanian workers (Kikulski was fluent in both languages, as well as English). Kikulski established five separate immigrant locals, and was largely responsible for the union's enormous success among Slavic workers, some twenty thousand of whom joined the SLC by 1918.[74]

The campaign represented a veritable revolution in the stockyards. In a mere two months, Foster and the council had deflated the packers' threats of arbitrary firings and wage fluctuations, neutered the importance of company spies, broken down barriers of race and ethnicity, and built a strong, unified campaign of skilled and unskilled workers. By the end of the year, the SLC had organized some twenty-four thousand stockyards workers—fully 40 percent of the total workforce in the city's meatpacking industry. In 1918, that number would rise even further, with some departments claiming 100 percent organization of the skilled tradesmen and greater than 90 percent membership among the unskilled.[75] Perhaps the campaign's greatest achievement was its organizing of black workers. It is estimated that of the twelve thousand black workers in the stockyards, at least half belonged to the SLC at some point.[76]

The overwhelming response of workers vindicated the faith of Fitzpatrick and Foster in federated unionism, and they quickly moved to consolidate their influence over the stockyards. In November, they hashed out a list of demands to be submitted to the packers. First and foremost was recognition of the union, as well as demands for a guaranteed eight-hour day, paid holidays, and extra pay for overtime. The newfound influence of the AMCBW was in full effect, as the union also demanded more sanitary working conditions, abolition of mandatory participation in "sick and death benefit associations"—essentially, company insurance programs—and a maintenance of current guaranteed weekly hours.[77] These demands reflected the ways in which the SLC had redirected the city's unions away from old-style craft union organizing and toward a federated model. The union demanded not only an increase in the hourly rate, but an equivalent percentage increase for "piece workers"—the mass of overwhelmingly unskilled workers who performed one segment, or piece, of a particular process. Additionally, the union asked for "equal pay for men and women doing equal work," a tremendously progressive proposal for the time. The message was clear: the diverse mass of unskilled workers would have as much of a voice as skilled operatives.[78]

The revitalized CFL had made a number of major breakthroughs. By redefining itself as a federated union, it was able to transcend the barriers of ethnicity and craft and reach the great mass of unskilled workers. It engaged in a major, and largely successful, assault on the open-shop fortress of the Chicago stockyards. It had even swept away decades of white supremacist doctrine within the AFL and made legitimate inroads among the city's African American population. Yet despite the inroads the SLC had made in the yards, the demands produced by the AMCBW and mechanical trades conferences had been ignored by the packers. The stage was set for the SLC to confront the packing industry head-on.

With the organizing campaign progressing, Foster felt confident in submitting a list of demands to the packers in November. The packers, unwilling to negotiate with organized labor, refused even to read them. Foster, undaunted, assembled a committee and requested an audience with the packing bosses. Again he was rebuffed. But Foster understood that the SLC was a major force in the meatpacking industry and would not be ignored. Late in November, the SLC called a strike vote of its members. It passed with 98 percent approval. The union alerted AFL leadership to the strike vote, to the horror of AFL president Samuel Gompers and other conservative AFL leaders. Gompers was in an untenable position.

If the strike failed, unionism would be driven out of a basic industry in a major city. If the strike succeeded, it would be a major victory for federated unionism and, potentially, a threat to the power of the AFL's craft-organizing model. Using his political contacts, Gompers managed to secure an audience in Washington for the SLC.[79]

The meetings in Washington were a testament to the tremendous organizing work the union had accomplished in mere months. The committee enjoyed an audience with both president Woodrow Wilson and secretary of war Newton Baker. The committee convinced them that the threatened strike was a very real possibility, and that its consummation could cripple the meatpacking industry—a major fear of the administration as the nation prepared to enter World War I. Wilson ordered the President's Mediation Commission to Chicago. The meeting schedule reflected the urgency of the situation: the two sides met deep into Christmas Eve, finally concluding talks at 3:30 A.M. Christmas morning. The commission arbitrated a number of concessions to the SLC, including a dollar a day wage increase and an eight-hour day. The packers, however, refused to abide by the agreement, with at least one report holding that they stormed out of the room when the decision was handed down. Stockyards workers, meanwhile, complained that they were suffering more abuse than ever. Libby dismissed twenty union men without cause, and refused to allow them to discuss the matter with their foremen or superintendents. Rumors emerged that "a number of girls had been approached and told that if they would take off their buttons and tear up their union cards they would be given [a] substantial increase in wages."[80]

Infuriated, the committee returned to Washington and issued an ultimatum to the president: take over operation of the packinghouses, or the SLC would go through with the strike. Wilson managed to talk the union off its threat and offered to listen to their concerns. The union submitted a list of eighteen demands. Wilson brokered a compromise: if the SLC agreed not to strike, Wilson would refer six of the union's demands to a special session of the President's Mediation Commission. Unlike the previous meeting between the SLC and the packers, this new arbitration would involve extensive testimony by both packing representatives and rank-and-file workers. More importantly, the resulting decision would be binding and carry the full weight of the federal government. As the previous administrator had since resigned (and had proven ineffectual in any event), the union would have input into the selection of the arbitration's new head. Finally, and most critically, Wilson agreed to immediately grant twelve of the union's demands. Several of these represented major breakthroughs. Wilson agreed to establish a formalized grievance procedure and seniority system, stipulated that workers could only be fired for just and demonstrable cause, declared that union membership was not grounds for dismissal, and won the right to "proper dressing rooms, lunch rooms, wash rooms, and toilets," a major victory for workers inured to toiling in the fetid filth of the meat industry. Perhaps most importantly, the union placed the concerns of black workers at the center of their proposal, and successfully pushed for a clause banning "discrimination against any employe[e] or prospective employe[e] because of creed, color or nationality."[81]

Though this second round of meetings was a major victory for the union, the real work lay ahead. The six unresolved issues were the most crucial to the stockyards workers, as most of them dealt with wages and other monetary concerns: a wage increase for both hourly and piece workers, equal pay for men and women, an eight-hour day, overtime pay for Sundays and holidays, lunch breaks, and a minimum guarantee of weekly hours. With the agreement of both the union and the packers, Wilson appointed federal judge and Chicago native Samuel P. Alschuler as administrator.[82] Alschuler's task was an immense one. The decision of this new iteration of the President's Mediation Commission would determine not only the battle between the packers and their employees; it would also reflect the degree to which the SLC had succeeded in its campaign. Though the mission of the President's Mediation Commission was to avoid conflict and ensure smooth functioning of the wartime economy, a victory for the SLC would confirm the union as a major force in the industry and guarantee it recourse against the abuses of the packers— not to mention improve the lives of tens of thousands of workers. On February 11, 1918, the hearings that would determine the future of the stockyards began.[83]

The hearings were a dramatic affair. For three weeks, the commission, along with representatives of the packers and the SLC, huddled in the Chicago Federal Building and conducted interviews with hundreds of subjects, ranging from CEOs of the packing companies to superintendents and foremen to unskilled piece workers. For many workers, the hearings came to define the battle between labor and capital, with real-life heroes and villains clashing in the Federal Building for supremacy at the yards. The SLC's hero was lead counsel Frank P. Walsh, a self-taught attorney from Missouri, who gained national renown as a champion of progressive causes. As head of the federal Commission on Industrial Relations, Walsh had critiqued the low wages and poor conditions under which most workers toiled, as well as the massive and centralized profits that resulted, referring to American industry as "industrial feudalism."[84] Walsh was so dedicated to the cause of the SLC that he counseled the union free of charge, declaring that assisting the SLC was "a service to humanity."[85]

Walsh adroitly recognized that he could play the profit-obsessed coldness of the packers to his advantage. To that end, Walsh took the hearings outside the Federal Building and into the yards. He guided Alschuler and the commission through numerous tours of packing plants, showing them firsthand the grueling physicality, the unforgiving pace, and the relentless monotony of stockyards work. Walsh's gamble succeeded: Alschuler was horrified. One worker who accompanied Alschuler recalled their attempt to visit a plant's offal processing center: Alschuler reached the entrance, stopped, and reversed course, as his "sense of smell would not permit him to go any further."[86] The commission also visited Packingtown, witnessing the disease-ridden squalor in which the mass of low-paid unskilled workers lived. One by one, as contemporary scholar Edna Louise Clark explained, "characters [from] 'The Jungle' appeared before the arbitrator and . . . exposed the dreary, hard lives they were forced to live."[87] These sojourns helped turn the tide of the arbitration.

As witnesses, Walsh prioritized unskilled workers, men and women who performed the lowest-paid and most unpleasant work at the yards. Both on his tours of the yards and in testimony at the Federal Building, Alschuler was confronted with a staggering level of human misery. The judge encountered black employees working more than twelve hours a day for the common labor rate of twenty-seven and a half cents an hour. By some standards, these workers had it easy; at Armour, Alschuler spoke to a man "about sixty-five years of age," who was working eighty hours a week in the subzero pickling room for the same rate.[88] Alschuler's experience in the yards was perhaps best summed up by the words of a local carpenter, who claimed he would "rather be a janitor in hell than a worker in the Stock Yards."[89] With the destitution of Packingtown and its residents firmly in the mind of Alschuler and the commission, Walsh could make his case for the SLC.

Perhaps the most damning testimony came from the packing bosses themselves. Walsh relentlessly grilled packing executives, explaining to J. Ogden Armour that he could double his employees' wages and still make a hefty profit. The packers responded to such lines of questioning with shocking coldness. During the examination of a Morris executive, Walsh inquired about cost of living. When he produced an average household budget, the conversation became increasingly awkward. Noting that the budget only allowed for one hat per year, Walsh asked whether the executive believed "one hat [was] too much for one year." The executive replied flippantly, "I don't wear any myself." Infuriated by the executive's indifference, Walsh demanded: "In ... determining what you are going to pay these people ... don't you consider what it costs them to live at all?" Against all available evidence, the executive insisted that his employees "seemed to get along all right." Walsh, seeking to get to the heart of the matter, referred to the budget for a final, poignant question: "Do you think that three pairs of shoes for a child for a year would be too much?" The executive sealed his own fate by coolly replying, "Off hand it would look like it might be one too much."[90]

With Alschuler fully aware of the horrors of the yards and of Packingtown, and of the cold indifference of packing bosses to the suffering of their employees, Walsh proceeded to his closing argument. His address was a stirring five-hour oration that encompassed the history of the United States, the ways in which unions brought together workers from disparate ethnic and racial backgrounds, and the ways in which a living wage could secure American liberty. Walsh's argument also reflected the values of the SLC. In discussing perceived splits among workers along the lines of skill and race, Walsh claimed, "I see in the packing houses the men and women siting side by side ... in the greatest harmony." For Walsh, as for the SLC, "the whole question of discrimination between the races is a financial and economic question." Racial discrimination, which caused Walsh's own "emigrant ancestors ... [to be] called 'Micks,'" and modern packinghouse workers to be insulted as "damn Polocks," was a product of Irish and Polish workers being "forced down in the social scale."[91] The elimination of economic barriers—the organizing of skilled and unskilled, white and black, native and immigrant into a single union would ameliorate social conflict and make for a more prosperous nation.

Significantly, Walsh took great care to address the situation of black stockyards workers, declaring that they were the heart of the SLC's new unionism. The entrance of masses of black workers into the SLC was a revolution in the labor movement, Walsh argued, telling the packing bosses that interracial unionism broke down "the last barrier in your defense against the American working men." Reiterating the SLC's argument that unions were the most efficacious way for African Americans to achieve social and economic freedom, Walsh noted that "colored men brought from the south are going into these unions by the hundreds" and that unions, in turn, pledged "to stand shoulder to shoulder and side by side to get [for them] the same financial benefit and . . . the same economic benefit as the white man."[92] Indeed, some of Walsh's address had the air of a recruiting speech given in the Black Belt: "From this point on the white man's unions are going to show that they are as loyal to the rights of the black man as they are to a white man." But whatever Walsh's rhetorical flourishes, his argument echoed that of the SLC: as a result of interracial unionization, the packers would be forced "to emancipate them with the white people." Walsh concluded his address with an air of confidence. The packers' power "is slipping," he claimed. With African American workers joined in the SLC organizing drive, "every negro is going to have a grievance, every negro can make a fight." To back his words, Walsh brought dozens of black workers into the hearings to testify to the discrimination they had faced from packing bosses, and the ways in which the union had ameliorated it.[93] Walsh's speech became legendary in labor circles. When Alschuler's decision was handed down, many unions printed copies of it alongside a full transcription of Walsh's address.

Walsh's tactics worked. On March 31, 1918—Easter Sunday—the commission issued its decision. It was a total victory for the union. Alschuler granted an immediate pay increase (to be followed by another increase in May), equal pay for men and women, an eight-hour day and a forty-hour week, overtime pay for Sundays and holidays, lunch breaks, and proper dressing rooms. Most importantly, Alschuler established a revised grievance procedure under which the President's Mediation Commission, and Alschuler himself, would be the final arbiter of labor-management disputes. Chicago workers were jubilant. Even in its wildest dreams, the SLC could not have predicted such a resounding victory. Walsh praised Alschuler by saying that if the judge were made labor administrator of the United States, Walsh and other labor activists "could all go home, quit our foolishness, and go to work."[94] Unlike the ill-fated Christmas arbitration, the Alschuler award was a firm declaration of worker rights. There would be no packer shenanigans—no summary dismissals, no cajoling to remove a union button, no threats against organizers. Smaller packing companies initially resisted the award and refused to abide by it; in June, Alschuler summoned them to a meeting and quickly brought them to heel. The award also had a material effect on the SLC. Almost immediately, the union claimed credit for the award, energizing meat-packing organizing in Chicago and beyond. By November 1918, nation-wide membership in the AMCBW had reached nearly seventy thousand.[95]

Workers' reaction to the award reflected the success of the CFL campaign. The crowning achievement of the organization of the black workers was a massive interracial parade and demonstration in July 1919, to commemorate the award's expiration. At LaSalle and Thirty-Third Streets, in the Black Belt, a series of speakers exhorted the assembled crowd to organize. SLC secretary J. W. Johnstone remarked on the "checkerboard crowd," a mass "not standing apart in groups, one race huddled in one bunch, one nationality in another," but rather "standing shoulder to shoulder as men, regardless of whether your face is white or black."[96] Other speakers followed—T. Arnold Hill of the Chicago Urban League, CFL organizers Andrew Holmes and John Kikulski, and the wife of imprisoned labor *cause célèbre* Tom Mooney—and the rally ended "with three rousing cheers of '100 per cent union or bust.'"[97] Despite the racial tension that wracked the city, it appeared that the CFL had succeeded in creating an atmosphere of interracial cooperation and solidarity.

The Alschuler award represented the first major victory of the SLC, and it was well earned. Though Judge Alschuler had proven sympathetic to the plight of stockyards workers and their families, the union's tireless organizing, as well as the declaration of its principles by attorney Frank Walsh, was similarly instrumental to the victory. Though it required assistance from the federal government, the SLC had built a union movement on its terms—dynamic, diverse, and democratic—and won major concessions from the packers. The coming challenge of the CFL would be to maintain the gains proffered by the award, to consolidate their inventive union structure, and to hold together their multiracial coalition. The federation's most immediate task, however, was to mobilize politically.

The creation of the Labor Party was perhaps the most heretical act of the CFL. Interracial unionism was one thing—the AFL expressly forbade racial discrimination, and both individual AFL unions and the AFL itself had made real, if clumsy, overtures toward racial inclusion. But Gompers was steadfast in his opposition to independent political action. As early as 1891, the federation recommended that unions "stand by the advocates of labor measures and reward them . . . or punish at the polls those who are inimical to their interests," but claimed that an independent political party "has no right to representation in the Trade Union councils." This policy was firmly in line with the AFL's prioritizing of craft union autonomy and supremacy. For Gompers and other leaders, "the economic function and power of trade unionism" itself was "by far its greatest instrument for good," and could not "be endangered by the attempt to identify it with a partisan political movement."[98] This stern opposition did not deter the CFL.

The Labor Party's mission and structure openly defied the AFL's long-standing opposition to both independent political action and organization of the unskilled. The party was organized similarly to the SLC. It was a relatively weak coordinating body whose power—both human and financial—rested entirely with local unions. As a result, the party focused much of its energy on engaging the sympathies of rank-and-file workers. Local unions affiliated with the party by paying yearly dues, so members of those locals were automatically members of the party. Party officials never ceased reminding membership of the inclusiveness of the group. The *New Majority,* established as the official organ of the party in 1919, referred to members as "real citizens of Chicago." Party propaganda established the Labor Party as the ultimate "big tent" political organization. Party literature boasted that its membership consisted of "all men and women who perform useful labor with hand and brain," including "mothers and workers in the homes and all workers on the farms." The only people excluded were "the shirkers, parasites, and plutocrats" who had spent their lives "fattening [themselves] on the labor of others."[99]

But Labor Party leaders also actively sought to involve workers in the political process, recruiting them to serve on local ward committees and attend party conventions. One of the earliest actions of the party was to hold a speakers class "for all who are 'up and coming'" with the party's campaign. The party hired a former University of Chicago professor to tutor party members in oratory, allowing them to host meetings, create and disseminate literature, and thus "over-come the conspiracy of silence ... which the...press and old party politicians are maintaining toward the Labor Party." No qualifications were necessary; in fact, "every man and woman who desires to speak and to work for the Labor Party in this campaign" was strongly urged to attend.[100]

Much like the SLC had done in its stockyards campaign, the Labor Party paid particular attention to the concerns of black voters. As in the stockyards, blue-collar African Americans represented a powerful and influential group within city politics. Moreover, much of the militant cadre within the CFL, particularly the SLC, was composed of recent immigrants who were ineligible to vote. As a result, the importance of black voters was greater than their proportion of the population. Just as crucially, black Chicagoans quickly developed a sense of racial solidarity and tended to vote in a bloc; securing their votes, as a result, could easily swing an election. Perhaps, most importantly, the party recognized the fact that the ballot box represented a critical symbol of freedom for African Americans—particularly migrants from the South who had long been denied the franchise. If party leaders could tap into the black community's racial solidarity and political engagement, they could build a crucial and lasting power base in the political life of the city.

As a result, the party appealed directly to African American voters whenever possible. In addition to the party's avowed antiracism and its support for social and economic equality, the Cook County party's first executive committee included black AFL organizer John Riley, while the 1919 Labor Party slate included an African American candidate for alderman: William Robert Wilson, president of a black local of the Coopers' International Union. Party officials also attempted to drum up support from within the black community itself. A black member of the national Labor Party, in Chicago on business, was recruited to write a guest editorial in the *Chicago Defender*. In it, he claimed that "we as a Race have been used long enough as a political issue," and claimed that African Americans could gain "every right ... politically, civically and economically," through support of the Labor Party."[101] Much like the SLC, the Labor Party defined itself through its direct engagement with rank-and-file workers, including African Americans.

That engagement paid almost immediate dividends. By March 1919, 175 local unions had affiliated with the Illinois Labor Party. Most of those were based in Chicago, where party organizing had been a rousing success: 116 local unions composed of nearly 60,000 members had affiliated with the Cook County party. That membership was meaningless, however, unless it could be put to use at the polls. The party had a chance to test its strength in the municipal elections of 1919. CFL officials were hopeful that fighting between the candidates would split the mayoral vote and hand Fitzpatrick a plurality. This was certainly possible; the administration of Republican incumbent William Hale Thompson was wracked by charges of corruption, and Democrats remained divided after a bitter primary campaign left Robert Sweitzer as the party's nominee and fellow Democrat Mackay Hoyne as an independent challenger. Party leaders were also buoyed by their success in organizing the city's workers into the SLC and hoped that such energy would cause a late groundswell of support for the party. As early as 1918, CFL secretary Edward Nockels predicted that the party would receive "at least 300,000 votes."[102] Nockels was far too optimistic. Thompson retained office by earning a 37.6 percent plurality, barely edging Sweitzer's 34.5 percent but trouncing Hoyne's 16 percent. Fitzpatrick had polled only 8 percent of the popular vote.[103]

But Fitzpatrick's campaign was by no means a failure. Though his share of the vote appeared unimpressive, that percentage represented the votes of nearly fifty-six thousand Chicagoans. In the areas of the CFL's greatest influence—namely, the city's heavily blue-collar northwest and southwest sides—Fitzpatrick competed gamely with the other candidates. In the Fifth, Twenty-Ninth, and Thirtieth wards, which encompassed the stockyards and its environs, Fitzpatrick earned 11 percent, 16 percent, and 13 percent of the vote, respectively. Other candidates performed respectably as well. SLC president Martin Murphy gained 20 percent of the vote in his aldermanic campaign in the Twenty-Ninth Ward. In the far southeast Eighth Ward, home to thousands of steelworkers, South Chicago Trades and Labor Assembly president T. J. Vine earned 13 percent of the vote in his campaign for alderman, while Fitzpatrick earned 12.5 percent.[104]

Though disappointed with their lack of victories, party officials took heart in the strong response from working-class communities. The campaign had clearly succeeded in securing support for the party and its candidates among SLC and CFL members. By defining itself as an organization dedicated to the support of rank-and-file workers, the Labor Party had created a base of support within the city's union community. Additionally, party leaders had reached out to African Americans and attempted to convince them of the efficacy of independent political action. The party's respectable but disappointing showing at the polls in April 1919 displayed the party's need to broaden its base beyond the existing CFL membership and to engage more fully with the black community—problems that would soon come to define the SLC as well.

Chicago's workforce was transformed between 1904 and 1916. Packing bosses brutally consolidated their power, rolling back union gains, preying on ethnic and racial differences, and crushing unionism out of the stockyards entirely. The increasing diversity of the yards as a result of mass immigration from southern and eastern Europe and the Great Migration of African Americans rendered attempts at organizing the yards unsuccessful. But in 1916, John Fitzpatrick and William Z. Foster reconstructed the CFL as a dynamic, progressive federation with mass appeal. By transforming stockyards unionism from a collection of skilled locals into a federated committee of unions representing all workers, the CFL was able to organize the huge numbers of unskilled workers who had previously been neglected. Just as importantly, the CFL actively recruited black members, and sought to define unionism as an agent for interracial unity as well as class solidarity. The CFL's efforts to create a large and powerful union succeeded to such a degree that the federation defeated the meatpacking bosses in federal arbitration and won many of their demands. With a strong showing by the Labor Party in the 1919 municipal elections, it appeared that the CFL was on the rise.

But buried within this success was the germ of discontent. As chapter 3 will demonstrate, the federated structure of the CFL replicated rather than surmounted many of the racial issues that had long plagued the AFL. Such issues helped stymie the union's efforts to create a truly interracial labor movement in Chicago. Moreover, as chapter 4 will reveal, many black workers initially responded with enthusiasm to the CFL appeal, but became disillusioned and left. Other African Americans distrusted the union and its message from the beginning and declined to join at all. The CFL had staked much of the success of its campaign on the organizing of black workers, and on an alliance with the black community. Despite its earnest efforts, those goals would prove increasingly elusive to the CFL and its leaders.

3.

"DEMORALIZED BY ITS OWN WEAKNESSES": THE STRUCTURAL LIMITS OF FEDERATED UNIONISM, 1916–1921

John Fitzpatrick's dream of creating a militant, diverse, interracial union centered on a reimagining of craft unionism—a set of reforms intended to replace trade union exclusionism with cooperative federated control. Such a system allowed the CFL to make major headway in Chicago's stockyards and secure a victory with the President's Mediation Commission. Particularly given the union's inroads with black workers, it appeared that federated unionism might permanently alter the labor landscape of Chicago.

In fact, however, the CFL was unable to permanently organize a significant number of black workers. Estimates of the total black membership of the SLC vary, with some claiming that as many as 50 percent of black stockyards workers—around six thousand—were members at some point. In 1920, however, the union itself estimated that "the percentage of the organized colored workers has been very insignificant" and had not exceeded "15 per cent at any time." More damning was the fact that white membership was estimated as peaking at close to 90 percent.[1] Membership data for individual locals does not exist, but the primary local union of black workers, Local 651, rarely exceeded a thousand members. A sister union composed of black women, Local 213, maintained a membership of less than two hundred.[2]

Those African Americans who did join were often less than enthusiastic in their embrace of unionism. Many joined the union and quickly defected, realizing that the guarantees of the Alschuler award applied to them regardless of whether or not they remained members of the union. Membership estimates bear out this sad fact. It is entirely possible that six thousand black workers joined the union at some point, but the membership rolls for Local 651 reveal barely two thousand "members in good standing"—that is, members who were current on their dues payments. This suggests, as James Grossman has argued, that "black workers joined readily, but let their dues lapse just as freely," indicating that "they were interested in unions, but not committed to them."[3]

The following two chapters explore the reasons for the CFL's failure to organize black workers. The first issue discussed lay in the structure of the CFL's organizing campaign and its roots in the AFL's tradition of federal labor unions (FLUs)—local unions of unskilled workers affiliated not with an international union (such as the carpenters or teamsters) but with the AFL itself. The CFL adopted this system to organize the unskilled workers of Chicago's packinghouses, modifying it to allow the creation of "neighborhood locals" linked to specific areas of the city. But the use of neighborhood locals was enormously problèmatic. For one thing, affiliating the neighborhood locals with the SLC decentralized decision-making in a cumbersome way. As a result, the neighborhood locals had little power on the shop floor and were vulnerable to the predations of packinghouse foremen, who intimidated and threatened union organizers and members and actively sought to hire nonunion workers. Rank-and-file SLC members engaged in a series of failed wildcat strikes that reveal both the depth of workers' anger and the powerlessness of neighborhood locals in the face of an employer counteroffensive. More importantly, the use of neighborhood locals resulted in the creation of a de facto segregated SLC local, Local 651. Black workers in Local 651 found themselves marginalized and powerless to help shape the union. When they aired their complaints to CFL leadership, white union leaders responded with defensiveness and petulance. The segregation and resentment that resulted from the neighborhood locals system undermined the CFL's claims to interracial organizing and unity, and provided yet another barrier to the organization of white and black workers.

Despite the CFL's numerous breaks with the AFL, the structure of Fitzpatrick's federated unionism owed much to AFL traditions, a concession that would prove costly later on. Although racism and organizational inertia suffused the AFL's leadership and member unions, the AFL realized that black workers could not be totally neglected. Progressives within the AFL vigorously protested the federation's ongoing policy. Leaders of various unions harped on the ability of employers not only to hire black workers to compete with whites, but to foment racial discord on the job.[4] The problem of *how* black workers could be organized, however, remained a sticky one. Most black workers were unskilled and thus had no place in AFL craft unions. Several unions proposed the possibility of industrial unionism—that is, the organization of all workers in a given industry into one union, regardless of craft boundaries. Thus all workers in a meatpacking plant, from butchers to tanners to blacksmiths, would be under the jurisdiction of a single union that controlled the entire industry. Each of these proposals, however, was rejected; Gompers contemptuously dismissed industrial unionism as an abdication of trade union principles to mob rule. Still another alternative was the organization of all-black unions in crafts where existing trade unions excluded African Americans from membership. Though some trades organized all-black unions, local central committees often refused to seat African American delegates.[5]

The compromise solution was the creation of what were called federal labor unions. These organizations were small local unions composed of unskilled workers that were affiliated not with a specific craft union—butchers, coopers, etc.—but with the American Federation of Labor itself. The AFL had made use of FLUs since the 1880s, primarily as "recruiting stations for the trade union movement," as Gompers put it, among unskilled white workers.[6] Though they were not specifically designed to house black workers, FLUs allowed the AFL to honor its dedication to craft autonomy while recognizing the importance of African American labor. The mechanism of FLUs was simple: the AFL established city central bodies "composed of representatives of negro workers' unions exclusively" to organize black workers, then chartered the resulting FLUs through the AFL executive council rather than specific international unions.[7] Such a solution circumvented the thorny questions of racial exclusion and craft jurisdiction: the AFL essentially took responsibility for the organizing and governance of black workers, thus making an end run around unions that refused to deal with them. As a result, FLUs gave African Americans the ability to "protect and defend themselves against the rapacity and cupidity of their employers" while preserving the rights and privileges of white unions and fulfilling the federation's dictum to organize regardless of "creed, color, nationality, sex, or politics."[8]

Despite the seeming ingeniousness of FLUs, they were rife with problems. For one thing, the federal unions did nothing to materially change the central issue: the institutionalized racism that pervaded AFL unions. If anything, the decision to relieve international unions of responsibility for organizing African American workers was a tacit endorsement of those unions' racially exclusive policies.[9] Indeed, Gompers made it understood that the federation was in no way supporting social equality: "we do not necessarily proclaim that the social barriers existing between the whites and blacks could or should be felled with one stroke of the pen," he argued.[10] FLUs, in other words, were organized not to uplift African Americans to a new standard of economic, let alone social, opportunity; rather, they were a convenient way to preserve the power and jurisdictional boundaries of white craft unions against the perceived onslaught of unskilled African American workers.[11]

Gompers's narrow-minded approach to the racial problem—his feeling that racial exclusion was, as he put it, merely an administrative "anomaly" that required correction—was also reflected in the relative powerlessness of the FLUs themselves. Because the AFL's governance was based on the autonomy and control of the international unions, the FLUs' affiliation with the AFL executive council rendered them practically impotent. Unlike international unions, federal unions had little say at conventions and little power over AFL affairs, including their own. Although the AFL was ostensibly responsible for organizing black workers, negotiating their contracts, and handling their grievances, the executive council's efforts in these areas proved desultory at best. Disputes were generally referred to the international union that claimed jurisdiction within the industry; since the exclusionary policies of these unions were the reason for the creation of FLUs in the first place, it is unsurprising that they rarely ruled in favor of black workers.[12]

Just as critically, the structure of the FLUs made them virtually powerless within their own communities. The central bodies that governed union activity in most cities were composed of delegations from union locals. Because black workers were affiliated with the AFL rather than those locals—and because the AFL constitution forbade the establishment of more than one central body in a given city—FLU members had no representation in these bodies and were subject to the whims of white unionists at the local level. Consequently, black workers, despite holding membership in the AFL, were regularly pushed out of jobs where their presence might threaten white workers.[13] In short, black FLU members were technically affiliated with the American Federation of Labor, but remained in all practical respects outside the labor movement. Lacking the power conferred by an AFL international charter, FLU members—segregated and marginalized into a small, powerless corner of the federation's vast structure—languished. Inevitably, black workers, growing wise to the AFL's scheme, quickly lost interest in the federation's unkept promises. In 1919, the AFL reported a total of 92 FLUs nationwide. That number jumped to a high of 136 in 1922 and quickly declined: 79 in 1923,

67 in 1925, and 38 in 1926. By 1927, the AFL reported only 21 federal unions still in existence.[14] This fate was not surprising. FLUs were created solely as a pragmatic compromise. Their structure and function sought to appease the federation's longstanding tradition of white supremacy while mitigating the threat posed by unskilled black workers. In this task, they were, if anything, all too successful—FLUs were utterly powerless within the AFL, and soon grew defunct. In the words of a blistering *Chicago Defender* editorial, segregated unions allowed the labor movement as a whole to be "demoralized by its own weaknesses."[15]

Though major differences existed between the AFL and the CFL, including on matters of basic philosophy and ideology, the AFL's experience with black workers presaged the struggles of the CFL to build an interracial labor movement. The CFL would begin its campaign from an entirely different ideological orientation than that of the AFL, but Fitzpatrick and the Chicago movement would borrow heavily from the structure and spirit of FLUs in structuring their campaign, with similarly problematic results. Despite the differences between the AFL and CFL, the latter quickly recognized the potential of federated unskilled locals. Since the majority of the unorganized workers in the stockyards were unskilled, the CFL had no need to create a special class of organizations such as FLUs. Instead, SLC leaders borrowed the spirit of FLUs—their federated structure, their organizing of the unskilled, and their openness to ethnic and racial diversity—and channeled it into the formation of so-called neighborhood locals that represented the values of the CFL. Fitzpatrick and Foster's federated model prioritized mass organization over craft autonomy, an ideal positively embodied by FLUs. Finally, the CFL saw the organization of African Americans as a central goal of its campaign—a goal that could be best accomplished through the mass organizing of the unskilled permitted by organizations like FLUs.

As a result, the CFL pursued federated organizing through a modified form of FLUs: neighborhood locals tied to local ethnic or racial communities. Such locals allowed the CFL to avoid the division and disempowerment of traditional craft organizing, which Foster felt had led to the "disunity and 'scabbing'" that had undermined the 1904 stockyards strike.[16] Not only did craft unionism divide workers by skill and department—thus reducing solidarity throughout the yards—it also excluded unskilled workers entirely. The use of neighborhood locals allowed the CFL to circumvent concerns of craft autonomy in favor of an organizing campaign that included all stockyards workers. Such a campaign would ultimately permit mass solidarity and, it was hoped, worker governance of the yards.[17]

The CFL's neighborhood locals also allowed the union to tap into the energy and solidarity of local ethnic and racial communities. CFL leaders felt that traditional craft organizing not only separated workers from one another at the workplace; it also broke critical ties to their neighborhoods and communities. Fitzpatrick and Foster recognized that given the recent arrival in Chicago of many immigrants and African Americans, workplace relations would be far less significant than neighborhood networks based on ethnic or racial kinship. Consequently, the neighborhood organizations were headquartered in blue-collar communities and organized by ward. Many of the locals retained foreign-language organizers and even conducted official business in Polish and other languages. Perhaps the greatest testament to the SLC's dedication to organizing ethnic neighborhoods was made in its choice of headquarters: Columbia Hall (better known to Polish workers as Slowacki Hall) at Forty-Eighth and Hermitage Streets in the heart of the city's growing Polish community.[18] Though akin to the AFL's use of federal labor unions, neighborhood locals afforded the CFL the flexibility to create a union that not only recognized, but built upon, ethnic and community connections.

Despite the progressive spirit that animated the neighborhood locals, they were never able to harness the militancy of stockyards workers, and in fact proved to be largely impotent in defending worker rights, for several reasons. For one thing, the SLC's use of neighborhood locals redirected the energies of class-conscious unionists from the workplace to the community. As Paul Street has argued, such a structure deprived the SLC of "the militant shop-floor presence" that had animated the AMC-BW's 1904 campaign. Though local unions based on neighborhood and ethnicity served to unite workers and elide the importance of craft divisions, they also diluted the importance of job control and workplace militancy. As a result, the energy of the organizing campaign never translated into increased control over the workplace, making workers easy prey for the informal oppressions employed by discriminatory foremen and superintendents. The Alschuler award further complicated the union's position. The formalized structure of the award served to normalize relationships between workers and employers, co-opting the militancy of the union itself. Moreover, the award pushed the center of working-class activity even further from the shop floor. By relying on the government for the resolution of grievances, workers redirected their energies toward the hearings at the Federal Building—not toward the construction and maintenance of a militant cadre of rank-and-file unionists who could aggressively govern the shop floor.[19] Though the Alschuler award had been a major victory for the union, it had also sapped much of the vital organic energy required to build a powerful, long-lasting labor organization.

A second issue was the packers' aggressive posture in dealing with the union. Sensing its lack of energy, packing bosses assailed the SLC at every turn. Although the Alschuler award had provided union members with protection from unfair discharge, employers used a variety of informal means to circumvent the award and intimidate workers. As Fitzpatrick said during an investigation into the packers' behavior, "ever since the United States Government has taken the question of the packers dealing with their employes [sic] out of the hands of the packers . . . still there is a decided fear among the employes [sic] . . . up in the stock yards." Many meatpacking workers, Fitzpatrick argued, "have not got the courage to put on the Union button."[20] Fitzpatrick's suspicions were borne out by the testimony of stockyards workers. AMCBW officer Dennis Lane complained that "non-union men are protected by the company," but that "the union man is made to toe the mark . . . so far as the privileges of the [Alschuler] agreement will allow him to extend himself."[21] Union workers frequently received the worst assignments, while nonunion men were promoted and even protected from punishment. Lane recalled a case in the Wilson plant in which a nonunion man broke the jaw of a union member with an iron pipe. After recovering from his injury, the packers had the union man arrested; the nonunion man was defended free of charge by the company attorney and acquitted.[22]

Packers also openly disregarded the benefits of the Alschuler award. B. H. Rendell of the machinists' union complained that "men are intimidated from the fear of losing their positions." Despite the Alschuler award's guarantee of protection for union workers, Rendell claimed that foremen and superintendents constantly threatened him and his coworkers, claiming that one told him, "You had better keep your mouth shut if you want to hold your job." Any employee who was found to have "a little more independent spirit" was immediately discharged. Foremen defied the award's orders, "advertis[ing] through the shop" that offending employees had been fired for union activity.[23] Discharged union activists were frequently the victims of violence as well. A CFL delegate lamented the presence of company guards, who were "officered in the uniform of policemen and carry clubs." When a union activist was fired, he claimed "he is escorted to the gate and if he makes any effort to get a consideration of his grievance he gets a rap over the head with a club." Union officials complained of the difficulty of attempting to get past such guards. "It is absolutely impossible to get up where the business end is run," one delegate said, wearily concluding, "We are not able to negotiate."[24] Packing bosses used both informal intimidation and open defiance of the Alschuler award to weaken the union's influence on the shop floor and drive its members out of the yards.

Finally, and most critically, the union was unable to respond effectively to such aggression. Though the Alschuler award had provided a number of benefits to the union, the union shop was not one of them. Because the union could not negotiate such rights and benefits, it was powerless to prevent the unemployment of nonunion workers. Even open defiance of the contract by the packers involved a cumbersome grievance procedure arbitrated by the President's Mediation Commission. Lacking the ability to negotiate directly with the packers, and unwilling to await the decisions of Judge Alschuler, workers regularly engaged in spontaneous job actions to protest both the presence of nonunion workers and the powerlessness of their leaders. In June 1919, a union official in the hog offal department at Hammond complained to foreman S. C. Calef that two men in the seventy-five-man gang were not members of the union, and that Calef must "get them to join or discharge them." Calef responded that workers could not be compelled to join the union, that the company "could not discriminate for him," and that the company would have no hand in organizing workers. The SLC could organize on its own time. In response, the entire gang walked off the job. Within an hour, the entire pork house—between seven hundred and nine hundred men—joined them in protest.[25]

Similar events took place elsewhere. At Wilson, the union steward of the cellar gangs complained that several workers from the sweet pickle and dry salt departments were nonunion. The union members demanded their dismissal and threatened to stop working if the nonunion men were kept on. When the superintendent refused, union members shut down the machines in the dry salt department and told their coworkers "to stop work at once." SLC leaders Martin Murphy and J. W. Johnstone arrived and ordered the men back to work, but the strikers remained out, and even recruited other men from the freezer and sausage rooms to join them. A beef killing gang posted a sign on the shop floor that read "Final Notice:

Everybody must have their union button on [tomorrow] morning when they come to work or they cannot work. . . . Go to the hall and get your buttons tonight. This means everybody."[26] The workers' own words reflect their growing frustration with the presence of nonunion workers. Louis Michora, who helped lead the wildcat strike in the dry salt department, complained that despite the organization of nearly five hundred men in his department, the sixty-three nonunion men were able to undermine their work. Michora complained that these workers took too many sick days, cursed at union members, and even pulled knives on union organizers.[27] Though Michora recognized that the wildcat strike was illegal, and tried to stop it, it was to no avail: "everybody say 'stop the scab' . . . [they] no want to go and work with the scabs."[28] The packers' intimidation of union employees provoked ferociously bitter actions by the workers.

These wildcat strikes reflect the relative powerlessness of the union as an agent of shop-floor protest and collective bargaining. All of the strikers were eventually ordered back to work by the SLC, with no substantive changes made. Despite the efforts of the SLC to create an independent, militant union, its federated structure and reliance on federal largesse left rank-and-file workers powerless against the predation of employers. As John Kikulski testified as to the anger of the rank-and-file workers, who "never voted" to approve the no-strike pledge within the Alschuler agreement, many of the union members had begun to feel "that they have no rights." The rank-and-file, Kikulski concluded, "want to have something to say about their own future instead of leaving it to their officers."[29] The failed wildcat strikes, then, reflect the anger of workers at the packers, but also at the impotency of their organizations. That anger would soon be turned against nonunion employees, particularly African Americans.

The organization of Chicago's black workers presented a unique problem. Because many of the skilled stockyards locals were members of discriminatory international unions that excluded black members, the SLC considered it problematic to organize them into established neighborhood locals. Much like the AFL, the SLC came to a compromise. A neighborhood local known as Local 651 was established in the Black Belt with a "monster meeting" in late November 1917.[30] In theory, Local 651 served the same purpose as the other neighborhood locals: it served a specific community and organized its membership accordingly. SLC officials initially maintained this impression, referring to Local 651 as a "miscellaneous" neighborhood local. In reality, of course, 651 was an all-black union. Because it was headquartered in the Black Belt, its "neighborhood" constituency was necessarily African American workers. For this reason, the union was widely known as Colored Local 651. Though the SLC's organization of black workers followed a similar structure to that employed by the AFL, its racial policies were far more progressive. As such, Local 651 was not technically a segregated union—because of the SLC's federated structure, stockyards workers were free to join any SLC local, and in so doing received membership in the council as a whole.[31] Given its racial progressivism and its structural flexibility, it is tempting to believe that the CFL had solved the problem that plagued the AFL—the organization of a racially and ethnically diverse group of unskilled workers into federated locals.

Unfortunately, CFL leadership was operating from a faulty premise. The ultimate failure of the neighborhood locals was due in large part to a narrow-mindedness regarding the causes of, and solutions to, tensions between white and black workers. CFL leaders presented racial discord as essentially a material problem: employers had fomented racial conflict through differential wage scales, employment of black strikebreakers, and racially charged antiunion propaganda. The solution, then, was interracial union organizing; if black and white workers were organized together, the thinking went, the divisive tactics of employers would be neutralized and racial tension would naturally dissipate. The CFL's campaign was thus presented not only as an effort to strengthen the labor movement, but also to uplift the city's African American workers. Indeed, CFL officials made clear that the abuses suffered by black workers would go on unabated unless they organized. "Of course the colored people are just as good as the white people," read a resolution at the 1917 convention of the Illinois Federation of Labor. But "unless the trade unions help them they will not get fair play."[32]

Such rhetoric was often centered on the union's idea that a shared experience of class would inevitably transcend differences of race. Since black and white workers were both exploited by employers, it was felt that union organizing would allow them to shed racial preconceptions and organize together. Fitzpatrick made this point most clearly in an early meeting with black stockyards workers. His appeal was simple: an interracial union would lead to interracial cooperation. Black workers, he asserted, should join the union "to deal with the bosses as we do."[33] An editorial in the progressive black newspaper, the *Chicago Whip*, made the case for interracial unionism, noting that the SLC campaign was critical since "more of our group are employed in the Stock Yards than in any [other] industries." More importantly, the editorial argued, "the Negro . . . has more in common with organized labor . . . than he does with capital."[34] The CFL viewed racial discord as the result of material relationships at the workplace. As a result, it cast itself as the primary means toward equality and uplift for black workers, and interracial cooperation for all workers.

But Local 651 suffered from many of the same pitfalls that plagued the AFL's federal labor unions. For one thing, its structure ensured that black workers' power and influence within the SLC was nowhere near that of whites. In a procedural complaint that speaks to the relative powerlessness of Local 651, many black members claimed that the union's claim of federated reciprocity—that membership in one local was as good as membership in the next—was a lie. A number of black workers complained that they were unable to use their union cards in shops outside the yards; that is, members of Local 651 who left the stockyards and sought employment in other butcher shops were not recognized as union members by external AMCBW locals unaffiliated with the SLC. Members of the white neighborhood locals, meanwhile, could obtain employment at any union shop and be recognized as AMCBW members in good standing.[35] Similarly, because of the federated structure of the SLC, its leaders could not compel individual unions to admit black members. Nor could their grievances be handled by a local delegate; instead, they had to be brought to the council itself, where they were arbitrated by the leaders of the white locals. In one infamous case, a black union official was unavailable for a meeting, so in his stead the CFL called on white organizer Joe Bell, who was assisting with the organization of the black stockyards workers, as a representative. Though CFL leadership defended the decision as being purely one of convenience, the black workers were incensed by the federation's apparent mistrust of its black members' ability to represent themselves.[36] Thus, Local 651 remained in an agonizing in-between state: affiliated with the SLC, but subject to de facto segregation within it and lacking the power to affect change.

Among black workers, reaction to the creation of Local 651 was decidedly mixed. Though a number of African Americans joined the union (particularly during its most successful periods—the drive that accompanied the founding of the SLC, and the aftermath of the Alschuler award), many were angered by the fact that Local 651 was essentially a segregated union. Foster later remembered the difficulty that the SLC campaign encountered when organizing black workers. "The Jim Crow cry was raised that the whites wanted the blacks to herd by themselves," Foster recalled.[37] Indeed, the accusation that Local 651 was a "Jim Crow local" became pervasive within the Black Belt. Foster noted that 651's headquarters on State Street was the subject of derisive snickering among locals. "It was quite general along State Street that [Local 651] was a 'Jim Crow' proposition," he argued. Regardless of the CFL's efforts to convince black workers of the sincerity of their interracial ideals, Foster recalled that "it made no difference . . . there was always an argument against it."[38]

These suspicions are amply conveyed by the minutes of a Chicago Commission on Race Relations conference held in 1920. The conference, held between various members of the commission, black community leaders, and local union officials, concerned "Trade Unions and the Negro Worker." The commission and black community leaders asked a series of questions of each union leader. The questions themselves are inflammatory, even accusatory, and reflective of the suspicions black workers held toward the CFL's neighborhood locals. George W. Perkins, president of the Cigar Makers International Union, was asked about FLUs:

2. How many of the Internationals or Nationals bar the Negro by constitutional provision or in practice?

3. a. What is the purpose of a Federal or auxiliary union?

3. b. Are there not at present a large number of Federal and auxiliary unions?

3. c. Do you think organizing the Negro in these cases into Federal or auxiliary unions will really break down the bars in these National and International unions which exclude him? In what way?

3. d. Will the Negro obtain just as fair treatment in these Federal and auxiliary unions as the whites do in their own unions?[39]

The first question reveals the lingering resentment of racial exclusion in craft unions, but the other questions—particularly the latter two—are even more revealing. The phrasing used, specifically the interrogation as to whether or not FLUs would "really" ameliorate racial discord among workers, reflects significant doubts regarding both the equity and the utility of the federated union structure. Another question, posited to Illinois Federation of Labor secretary-treasurer Victor Olander, undermined Foster's claim that black workers desired to be organized into segregated all-black local unions: "Is there any basis for the statement that Negroes prefer their own separate locals?"[40] Once more, the questioning revealed the narrowness of thinking that led to the creation of a segregated body in the first place, and implied that Foster's justification was merely a retroactive rationalization of a decision made out of convenience.

John Fitzpatrick was similarly needled. The commission stated that "there seems to be a common impression among colored people today that they cannot get a square deal from the unions," a sentiment based primarily in the bitter legacy of the 1903 waiters strike. Though the commission invited Fitzpatrick to defend the CFL from accusations that black waiters were "double-crossed," it also noted "the fact that Negroes are not taken into the Waiters' union today" as a point that would "tend to confirm this impression" among black workers. Like Perkins, Fitzpatrick faced questions regarding the usefulness of neighborhood locals. Specifically, the commission asked, "Is not local [C]olored #268, (Sleeping car porters and diners) a sort of 'Jim-Crow' union, from the Negroes' point of view?"[41] These questions reveal the cynicism with which Chicago's African Americans viewed FLUs, neighborhood locals, and the prospect of interracial unionizing more generally.

Even more revealing are the words of black union members themselves. The separation of white workers from black workers charged otherwise ordinary grievances and disputes with racial peril. Many black workers accused the union of "Jim Crow unionism," claiming that the CFL sought to preserve white trade unions above all else, and turned against the SLC altogether. At a July 1918 CFL meeting, black workers railed against the body's refusal to grant charters to dozens of majority-black unions, including brakemen, machinists, and laundry workers. The discussion became a general critique of segregated unionism. "The colored workers themselves are the first to object to Jim Crow organizations," one delegate argued. "They insist, and rightfully so, that if they are to come into the trade union movement they should come into it upon the basis of equality," and not through segregated locals.[42]

Indeed, black workers repeatedly and stridently criticized the structure of the CFL and its campaign as inimical to the organization of African Americans, let alone the construction of interracial unity. At another CFL meeting, a black delegate named Sims, who was organizing an all-black local of waiters and bartenders, claimed that "since their organization was chartered . . . they had met with considerable difficulty" in organizing and maintaining their local. With little monetary or moral support from the CFL, their local was forced to fend for itself against the predation of employers and the discrimination of their white coworkers. Sims declared that "this Federation of Labor was defeating the purpose of their efforts to organize the colored workers," noting that white leaders had asked him to leave the organizing campaign. The creation of Local 651, he declared, was done only out of "a ghoulish desire for the income that the [AMCBW] International would get out of such a local organization." Both Sims's comments and the official meeting notes' claim that his comments were met with "approval" from other delegates, evinces black workers' deep resentment of all-black locals.[43]

Another resolution provides similar insight. Introduced by a series of black locals, including Sleeping Car Porters, Railroad Coach and Car Cleaners, and Local 651 itself, the resolution condemned the use of FLUs, and segregated unions more generally. Federated charters were issued, the resolution claimed, only because "the . . . body having jurisdiction over [the FLUs] are [sic] so blind to justice, and so imbued with that kind of spurious unionism which has retarded the American labor movement." The black locals resolved that the CFL approve "this progressive move of these militant locals to enhance their power to combat the unscrupulous forces that would deny them life." Taking aim at the CFL, the resolution concluded that the federation must "suggest ways and means of intensifying the interest these workers are showing in the labor movement, to the end that they will be granted a status in the labor movement equal to any other group of wage earners."[44] Black workers were clearly aware of the limitations of a federated structure, particularly the ways in which it countervailed the CFL's interracial ideals by segregating white and black workers.

Making matters worse, white CFL leaders responded to these claims with defensiveness and even anger. In response to delegate Sims's complaint, the meeting's chairman claimed that if Sims "had come here as the direct agent of the packers . . . he could not have been of more service to them." Sims himself was accused of being "the biggest obstacle in the way of the organization of the colored workers in the Yards," and that his "policy was to rule or ruin an organization."[45] CFL leadership's resultant attacks on black workers are even more telling. A teamster argued that the CFL "had endeavored to get the colored workers in the Yards here to become a part of the labor movement but that they had not taken advantage of the opportunity offered them." Meanwhile, he claimed, in other meatpacking centers—Denver, Omaha, Kansas City—"the colored workers belonged to the established unions and were wearing their union button." Sims attempted a rebuttal, but the chair refused his appeal and denied him the floor for the remainder of the meeting. The CFL minutes report that he was later removed from office.[46] Sims's criticisms reflect the very real concerns of black workers that the CFL's use of neighborhood organizations did not match its stated commitment to truly interracial organizing. Similarly, the quickness with which CFL officials blamed African Americans themselves for failing to join the union reveals a basic misapprehension of the potentially divisive nature of neighborhood locals.

Indeed, such comments were commonplace at CFL meetings. During a discussion of an organizing campaign among waiters, several delegates made pointed note of the hotel industry's strategy of employing "alien enemies" at low wages to help break the campaign. A delegate from Local 651, sensing that the waiters' prejudices might be sabotaging their efforts, meekly asked whether any of their organizations discriminated against African Americans. Various white CFL members leapt to the defense of the union, noting that "it has been explained to the colored workers [that they] might improve their conditions by joining the union," but that black workers allowed themselves to be "used by the employers against the organized workmen."[47] In a far harsher rebuke, CFL secretary Ed Nockels—in what appeared to be a direct shot at the concerns of Local 651—claimed that "every effort has been made to organize the negroes and show them that their only hope of emancipation is to join the labor movement and they have not responded." Evincing a total failure to grasp the problems of neighborhood locals, Nockels noted that "only 2,500 of the 12,000 [black workers] in the Stock Yards belong to the organization and it cannot be said that they have been discriminated against in any manner." The fault for this state of affairs, CFL leaders concluded, fell on both black workers themselves and on black "preachers and politicians," as well as the packers, "who have used the Y.M.C.A. to influence them." In a similarly paternalistic tone, Foster argued that black workers preferred "their own local meeting with their own local officials in charge," despite the lack of any official or unofficial statement of such belief by black workers themselves.[48] Such responses only enflamed widespread resentment of the CFL's structure and further marginalized African Americans from governance of the federation.

The CFL's efforts to build a diverse, interracial union were complicated by factors within the organization itself. The history of interracial unionizing was fraught with the problematic efforts of the AFL, which used federal labor unions to organize black workers. FLUs, however, came with a price: they were largely powerless within the larger structure of the

AFL, and they tended to reinforce segregation rather than undermine it. Despite its decidedly more progressive policy regarding race, the CFL suffered similar pitfalls. CFL leaders took their inspiration from FLUs, particularly in their organization of "neighborhood locals" among racial and ethnic communities. Like the AFL, the CFL quickly confronted the shortcomings of federated organizing. Neighborhood locals not only exerted little power within the CFL, resulting in resentment and rebellion from the rank and file, they also tended to reinforce existing patterns of racial segregation. As a result, African Americans resented the federated structure and questioned the legitimacy of the CFL's dedication to interracial unionism.

The most critical error made by the CFL was its view of union organizing as a means of eliminating racial conflict. White unionists viewed racial discord as a class problem—an issue of employment and wages and conditions. If these inequalities were leveled, it was thought, racial prejudice would be eradicated. Such an idea was dangerously naïve. This was reflected in the union's problematic structure: though nominally the same as white locals, Local 651 was composed only of black members and had lesser power within the SLC. The CFL, then, had greatly misapprehended the fact that black workers would not respond favorably to what was, essentially, a purely class-based appeal. This was particularly true within the context of a union whose structure resulted in segregated and marginalized black locals. In addition, as the next chapter will show, the enduring mutual distrust between white and black rank-and-file workers only emphasized the shortcomings of the CFL approach and widened the gap between the races.

4.

"BETWEEN TWO FIRES": WHITE
AND BLACK WORKERS CONFRONT
INTERRACIAL UNIONISM, 1916–1921

The CFL's use of a federated structure proved a major impediment to the organizing of African American workers. But the problems of the federation ran deeper than the construction of the union. The racial divisions between white and black workers were rooted in conflicts among the union's rank and file. Traditional white attitudes regarding African Americans, particularly in regard to work and union membership, resulted in discrimination among white unionists. Despite the efforts of Foster and Fitzpatrick to improve race relations in the stockyards, many white unionists derided African Americans as a "scab race."

Such divisions were only deepened by the actions of employers. Sensing an opportunity to divide the CFL, packing bosses spread antiunion propaganda among African Americans, both in the stockyards and in the black community. The antiunion, proemployer stance of many middle-class black community leaders seemed to vindicate blue-collar whites in their feeling that African Americans were a "scab race" seeking to destroy unionism altogether. The packers also made extensive use of nonunion black labor, hoping not only to undermine the union but to ignite racial conflict as well. The hiring by the packers of nonunion black workers, including a number of so-called antiunion "agitators," only augmented this perception and complicated the CFL's efforts to recruit black workers. Ultimately, such divisions manifested as violent workplace conflict that only heightened white workers' prejudice against African Americans. The success of the packers' strategy, particularly in the context of a series of violent racial confrontations at the workplace, was a testimony to the CFL's failure to effectively recruit black workers.

Most damningly, CFL members and leaders disparaged black workers for failing to join the union in sufficient numbers, creating a loop of prejudice: African Americans were derided by union members, then derided further for not joining the union. As a result, black workers, alienated by white intolerance, turned away from the union's class-based organizing and toward racial organizations—a phenomenon typified by the Labor Party's utter inability to recruit black voters in significant numbers. With rank-and-file workers battling one another on the shop floor, the CFL faced yet another blow to its efforts to organize an interracial union.

The CFL's ideals of interracial cooperation were not always shared by its white members. Many of these prejudices were based around what historian Eric Arnesen has dubbed "the specter of the black strikebreaker," a pathological array of racial ideas regarding black nonunion labor as "alternately . . . ignorant and aggressive, manipulated and defiant, docile and violent." In actuality, African Americans represented but a fraction of strikebreakers—as Arnesen notes, "white native-born and immigrant workers constituted a clear majority"—but African Americans' racial identity charged strikebreaking with volatile prejudice. Black workers were thus despised not only because they were perceived as job thieves, but because they were associated with a broad array of pathologies that made them unfit for inclusion in visions of independent white manhood.[1] As a result, the most enduring and dangerous bigotry confronted by the CFL resulted not from black strikebreaking, but the *specter* of black strikebreaking; not from the black community's opposition to unionism, but fears regarding the implications of such opposition; not from racial violence, but terror regarding the possibility of its spread. Such ideologies both stymied the CFL's attempts to create an interracial union and resulted in whites "hanging the charge, like a proverbial lynching rope, around the neck of the [black] race."[2] These rank-and-file attitudes and their roots are crucial to an understanding of racism within the CFL, and mirror the union's difficulties in building interracial unionism.

Events outside the city gave fears regarding black strikebreaking a gripping immediacy. The bloody race riot that seized East St. Louis, Illinois, in July 1917, in which dozens of black citizens were brutally murdered by white mobs, typifies the attitudes of white workers toward black labor. The fury that fueled the riot was rooted in the ferocious resentment of blue-collar whites against black workers, who had been "imported" from the South to break a strike at the Aluminum Ore Company and forestall union organizing.[3] The Illinois State Defense Council report, prepared by a committee headed by Illinois Federation of Labor president John Walker, claimed that the riot was "a warning to Chicago and other northern cities to which Negroes have emigrated."[4] Walker grimly noted that 35 percent of black laborers who came to East St. Louis displaced white jobs. "The services of negro workers," the report claimed, were "used to destroy the standards of work established by organized labor." Such displacement was the result of an active campaign by bosses to undermine the union and create "a surplus of labor on hand in order that white labor might continue to be kept under the heel of the employing interests."[5]

Even more instructive is the report's opinion on black workers themselves. Though the committee blamed the "devious methods" of employers for enflaming race hatred and "preventing the negro [from joining] ... the white man's union," it also evinced the widespread feeling that black workers were simpletons who were largely unfit for union membership.[6] Walker claimed the riot occurred because of employers' practice of "deluding and inducing poor ignorant colored men to leave their homes and spend their last few dollars to come to East St. Louis." The 1917 convention of the Illinois Federation of Labor noted that with immigration closed off due to World War I, the employers could no longer recruit the "uninformed working men of Europe" and instead resorted to exploiting "the poor, unfortunate negro," an "uninformed, unskilled, helpless" worker who came from "the cotton farms and the plantations, away from the industrial centers" and was "uninfluenced by the trade union movement." Most damningly, Walker's labor committee—with the approval of other labor leaders—recommended the passage of emergency legislation "to discourage southern Negroes from emigrating to industrial centers of the north, and prohibiting northern employers from inducing them to do so."[7]

In Chicago, these ideas quickly took root. The East St. Louis riot, which occurred just three hundred miles from the city, was a major story in local newspapers, and the committee's conclusions regarding black workers found a receptive audience in union members still stinging from the racial violence of the 1904 packinghouse strike and the 1905 teamsters strike. Despite the fact that the majority of strikebreakers deployed in both conflicts were native-born or immigrant whites, it was black workers who were most bitterly remembered as a "scab race." Such distorted memories, combined with the cautionary tale of East St. Louis, made white union workers wary, even resentful, of the presence of any African Americans among their workforce. As the Chicago Commission on Race Relations argued, the historical role of black workers as strikebreakers "center[ed] upon them as a racial group all the bitterness which the unionist feels toward strike breakers as a class." African Americans' role as strikebreakers confirmed existing suspicions that black workers were tools of capital who could be easily duped into undermining unionism.[8]

Such attitudes toward strikebreakers were relatively common. Chicago's labor movement, even its most progressive adherents, regularly derided black workers as dupes.[9] In an editorial, a *Butcher Workman* writer summed up the situation of the black strikebreaker:

> He soon learns that he has been made a victim of deception, but the show that is made by having the colored man on the ground has been the undoing of the foreign workman, who has struck for an improved condition, and the strikers go back to work, and the employer's object has been accomplished. Then the colored man is turned out upon the world to shift for himself, and in nine cases out of ten becomes a victim of the hospital and an object of charity, and the general public is contributing millions from year to year in support of these cases. When the colored man finds himself stranded in a strange country, with no home or friends, he becomes an easy prey to the sharks in all walks of life and compelled to accept any position or condition that will prevent starvation, and fall an easy victim to the political shark who uses him to stuff the ballot box at election time.[10]

At a stroke, the *Butcher Workman* summed up an array of white attitudes toward nonunion African Americans. Black workers, ignorant of the work they would be asked to do, were brought to northern cities with the promise of a steady job, only to find they'd been tricked into breaking a strike. With the strike defeated, black workers were immediately dismissed, leaving a legacy of hatred and resentment among white unionists. Devoid of the skills necessary to survive in the urban North, they quickly joined the public dole and became easy prey for the "sharks" of both the red-light district and City Hall.

Similar ideas were commonplace, even among the comparatively racially progressive CFL. For white union leaders, racism was the result of material economic conditions and the calculated attempts of packing bosses to prey upon unlettered black workers. Interracial organizing, it was thought, would not only defeat capitalist schemes, but also protect African Americans from their supposed predisposition toward being manipulated and exploited and sinking into a life of degeneracy. As one union member testified, "The non union man . . . [is] so weak in mind that he doesn't have principle enough . . . to say, 'I will join the butchers, and try to tear down this brutal way of living, and try to make an easier way of living for ourselves.'" A scab, he went on, simply "hasn't got the brains to think that way."[11] Such attitudes reveal the innate paternalism of the CFL's vision:

white workers—even those who supported interracial unionism—largely viewed African Americans as a naturally "servile race" that required the custody and care of union organizing to protect them from succumbing to the predation of employers and the temptations of the city.[12]

These arguments reflect a growing paradox: despite the many barriers to African American participation in the CFL, union members often blamed black workers themselves for being resistant to the union call. The Chicago Commission on Race Relations recounted an encounter with white union members who felt that "union action and union money" had made the Alschuler award possible, but resented the fact that the agreement applied to all stockyards workers, whether they were union members or not. During a dues collection meeting, a CCRR investigator noted that "a number of the white members . . . showed, quite unsolicited, that considerable feeling existed because the Negro workers were not coming into the union" in sufficient numbers, allowing them to enjoy the benefits of the award while incurring none of the risks.[13]

Such feelings were at times manifested as open hostility toward black workers, who were viewed as pawns of the packers. A CFL delegate lamented the packers' attempts to keep "these ignorant colored men" from joining the SLC.[14] Black antiunion agitators were derided as "simply . . . ignorant and low-minded" tools of the packers' avarice.[15] At one point, the union even abdicated responsibility for organizing black workers, claiming it had done enough: an article in the *New Majority* detailing the mass interracial parade in July 1919 opened, "If the colored packing house worker doesn't come into the union, it isn't the fault of the Stock Yards Labor Council."[16] Despite their derision for black workers as a threat to public welfare, as tools of capital, as competitors for work, and even as violent enemies, white workers blamed African Americans for their reluctance to join unions, making their prejudices a grimly self-fulfilling prophecy and reinforcing the historical context for racial discrimination within unions.

These fears were augmented by pervasive prejudices against the perceived immorality of African Americans, particularly southern migrants. Local newspapers reported that black migrants brought tuberculosis and sexually transmitted diseases with them to Chicago. As a result of "displaying a childlike helplessness in the matter of sanitation," the migrants lived in "conditions . . . that threaten the health of the city."[17] Black newcomers were also portrayed as deviant and immoral. Whites were scandalized by reports of "six or eight" unmarried male and female migrants sleeping in the same room, and of the "nightly capers for dice, monte, and card games" that took place within the Black Belt.[18] Such reports conjured memories of the "degeneracy" of conditions within the stockyards, where black strikebreakers were lodged during the 1904 strike, and seemed to confirm whites' opinion of African Americans as unfit for city life.

Public spaces such as elevated trains became the site of racial discord. Whites regularly complained to city transit authorities about the conduct of black passengers, resulting in a commissioned report about the use of public transit by white and black riders. Loud talking and laughter, foul language, and lounging in all areas of the car were cited as common complaints. Black stockyards workers were also castigated for neglecting to change clothes before leaving the yards. Passengers on elevated trains complained of the odor of the men's filthy clothes, which further cemented ideas of black migrants as unclean and dissolute.[19] The *Defender* informed migrants that "it is not the custom in Chicago for people to wear overalls . . . in places such as ice cream parlors, dance halls and theaters."[20]

The most damaging white fears about black deviance were centered on the world of work. CFL leaders recognized that the success of their campaign depended on their ability to organize newly arrived black migrants. This was particularly true in the case of the stockyards, where northern-born black workers supported the SLC campaign at roughly the same rate as whites; it is estimated that more than 80 percent of northern-born black workers, and possibly as much as 90 percent, were members of the SLC.[21] But white workers recognized that northern-born African Americans were both experienced in industrial work and familiar with the idea of unionization, if not its specifics. Southern migrants, on the other hand, had little experience with nonagricultural work, and practically no exposure to unions. Most of them traveled to Chicago from the rural South, and had lived their lives as farmhands. Those few who came from industrial cities—the steel center of Birmingham, Alabama, for example—had an overwhelmingly negative impression of unions. In the South, trade unions were even more discriminatory and exclusionary than elsewhere; to black southerners, unions represented nothing more than a system by which whites retained the highest-paying jobs at their expense. The CCRR interviewed a black paper worker who traveled to the city from Georgia in 1919. "Unions would be all right," he argued, "if they let all of the men in who would do right, but when they don't, they do more harm than good."[22]

These attitudes served to reinforce white prejudices. Viewing them as victims of what William Tuttle has called a "rural psychology," whites derided black workers as lazy and slipshod, with no conception of fair wages, class solidarity, or the principles of labor organizing.[23] African Americans were thus feared as an invading army of low-cost workers immune to the union appeal. The *Defender* attacked many of the migrants hired by the stockyards as "no-account," men who "work three days a week and lay off" the rest. The migrant "newcomers" needed to learn "that in this section of the country three things go to hold a job, thoroughness, promptness and steadiness."[24] A survey by the CCRR found similar complaints among whites, who resented black coworkers as "irresponsible and shiftless." The manager of a millinery house claimed that "our white people resented very much the fact of employing colored people in our business" to the point that he "couldn't overcome the prejudice enough to bring the people in the same building, and had to engage outside quarters for the blacks."[25] White fears of black immorality and degeneracy were generalized into prejudices regarding African American work habits, further dividing white and black workers from one another.

The specter of the black strikebreaker proved to be the most durable and lasting of a tangle of prejudices held by white workers. Believing that black migrants were dirty, uncouth, and unaccustomed to life in an industrial city, white workers were skeptical of African Americans' place within the labor movement. Accordingly, their ideas about black unfitness for union membership extended into the workplace, where black workers were criticized as lazy and undedicated. These prejudices would prove to be a major boon for employers, and extraordinarily destructive to the CFL's efforts to organize an interracial unionism.

Chicago employers eagerly sought to take advantage of these divisions between white and black workers. Packing bosses in particular made great efforts to spread antiunion propaganda among black workers. The packers did not just employ black workers as chess pieces to use against the union. Bosses also actively sought to drive African Americans away from union membership. Once hired, a CFL delegate claimed, the packers made every effort "to prevent the organization of the colored workers." To that end, "all kinds of propaganda was being distributed among them and every conceivable method used to keep them out of the labor movement."[26] Indeed, the packers engaged in a wide variety of activities intended to win the fealty of black workers. Black workers were disproportionately hired in the killing rooms—the most powerful departments in the packinghouses. Though most black workers remained unskilled "common laborers," the packers made sure that a suitably strategic number were promoted to skilled knife tasks, promoting agitation between white and black workers.[27]

Such efforts to win the loyalty of African Americans extended outside the workplace as well. Packing bosses engaged in a wide variety of activities intended to make themselves—and not the CFL—a central part of black community life. Black SLC organizer Andrew Holmes noted that "many of the race's educational institutions were donated, and often times supported and maintained by capitalists," and that black union membership could easily "be interpreted as ungratefulness to benefactors."[28] In Chicago, those benefactors were particularly active in allying themselves with the black community. CFL leaders regularly blamed "welfare clubs, company Y.M.C.A.'s, glee clubs, and athletic clubs" as being "supported by employers as a substitute for a form of organization which they cannot control," and lamented "the subsidizing of [black] social movements and churches" as "one of the means employed by large employers to insure [a] reserve of strikebreakers."[29] The packers' patronage of two major social organizations—the Wabash Avenue YMCA and the Chicago Urban League—reflect the degree to which the packers sought to burrow into the life of the black community.

The Wabash Avenue YMCA was a major hub of social activity within the Black Belt. Sensing an opportunity, the packers poured funding into the organization once African Americans became a major part of their workforce. By the end of World War I, the organization was, for all intents and purposes, a social arm of the packers. Armour, for example, offered black employees (and only black employees) free membership to the organization after a year of employment. At the club, workers could enjoy their free membership by joining the Efficiency Club Program, where they could learn butchering skills and time management techniques—and be fed antiunion propaganda. The packers also sponsored glee clubs and baseball teams, always with the company name front and center. Wilson funded an organization known as the Wilson Club, which met at the YMCA.[30] Black SLC activist Frank Custer reported that the club was misrepresented among black workers as an all-black union and an alternative to the SLC. In reality, however, "all the men that belong to this club ... try to undermine the other men of their job."[31] SLC official J. W. Johnstone claimed that the club was nothing more than "a combination of non union colored men, where they are lectured and taught that the thing they have to do is to keep out of organized labor," while Custer complained that superintendents regularly walked among black workers on the shop floor and pressured them into joining.[32] Once they were members, black workers were charged with distributing antiunion literature and with monitoring the activities of SLC members and reporting their findings to bosses, who could use the information to discharge union activists.[33] Such tactics not only fostered black fealty to the packers, but also confirmed white suspicions regarding black labor and increased racial discord at the workplace.

The case of the Chicago Urban League is more complex. For much of the wartime period, the league's activities consisted mainly of securing employment for black migrants. The league's best interests were served by an avoidance of industrial conflict altogether. As a result, the league often attempted to stand "between capital and labor, insisting that each should recognize and do its duty by the Negro" and claimed that it "would welcome any effort tending to an amicable settlement of this vital problem."[34] The league held regular conferences with the CFL, the Illinois Federation of Labor, and the Women's Trade Union League.[35] Unfortunately, that middle course proved unsustainable. The league simply could not afford the bad publicity of entanglements with the increasingly militant SLC. To succeed, the league already needed to convince the employer "that it was to his advantage to use Negro labor." An alliance with unions would make such an argument impossible to sustain.[36] Moreover, an alliance with a mass movement like organized labor threatened the organization's carefully cultivated air of respectability. As the SLC campaign grew more powerful and contentious, the league began to extricate itself from the conflict altogether, preferring to resolve industrial disputes not through labor-management battles but through the intervention of the league's social workers.[37]

The packers also forced the league's hand. By the middle of World War I, the Big Five had become a major benefactor. For packing bosses, the league served not only as an easy way to procure black labor—and thus reduce labor costs and union activity—but also as "a conservative stabilizing force in the colored community," in the words of historians Sterling Spero and Abram Harris.[38] In 1917, for example—seeking to counter the community recruiting of "Colored" Local 651—the packers established the Stockyards Community Clearing House. A philanthropic organization with a heavy focus on the African American community, the Clearing House quickly became the second-largest single donor to the

Chicago Urban League. The effect was nearly immediate. In that year's annual report, the league announced that "efforts will be made to form a closer relation between the league and corporations employing large numbers of Negroes." No longer "standing between capital and labor," the league now sought only "to relate the interests of the employer and employe[e] so that mutual benefit will result."[39] By 1919, donations from Chicago's packinghouses were responsible for 20 percent of the league's total budget, destroying once and for all any connection between the league and the CFL; in 1921, the league willingly supplied the packers with strikebreakers during a meatpacking walkout.[40] Packing bosses' involvement in black institutions helped them cement a link between themselves and Chicago's African American community, while simultaneously undermining the possibility of interracial unionism.

Many black community leaders also increasingly rejected the prospect of unionism. A whole host of aldermen, social workers, and, especially, ministers, tended to side with influential African Methodist Episcopal Bishop Archibald J. Carey in his opinion that "the interest of my people lies with the wealth of the nation and with the class of white people who control it."[41] Employers, in other words, had given black workers their first opportunity in industry, and were thus owed their loyalty. The opposition of the black middle class was not universal. Reverend Lacey K. Williams of Olivet Baptist Church embraced unionism, though he was a dedicated antiradical. For all his bluster, Robert Abbott of the *Defender* supported those unions that opened their ranks to African Americans, while the progressive *Chicago Whip* carried a regular column from black AFL organizer John Riley. But for the most part, middle-class black leaders, when given the choice, tended to choose employers over unions.[42]

The CFL's rejoinders to such arguments only served to deepen racial discord. Labor leaders frequently derided middle-class African Americans for their refusal to support unionism. Foster lamented the "large and influential black leadership, including ministers, politicians, editors, doctors, lawyers, social workers, etc., who as a matter of race tactics are violently opposed to their people going into the trade unions."[43] He recalled that during the SLC campaign, "no sooner had organizers begun the work than they met the firm opposition of the negro intelligencia [*sic*]." These "misguided intellectuals" suggested that African Americans' "interest[s] lay in working with the packers to defeat the unions" and thus sought "to make a professional strike-breaker" of the black worker.[44] Black SLC organizer Andrew Holmes made a similar argument, claiming that the "duplicity of self-styled Race Leaders" was a major factor in black workers' reluctance to join the campaign.[45] In a 1918 resolution decrying the use of black strikebreakers, members of the waiters union claimed that "many race leaders condone, if they do not actually urge, strike breaking as a method of gaining entrance into industry."[46] Indeed, a waiters union delegate complained of the ease with which employers could summon strikebreakers from local black community organizations, particularly the YMCA and YWCA. Black community leaders, many of whom genuinely were allied with the packers, supported such institutions. "The politicians and colored ministers of the churches in the black belt" were "supported by the big business interests" and were "a great factor in keeping the colored workers in submission and restraining them from joining the trade union movement with their fellow workers."[47]

A discussion of the stockyards campaign at the 1917 convention of the Illinois Federation of Labor (IFL) typifies white union members' anxieties. IFL president John Walker noted that "there was considerable proof from colored men that circulars had been sent out to try and poison their minds against the trade union movement." Such propaganda was written by the packers, but circulated by "some few mountebanks of colored men" who "pose as saviors of the colored race" yet "poison ... the minds of their own people against the labor movement, and [make] it impossible for them to get together and work for their mutual protection." The leaders of the black community, Walker concluded, were merely "living off the colored race at the expense of the colored race" and represented the worst "of all the enemies of" African Americans. Another resolution claimed that the CFL, "in its great work, has not been able to make much headway in the black belt, and the reasons are that the colored leaders are ... preventing them."[48] These paternalistic responses by CFL leaders only served to deepen the divisions between the union and the black community.

More sinister was the growing feeling that black workers were engaged in an open alliance with capital. Many black workers were derided not merely as pawns in capital's mission of undermining unionism, but as partners. Such attitudes were most often expressed in response to the "importation" of black workers by white businesses. Particularly galling to the union was the stockyards' call for "10,000 to 14,000 men" to fill the labor shortage created by World War I. Even worse was bosses' subsequent claim "to guarantee food and lodging for one week to southern Negroes," which conjured memories of the 1904 stockyards strike.[49] In the minds of union members, such recruitment not only undermined the CFL's organizing campaign, it marked black workers as coconspirators with capital. At the first sign of trouble, one union writer claimed, "The employer immediately wires to his agents in the South and they ship on carloads of colored men" who "threatened" the city "in such numbers as to menace wage standards and union organization."[50]

The packers knew that such racial division represented perhaps the greatest weakness of the SLC, and exploited it mercilessly. Employers began to hire large numbers of black employees in order to foment racial discord. In this way, the packers hoped to reinforce the long-standing idea of African Americans as a "scab race" that actively undermined both white and union privilege at the workplace. The testimony of worker Frank Custer is instructive. "It seems as though Wilson & Company has a batch of men they can ship any place they want to," he claimed. Many unionists held similar suspicions that the packers held a captive labor force that they moved "from one packing house to another, in order to discriminate against the union man" and "break down the union power if they possibly can."[51] Evidence does indeed suggest that such efforts were highly coordinated. During the Alschuler hearings, Frank Walsh interrogated Swift superintendent John O'Hern, who admitted that the company moved employees throughout the country when necessary. "We have moved employes [sic] from one plant to another...both [white] and black," he acknowledged. Though O'Hern maintained such actions took place only in times of need for specialized work, such as fertilizer shipping, such actions confirmed for unionists the packers' deployment of a mobile force of nonunion labor to undermine organizing efforts. A letter from Louis F. Swift was far more damning. The letter explained the opening of a new employment bureau outside Swift's plant in Denver. The goal of the bureau was simple: "We shall start at once to increase the percentage of colored help [in] the plant with the intention of getting it to 15% or higher as soon as we possibly can."[52]

For white workers, such situations were viewed not in the context of black advancement but rather the breaking down of white unionism. Hair spinners at Wilson, for example, found themselves being supplanted by black workers; when they struck in protest, the company hired a full gang of African Americans as replacements.[53] Black union steward Robert Bedford claimed that foremen were "going through all the different departments, picking out non union colored men to put them in these men's places in the hair house" in order "to start white men to fighting colored men."[54] Those efforts were often successful. As organizer John Kikulski put it, the use of nonunion black workers only increased separation of and friction between the races. "At the noon hour," he claimed, groups of white workers would take their lunch break, leaving the black workers alone, furtively "looking out of windows and doors." The result, Kikulski claimed, was "a kind of moral effect that . . . creates a dis-harmony and hard feelings among the races."[55] The packers' hiring of increasing numbers of black workers, particularly to replace white union members, only increased distrust among the two races.

The actions of employers made the specter of black strikebreaking a living, breathing monster. Packing bosses spread antiunion propaganda through the workplace and, more importantly, through the black community. As a result, white workers saw African Americans as leaders at the head of a "scab race" that increasingly was not *non*union but *anti*-union. The perceived alliance between employers and African Americans became even more threatening as bosses hired—"imported," in the minds of many whites—large numbers of nonunion black workers. The very presence of nonunion African Americans was threatening to white workers, but employers augmented the effect of their presence both by employing them as strikebreakers and by recruiting antiunion "agitators" who could spread company propaganda throughout the workforce.

The efforts of employers to heighten racial tensions, combined with white prejudices, inevitably resulted in violence on the shop floor. A series of racially motivated wildcat strikes serve as proof that the SLC's message of interracial unity was not resonating among the rank and file. In July 1919, for example, a hog-killing gang at Wilson dropped their tools and refused to work unless the company removed a black nonunion worker from their gang. Rumors spread that other gangs might strike in sympathy, so the superintendent pulled the black worker into his office for the remainder of the day. After some thought, the superintendent fired two union leaders, George Kosek and Stanley Jinnicki, for threatening the strike. In response, the entire 125-man gang walked off the job, as well as gangs from the hog butchering and sausage departments. One superintendent estimated that close to four thousand men took part in the action at one time or another.[56] When it was explained that firing the black worker would violate the Alschuler agreement, Jinnicki replied simply, if "the colored fellow" was "going to work over there they ain't going to work." As a result, Jinnicki testified, the strike was a true wildcat affair. No one called the men out, rather, "the gang stopped itself."[57]

Jinnicki claimed that the workers' race was irrelevant. He argued that a scab was a scab, that it "it don't make [a] difference whether it is [a] colored fellow or [a] white fellow." But the workers' response to the black nonunion worker reveals deep-seated resentment. According to a black employee, at least one man suggested "that they should carry [the scab] off the floor and then the gang would go back to work." When the packers' attorney attempted to confirm that "the question was as to his being a union or non-union man," the witness intimated that other factors were at work: "I could not recall any particular man who said he would not work with him because he was not a member of the union."[58] Indeed, several different workers claimed that the issue was not a union issue at all. In fact, when the black nonunion worker relented and offered to join the union, workers responded by saying "we don't want him."[59] Seeking to avoid further tension, one union member offered to pay the man's dues for him, but his union comrades refused to accept it. Even with the non-union man sporting a union button, the union workers wanted the man thrown out. "We have so much trouble," they reportedly said, "we don't want him in."[60]

Other unionists turned to outright violence. According to a report received by Judge Alschuler, crowds of union members were gathering at the stockyards gates every night, vowing "to make the stock yards 100% union." This behavior was not a peaceable extension of the organizing campaign, however. The report claimed that nonunion workers were "threatened with bodily harm, if they do not show union cards or union buttons." Skilled workers and foremen were not immune to these attacks, and were ordered to join the SLC "or suffer the consequences."[61] Sworn affidavits claimed that "the minute [workers] . . . get outside of the gates," they were "hustled by force and duress against their will" into joining the union. Significantly, such attacks appeared to be particularly directed at black workers. Joe Hodges recalled that he "had a little trouble" with union members. Hodges left the yards during his lunch break and saw "6 or 7 or 8 Polocks grab . . . a colored fellow out there" and drag him by his neck onto a wagon. The union members yelled "you son-of-a-bitch, you will join the union." When they saw Hodges, one of the men grabbed him and asked "Where is your button?" When Hodges replied that he was not a union member, the union men shoved him back toward the plant, where "45 or 50" union members stood "cussin" Hodges as he walked by.[62]

Despite such attacks, white unionists generally blamed black workers for outbreaks of violence. The existence of violent racial conflict, even when it was perpetrated by black workers in self-defense, only confirmed that black workers were agents of chaos and violence. In response to Hodges's complaints, white union members claimed that Hodges had thrown rocks at a wagon full of union men and screamed "what are them sons-of-bitches doing around here." According to black union member Frank Custer, this was proof that Hodges "has it bitterly in his heart against the union men, and he means to get the [union] man out if he has to."[63] In another case, a nonunion black worker yelled "God damn that union" and claimed that black members were "a bunch of white folks' niggers." Eventually, black union worker Charlie Jamieson challenged the non-union worker to a fight, which ended with the nonunion man beating Jamieson into unconsciousness.[64]

Packing bosses exploited these tensions whenever possible. Union members frequently complained about black "agitators" who stirred up antiunion sentiment on the shop floor, reportedly under the orders of packing foremen and superintendents. Black union steward Frank Custer believed that such agitators were "imported" by the companies for that very purpose. Custer claimed that the packing companies were "taking my race up from Texas, using them as a big stick, using them as something to cut their own throats, to run themselves down lower than they are today."[65] Custer claimed Wilson had imported more than a dozen non-union black employees from Texas, who "for 18 long months" had provoked antiunion sentiment among the other African American workers. The use of such agitators caused union men to quit shop floor stewards' committees "simply because they [were] scared" of the consequences they would face from other black workers, who were clearly close with management. The union men, as Custer poetically put it, "were standing between two fires, the company on one side and the non union men on the other."[66] Negotiating a middle path between the two would prove torturous for the CFL.

Workers at Wilson frequently complained of such tactics. Two of the Texans, Joe Hodges and Austin Williams, apparently led most of the anti-union campaign. Joe Hodges told Bedford that he was "a God damn fool for joining that union" and claimed that he worked for the company, not the union, and would not sign an SLC card until company president Thomas Wilson did so.[67] These antiunion agitators increasingly became defined by their race as well as their connection to the company. White union member Walter Gorniak recalled that he was fearful of working with "Barneys"—white immigrant workers' term for black nonunion workers.

Gorniak claimed that a black splitter approached him and asked if he had a union button. When Gorniak responded that it was in his pocket, the black butcher called him "a fool," and claimed "I wouldn't put [a union button] on the end of my prick." Others, he testified, yanked union buttons off of members' shirts, threw them on the floor, and stomped on them. Stories circulated that some of the black workers regularly carried knives and guns to work.[68]

Incidents outside the stockyards further fueled white fears of black violence. During a 1919 strike at the Argo plant, the company hired six hundred African Americans—not only as strikebreakers but as armed guards. That summer, a protest by white workers led to a scuffle in which the black guards shot dead two white strikers. The CFL howled in response, upbraiding "the colored strikebreakers" for "gleefully staging [the] murder of strikers."[69] Such sentiments marked African Americans as traitors to their class and incapable of being trusted with union membership.

Of course, black workers were not drones manipulated by the packers for their own purposes. Standing astride these various conflicting parties and their increasingly contentious arguments, black workers made carefully considered choices regarding their allegiances. Unfortunately for the CFL, many African Americans, as the Chicago Commission on Race Relations found, simply felt that they had "more to gain through affiliation with . . . employers than by taking chances on what the unions [could] offer them."[70] Black workers lacked access to the white ethnic networks that hired so many immigrant workers, making their employment far more dependent on the largesse of high-level managers. As a result, African Americans often believed that employers, not unions, provided them the opportunity to enter Chicago's industries, and pledged their "first loyalty" to employers rather than unions.[71]

The replacement workers are an instructive example. These workers were not only "imported" from other cities or plants; many were plucked directly from the Black Belt. A number of them were hired to take the place of a white employee discharged for union activity, and were fully aware of that fact. Despite the efforts of the union, black workers still suffered from the discrimination of their coworkers, and many viewed strikebreaking as their only opportunity to enter the industry. As a result, they had little compunction about taking white jobs. The *Defender* summed up the attitudes of many black workers by recalling "the changing in hotels and restaurants from colored to white waiters." At first, the exclusion of black workers "seemed a hardship and an injustice." It quickly proved to be "a godsend," however, as it "drove [black] men into higher and better paying positions" in other lines of work. As for the union, the paper concluded simply "the world moves on and owes both black and white a living, providing we work for it."[72]

The same attitude prevailed in the stockyards. In 1918, a group of checkers in the car storers' department at Armour struck for overtime pay and more holidays. The packers moved quickly to entice black workers to take their place. A black foreman, J. M. Morse, was hired to organize a gang. Morse, a graduate of Talladega College, "lost no time and found the suitable men" from among the unemployed of the Black Belt. Despite the fact that his gang did not enjoy the advantage of the typical two-week apprentice period, the men "jumped in and made good" during their time on the payroll. After the strike ended, several were kept on, albeit in other departments. The *Defender* praised the men, lauding the situation as "simply another case where the opportunity came and the men were ready for it."[73] For black workers, the opportunity to gain a steady job at the stockyards was too good to pass up, regardless of the potential cost to the union.

As the issue of race came to define the CFL's campaign, black workers became less likely to identify with the union's class-based appeal. With white and black workers violently clashing at work, and white workers increasingly seeing black workers as allied with bosses, African Americans became defensive and even resentful toward the union. Despite his reputation as an antiunion "agitator," Austin Williams claimed that he had no personal problem with the SLC. "The union is all right," he said, "I have got nothing against the union." Williams's efforts to keep his fellow black workers from signing a union card were not due to a personal objection to unionism, but rather with the way unionism manifested itself among white members. "When [union members] put on a button," Williams argued, "it makes them think they are all of it." The vigor of the SLC's campaign, too, alienated Williams. Union members, he claimed, "try to run over you." In fact, Williams claimed he had decided to sign a union card on several occasions, but each time, he found SLC members "sticking up something on the [bulletin] board to bully you with."[74] Union propaganda claiming that "if you don't get in, we are going to put you out" not only antagonized Williams, it frightened off many black workers who lacked the money to pay dues. Confused by the union signs claiming "if you don't have a button in the morning, no work," many African Americans sought to stay out of trouble by avoiding the union altogether. The SLC, Williams concluded, would have more success "if they would go along easy."[75]

The increasingly racial component of the CFL campaign took its toll on dedicated unionists as well. Dedicated black SLC member Frank Custer argued vociferously that "the men are naturally working in fear . . . and the only way to get out of that fear is to get these agitators out of here." More revealing, however, is Custer's attitude toward race in regard to the union. "Supposing race trouble starts" as a result of the packers' efforts, he said, "I am a colored man, and love my family tree, and I ain't going to stand for no white man to come imposing on my color." Custer left no doubt as to where his loyalties lay. "If he is imposing on my race," Custer argued, "there is going to be a fight." Such racial pride transcended his loyalty to the SLC. "I don't care if the colored man wears a button or not," he said, "he has that love in his heart for one another."[76]

Though Custer remained a steadfast union man, other black workers shared his resentment at the increasing distinction between union membership and racial pride, and turned from the SLC as a result. For black Chicagoans, class organizing was insufficient; many African Americans felt that the path toward liberation lay not with class-based organizations such as unions, but with racial organizations of their own making. Indeed, the shared experiences of work and class that reinforced existing ethnic ties in Packingtown were replicated as racial unity within the Black Belt. A rejection of unionism was thus not a rejection of economically progressive principles, but a conscious choice to embrace race-conscious organizing, even at the expense of their involvement in unionism.

Indeed, many black Chicagoans, even those sympathetic to or even favorable to union organizing as a general principle, felt that the CFL did not serve their needs. The Chicago Commission on Race Relations noted that by the end of World War I, "a growing race solidarity" was evinced by the city's black residents. As Chicago Urban League president Robert E. Park wrote, "Race prejudice, in so far as it has compelled him to think always and everywhere in racial terms, has given the Negro a cause, and created a solidarity and a unity of purpose which might not otherwise exist."[77] Black workers participated extensively in campaigns to patronize only black businesses and joined neighborhood organizations that protected their interests and reaffirmed bonds of racial solidarity. The CFL's appeal was based solely on its intent to fight for black workers as vigorously as it did for white workers. For black workers— resentful of organized labor's troubled racial history, embittered by the continued bigotry of white coworkers, and energized by a growing racial consciousness—such promises fell flat. The weakened position of the neighborhood locals and their tendency to reinforce existing patterns of segregation made them unable to demonstrate that they were truly interracial institutions. Despite their stated goals of interracial solidarity, CFL unions were largely seen as white organizations.

Some black workers flocked to alternative, race-based unionism instead. One shadowy example of this phenomenon was organized by the mysterious Richard Parker, also known as R. E. Parker, owner of the so-called Race Publishing Company and editor of the black newspaper the *Chicago Advocate*. Despite his notoriety, no copies of the *Advocate* exist today, and specific historical details regarding Parker's life are maddeningly scarce. Parker was a frequent topic of conversation among union leaders, however, for his persistent and well-organized opposition to the CFL and its campaigns, particularly in the stockyards. Parker described himself as "the man who was always with his race, right or wrong." Frequently, that statement entailed a public opposition to unionization. A black worker familiar with Parker and his methods told the CCRR that Parker made an appeal "to Negroes . . . that white unions would not admit them on an equal basis and that white employers preferred Negro non-unionists to white unionists and would . . . [afford them] better treatment." Meanwhile, Parker went to white employers and "represented the Negroes as being opposed to . . . white men's unions."[78] In 1916, Parker distributed an estimated twenty thousand pamphlets throughout Packingtown and the Black Belt urging black workers to shun the CFL and instead join his American Unity Labor Union (AULU).[79]

Parker was frequently derided by unionists as a tool of the packers, and the charge was difficult to refute. Parker claimed to have worked as a labor agent for the packers, and boasted that he had brought more black southerners to Chicago than any other man from the city. In testimony before the President's Mediation Commission, bosses from several packing concerns claimed that they did not specifically remember employing Parker, though several recalled inquiring among the black community as to "who could handle" the black migrant workers. It is likely that Parker worked for at least one packing company as a labor agent, and that the bosses claimed not to remember him in an effort to avoid controversy with the union.[80] In any event, Parker had a well-deserved reputation for providing black workers to the packers by the time he founded the AULU.

Parker's AULU served as a de facto company union for the packers
and a fertile recruiting ground for antiunion black activists. Where SLC
organizers were frequently tossed from the stockyards, AULU recruiters
were stationed next to the timekeeper's office and encouraged to speak
with black workers as they punched in and out. Parker also pledged complete cooperation with the packers. AULU advertisements boasted, "this
Union does not believe in strikes." Instead, Parker argued, "We believe
all differences between laborers and capitalists can be arbitrated." Parker
even pledged to supply black strikebreakers to the packers in the case of
an SLC strike. For the AULU, the strike weapon was "our last motive
if any at all." Instead, membership in Parker's organization simply got
black workers "in line for a good job."[81] Ironically, the "good jobs" Parker
promised came at a steep cost to his members. Parker pledged that in
return for steady employment and loyalty to the company, the AULU's
skilled members would work for 15 percent less than the regular skilled
rate, while unskilled members would work at a 10 percent discount from
the common laborer rate. Black workers also faced the same intimidation
from Parker that they did from the dreaded union bulletin board. Though
the AULU did not regularly collect dues, Parker—with the approval of
management—told recruits that they risked forfeiting their employment
if they did not join.[82]

Despite his shadowy allegiances, Parker made several astute critiques
of the SLC. Through numerous advertisements in local newspapers,
Parker urged black workers to join "a union of your own race with officers of your own race," a union that would allow black workers to "get a
square deal with [their] own race." Parker promised that membership in
the AULU entitled workers to "a card to work at any trade or a common
laborer, as a steam fitter, electrician, fireman, merchants, engineers, carpenters, butchers, helpers, and chauffeurs . . . for Armour's and Swift's,
or other Packers." These cards, he claimed, were redeemable "in Kansas
City, Omaha and St. Louis, or any other city where the [Big Five] Packers
have packing houses."[83] Such rhetoric was a clear shot at the SLC and the
controversy over the redemption of union cards by black SLC members
in other AMCBW shops. When a black CFL delegate attended an AULU
meeting and presented a proposal that would have affiliated Parker's organization with the CFL, he was "hooted from the platform."[84] Parker's
racial rhetoric made a case for black organizing at the expense of the CFL.

Though Parker was seen by some black community leaders as a "public
nuisance" and a "soldier of fortune," his rhetoric did inspire action by

many working-class African Americans.[85] At one point, Parker led a group of unemployed African Americans to City Hall, where they demanded to see Mayor William Thompson. When they were told Thompson was out of the office, Parker responded, "Well, it's funny we can't find him," since "he can always find us . . . when he wants us to vote for his bond issues." Parker raged on, arguing that when Thompson needed black votes, "he promised jobs for all colored men." Now that the bill had come due, he was nowhere to be found. When Parker raised his voice, the chief of police ordered the men out, calling Parker a labor agent and claiming that his "army of the unemployed" were recent migrants from Louisiana. Parker claimed that the men "are from Chicago enough to vote for the mayor . . . why aren't we enough to get jobs?"[86]

The AULU also vigorously protested white racism in any form. When whites responded to the expansion of the Black Belt by bombing black homes, Parker held street-corner meetings demanding that Mayor Thompson apprehend the bombers, and assembled a "flying squadron" of cars to patrol black neighborhoods.[87] Parker also held a meeting to protest the establishment of a Ku Klux Klan chapter in the Chicago area. Parker exclaimed that if the Klansmen were to open a chapter in the city, they should do so in the heavily black Second Ward, where he said a "warm party" awaited them. If the mayor and governor would not "unmask every member of this order and drive them from Chicago," Parker said, "send 'em down to the Second ward and we will."[88] Such racial appeals, combined with Parker's alliance with the packers, allowed him to publicly undermine the power of the CFL.

Without any organizational records, it is impossible to estimate the strength of the AULU. Historians estimate the actual membership of the organization at no more than two hundred, with perhaps a few hundred more occasionally attending meetings.[89] But the reaction of Chicago's unionists to Parker's efforts is revealing. Parker's work recruiting laborers for the packers, combined with his antiunion campaign as head of the AULU, made him a feared enemy of the CFL. During a meeting, a CFL delegate colorfully referred to Parker as a "scab herder," and claimed that he was in charge of an effort "to create race riots and . . . to force conflicts between the races in the event of a strike." Such discord would furnish the packers with "an excuse to call in the militia to aid them in breaking the spirit of the packing house employees."[90] Singling out the Wabash Avenue YMCA and the Wilson Club, Johnstone called Parker "the organizer of all the troubles, practically speaking, between the white and black men in the stock yards."[91] Whatever numbers Parker was actually able to muster, he and the AULU stand as stark symbols of black workers' turn away from the CFL's class-based appeal and toward a politics of race.

But perhaps no phenomenon better typifies black workers' turn away from unionism and toward racial solidarity than the failure of the Labor Party. Despite its legitimately progressive platform, the party ultimately failed in its attempt to recruit black Chicagoans. The party's rhetoric and activity were centered on labor issues, and were unable to sever black workers' ties to the Republican Party, which directly served their interests. The failure of the Labor Party to recruit black workers typifies the CFL's inability to translate its message of interracial unity into a workable plan of action.

To be sure, there was some support for the party among segments of Chicago's black leadership. The party's stated (indeed, constitutional) dedication to interracial cooperation and an eradication of racism in all forms was appealing to many African Americans. Many of the Labor Party's central issues, such as public ownership of utilities, were also shared by the black community. A guest editorial in the *Defender* claimed that "we as a race have been used long enough as a political issue," and claimed that the only way for black workers to gain "every right . . . politically, civically and economically" was through an alliance with the Labor Party.[92] The *Broad Ax* claimed that "Colored citizens of Chicago will have nothing to fear at the hands of . . . John Fitzpatrick, the labor candidate for mayor." The Labor Party, the paper argued, has "[n]ever assumed a hostile attitude against the best interest[s] of the Colored people of this city," and argued that black Chicagoans must "not permit themselves to become the abject political slaves of any political party" and "should cast some of their votes" for Fitzpatrick.[93] Fears of African Americans as "enslaved" to the city's Republican political machine were common in the *Broad Ax*, which was an outspoken critic of Thompson. Although the paper acknowledged Thompson was "very popular" and even "idolized" by "poor, ignorant, misguided colored people," it criticized him for his failure to protect black citizens from house bombings.[94]

Unfortunately for the CFL, the Labor Party was unable to take advantage of the anti-Thompson insurgency. The party's avowed antiracism did not match its actions. Like the CFL, the Labor Party's feelings on race rested on the assumption that the city had "no Negro problem," only a class problem that happened to involve black workers.[95] Such a political approach had little appeal for black workers. Unlike the CFL, the Labor

Party made little effort to actively recruit black Chicagoans. Besides the inclusion of black AFL organizer John Riley on the Cook County party's executive committee, and the running of black cooper's union official William Robert Wilson on the party ticket for alderman, one would be hard pressed to find many concrete attempts to organize black voters. Racial equality was a part of the party's platform, but racial issues were never at the center of its rhetoric. The Labor Party had essentially staked its success on the success of the CFL: workers who were active in the union tended to be active in the party. With black workers displaying ambivalence regarding the SLC campaign, the Labor Party was never able to develop a cadre of black activists, nor could it articulate a platform that could appeal to black voters. This failure was blamed not on the structure of the party, nor on the unique discrimination faced by black workers at the hands of employers, coworkers, and city officials, but rather on the naiveté of black workers themselves, who were deceived by employers and "misleaders" in the black middle class.[96]

In reality, of course, black workers made considered choices regarding their vote. Much as they rejected the CFL in favor of race-based organizations, African Americans rejected the Labor Party's limp nods toward racial justice in favor of the Republican Party, which actively served the interests of the race. By the end of the 1920s, the city's black workers made up 4.4 percent of the plumbers, 5.7 percent of the teamsters, 8.2 percent of the elevator operators, and 27 percent of the janitors employed by the city—a testament to the power of black workers' alliance with Thompson and other Republicans.[97] As a result, black community leaders praised Thompson as "a straightforward, honest man with but one purpose, and that is giving everybody a square deal."[98] Despite being white, Thompson's cultivation of relationships with community leaders like Ida B. Wells-Barnett marked him as a "race man" who would provide for the needs of African Americans in particular. The *Defender* noted approvingly that Thompson was "unalterably opposed to segregation of the school children in the public schools." His opponents, on the other hand, were "unfit to be classed as law-abiding citizens."[99] Such rhetoric reflected the degree to which Thompson appealed to black voters in ways the Labor Party could not. Black workers backed such feelings with their votes. In each of the four primary elections of Thompson's reign as mayor, he received at least 80 percent of the votes in the heavily black Second Ward. In mayoral elections, Republican candidates regularly received more than 70 percent of the total vote in the Second Ward. These votes were often decisive, including in the 1919 election that featured the candidacy of John Fitzpatrick.[100]

The Labor Party's class-based appeal to African American voters left them unmoved, allowing Chicago's Republican machine to continue its longstanding alliance with black voters. Despite the party's efforts to promote a message of racial tolerance and cooperation, it was unable to make any significant inroads into the black community. As a class-based organization, the Labor Party quite simply had little to offer Chicago's African American population. Significantly, black Chicagoans did vote in significant numbers—but overwhelmingly for Republican candidates, who offered them immediate and tangible gains through government jobs and desegregation. The Labor Party's lack of attention to racial issues further reveals the limits of the CFL's appeal to black Chicagoans.

The discrimination of white union workers, the paternalism of packing bosses, the opposition of black community leaders to unionism, and the violence that resulted all combined to reduce the effectiveness of the CFL campaign. The specter of the black strikebreaker was very real—not because African Americans were degenerate, or immoral, or a "scab race." Rather, the specter was real because a broad array of factors conspired to make strikebreaking "thinkable" to black workers, to borrow James Grossman's term. Though strikebreaking was, for white unionists, "unambiguously . . . evil," black workers were forced to confront racial as well as class oppression. As a result, strikebreaking and all its trappings—alliances with employers, participation in paternalistic worker welfare programs, an open rejection of unionism—were acceptable costs of securing employment. What white unionists did not understand was that for African American workers, "strikebreaking had to be considered seriously—even if rejected."[101]

The CFL's attempt to organize black and white stockyards workers, particularly its belief that such organizing would eradicate racial tensions, was complicated by the racial attitudes of white workers. Such attitudes represented a tangled bundle of fears and suspicions. The very presence of African Americans in the city was cause enough for many workers to view them as a "scourge" and a danger to Chicago itself. In the context of work, black laborers were considered both the helpless tools of, and the conniving allies of, capital. The spread of antiunion propaganda among the black community, and its propagation by black leaders, only deepened these feelings. As employers hired more and more nonunion black workers, such feelings became enflamed into violence. Not only did white workers attempt to expel black strikebreakers, they also resented acts of racial violence, such as the East St. Louis riot of 1917, as evidence that black workers were both non- or antiunion and dangerous to the existence of white unionism.

Though such feelings were rooted in perceptions and significations, CFL leaders' attitude toward the amelioration of racism was purely material—they felt that unionism was a prime solution for racial discord between workers. As a result, they failed to understand that black workers were reluctant to join organizations that so often vilified them; white workers interpreted such behavior as an expression of class, rather than race, consciousness, and blamed African Americans for their reticence, creating a destructive loop of discrimination and racial enmity. In short, white unionists perceived black workers both as intellectually infantile and as deviously shrewd, and resented them, paradoxically, for both. As black workers were pushed further from the union, many rejected unionism entirely and turned instead to racial organizations; such feelings account for the failure of the Labor Party to appeal to African Americans. The CFL's ability to organize an interracial union had encountered a series of devastating setbacks. In the summer of 1919, the federation would experience a brutal blow that would shatter Fitzpatrick's vision of progressive unionism.

5.

"PATIENCE IS NO LONGER A VIRTUE": THE CFL AND THE CHICAGO RACE RIOT OF 1919

————————

Though Chicago had withstood outbreaks of racial violence in the early twentieth century, nothing could have prepared the city for the brutality of the race riot of 1919. For seven days, black and white Chicagoans engaged in full-scale warfare, leaving thirty-eight dead, more than five hundred injured, and more than one thousand homeless.[1] During the riot, the CFL attempted to restrain its members from participating in violence. In this effort, it was successful: few union members took part in the riot's brutality. But the riot sapped much of the CFL's strength and all but ended its organizing drive. Several factors—including the sheer chaos of the riot itself, the costs of supporting members aggrieved by the violence, and the difficulty of reconstructing the workplace in its aftermath—can account for this defeat. Most significant, however, were the CFL's actions in the wake of the riot, particularly its attempts to control the reopening of the stockyards. Though a number of historians have examined the riot's effect on labor organizing in the city, the CFL's abortive protest against the deployment of militia in the yards has seen comparatively little scholarly attention. In reality, this final chapter of the riot was enormously consequential. The CFL's actions alienated black workers and exposed the union's vulnerability to employer predation. Additionally, white workers grew more resentful of black nonunion workers, while the black community grew increasingly convinced that racial unity—and not class solidarity—could best serve their interests. Workplace conflicts grew increasingly bitter as the gulf between Chicago's white and black workers widened into a chasm.

The explosion of Chicago's black population due to the Great Migration, the expansion of black residential areas into traditionally white neighborhoods, and the emergence of militant racial activism on the part of black residents all contributed heavily to the hatreds that exploded into violence in July 1919. In the span of a decade, Chicago's black population more than doubled, from 44,130 in 1910 to nearly 110,000 in 1920.

————————

Those numbers were augmented by the return of 50,000 black troops to the Chicago area after the Armistice in 1918—10,000 to the city alone. Though this flood of inexpensive labor helped fuel the economic growth of the city, it also strained resources and amplified tensions long extant in the areas of housing, politics, and labor.[2]

Because black Chicagoans were segregated in the city's Black Belt, housing options were limited, and the swell of black migration caused rents in the area to skyrocket. Faced with little alternative, black Chicagoans expanded their traditional residential area, spreading east and west into working-class Jewish and Irish neighborhoods, respectively, where rents were even more exorbitant.[3] Unscrupulous realtors engaged in "blockbusting"—selling a small number of homes in all-white neighborhoods to black families at enormous markups, then purchasing the homes of fleeing white families at a discount and flipping them to other black families, again at well over market price. This influx of black homeowners into white neighborhoods made interracial contact, which was relatively rare before World War I, inevitable.[4]

So-called "homeowner's associations" began to appear in newly diverse neighborhoods. Though ostensibly geared toward protecting their communities from "undesirables of whatever brand or color," such groups were thinly disguised white-supremacist organizations formed for the express purpose of cleansing their neighborhoods of African Americans.[5] Among the most vocal and vituperative of these groups was the Hyde Park–Kenwood Property Owners' Association on the city's South Side. Playing on traditional white fears, the group decried the possibility of "sex equality," an objective they claimed was "a universal ambition of the Negro race."[6] Another pamphlet, entitled "An Appeal of White Women to American Womanhood," reprinted a letter (of dubious veracity) from German women complaining of "the bestial ferocious conduct" of black troops during World War I.[7] The prospect of German citizens—who had been pilloried as brutish "Huns" in American newspapers during the war mere months before—being presented as innocent victims may seem incongruous. But in the face of an "invasion" of black homeowners, whiteness became a greater unifying factor than nationality. The group united under the slogans "Our neighborhood must continue white," "Stay out of Hyde Park," and "We base our rights on priority, majority and anthropological superiority," and repeatedly lobbied for the city to pass segregation ordinances.[8]

These attacks came amid an awakening of black protest in the city. As contemporary observers St. Clair Drake and Horace Cayton argued in their classic *Black Metropolis,* black migrants possessed a strong desire to advance economically; indeed, the promise of a better life was precisely the reason most had fled the South for Chicago in the first place. "Most Negroes," they claimed, "visualized the [Great Migration] as a step toward... economic emancipation."[9] The experience of World War I—both in the rhetoric of liberty on the home front and in the pride of black troops who served overseas—also raised new questions about the oppression African Americans faced within their own country. Black leaders and black publications exhorted African Americans to express their loyalty through military service, the purchasing of Liberty Bonds, and productivity in the nation's factories. But they also argued that in return, African Americans must be allowed to participate fully in the nation's social, political, and economic life. Black troops in particular felt the flush of resistance, feeling that they had earned a seat at the table of democracy.[10] Black Chicagoans were also increasingly active in local politics. Thanks to their fealty to mayor William Thompson, black Chicagoans saw some small measure of patronage from city hall, inducing them to vote for him in a bloc; the African American vote was particularly crucial in securing a hard-fought victory for Thompson in the 1919 election.[11] In return for largesse from the Thompson administration, the black community largely overlooked the administration's well-earned reputation for corruption.[12]

White Chicagoans ferociously resented African Americans' attempts to participate in the life of the city. Black agitation for equality was often (falsely) linked to hysterical fears of radicalism and foreign influence.[13] In an editorial in the *Chicago Defender,* former president William Howard Taft argued that "Negro leaders must certainly see that however great the injustice done to their Race through blind prejudice, 'direct action' is the worst possible remedy," claiming that "in the end the feeling out of which this evil has come will be increased."[14] Even the simple act of African Americans voting in their own interest infuriated whites, who sneered at the black community's habit of casting a "solid" vote "for the candidate who makes the best bargain with them."[15] With black and white Chicagoans having staked their positions, tensions increased throughout the summer of 1919.

That atmosphere soon became quite literally explosive. Between July 1, 1919, and March 1, 1921, fifty-eight bombs exploded in the homes of black residents; more than a dozen of these bombings took place in July 1919, in the weeks leading up to the riot. As if to leave no doubt as to their message, the bombers also targeted the homes and offices of realtors who sold housing to black families. The bombings killed two people, injured countless others, and damaged an estimated $100,000 worth of property. Despite the wanton brutality of these acts of terror, only two people were arrested. Neither was convicted.[16]

Awkwardly straddling this racial battlefield was the CFL. Having pledged its dedication to the principle of interracial cooperation, the federation spent much of the summer furiously attempting to prevent an explosion of violence. The Stockyards Labor Council took great pains to reinforce its message that class solidarity could supersede racial enmity—that black workers could find a safe haven within the CFL, where they would be "just another member." As violence against black citizens mounted, black and white SLC organizers held street-corner meetings in black neighborhoods, preaching the union's gospel of equality and solidarity. The council also consummated its own pledge to remain colorblind, passing resolutions reaffirming its commitment to the organization of black and white workers and expelling affiliated local unions that refused to accept African Americans on equal terms.[17] However, the machinations of employers combined with workers' own racial fears and resentments to prevent the CFL from maintaining racial peace. The CFL's celebrated parade of July 1919, discussed in chapter 2, serves as an instructive example. The event was successful in that it attracted a "checkerboard" interracial crowd of some thirty thousand white and black workers. At the same time, however, it revealed the fragility of the union's interracial alliance.[18] The event was originally planned as a mass interracial march, but meatpacking bosses concocted a story that African Americans were arming themselves and planning a massacre of whites during the parade. The police revoked the union's parade permit and forced white and black workers to march to the meeting site separately, humiliating the CFL and publicly undermining its message of solidarity.[19]

More telling was the CFL's furious response, which revealed deep schisms between the white leaders of the federation and the middle-class black leadership that they increasingly viewed as an enemy. Though the union's leadership blamed packing bosses for stonewalling the union's progress, they also turned their wrath against the black community. In a withering screed published in its official newspaper, the CFL excoriated the "negro politicians and negro preachers" who they claimed were "subsidized" by the packers and complicit in the creation of antiunion sentiment. The union claimed that the packers had paid off two black aldermen and purchased three hundred memberships in the Wabash

Avenue YMCA "and gave them to their [black employees] in order that they might go to the 'Y' and absorb the 'anti' union propaganda."[20]

Such feelings were manifest on the shop floor as well as in the union hall. As American industry demobilized following the end of World War I, a number of workers found themselves facing lower wages or outright unemployment. An estimated fifteen thousand employees were laid off from the city's meatpacking industry in spring of 1919. The insult of the mass layoffs was augmented by employers' decision to retain a high percentage of the nonunion labor, particularly nonunion black labor, hired during the wartime boom. Throughout 1919, the CFL repeatedly rebuked the packers for continuing to "import" black laborers from the South, keeping them "enslaved at low wages," and using them "to undermine union conditions."[21] Deploying the language of slavery reflected the union's divided feelings on black labor. On the one hand, it evinced a true rage at the avarice and brutality of packinghouse owners; on the other hand, it tied nonunion black workers to a whole host of white attitudes regarding enslaved people: namely, that they were simple-minded, uneducated, helpless, and in need of emancipation from a crusading army of whites.

Exacerbating these tensions were the packing bosses, who constantly reminded white workers of the ease with which they could be replaced. In June 1919, a group of hair spinners at the Wilson plant—members of a white-only union—walked off the job and were almost immediately replaced by nonunion African Americans.[22] The relatively small size of the stockyards' black workforce had mitigated the possibility of racial conflict in the prewar era, with the obvious exception of strikebreaking situations. With massive numbers of workers, both white and black, entering the yards during World War I, many white workers encountered African Americans in large numbers for the first time. The hatreds and resentments built in white communities were carried into the workplace.[23] Those hatreds and resentments fueled a series of workplace conflicts throughout the summer of 1919. Eight days before the riot, ten thousand stockyards workers walked off the job to protest the presence of black nonunion labor. In advising the men to return to work, SLC secretary J. W. Johnstone attempted to assuage the racial enmity that pervaded the yards and pleaded "for cool headedness and unity among the workers, white and black." The smaller walkouts that helped precipitate the July strike were nearly always occasioned by anger at black workers.[24]

These relatively minor conflicts reflected a growing crisis within the CFL's membership. At its peak, in 1917, the union claimed more than six thousand black members; by summer 1919 that number had fallen to less than two thousand.[25] The problem was simple: white workers still perceived their African American coworkers as members of a "scab race," while black workers took such perceptions as evidence of the unions' lack of true racial progressiveness.[26] The situation quickly descended into a tragic feedback loop: black workers left the union due to its de facto segregation and the racist attitudes of its members, which caused white unionists to deride black workers as class traitors, which only drove them further away. The CFL's inability to maintain a sizable black cadre had dramatic effects on shop-floor relations between the races. White workers grew more aggressive in their organizing tactics and decried as "agitators" anyone who refused to join, claiming that they were hired and retained merely to "raise a line of prejudice" against the union. Black workers, unsurprisingly, grew more resentful of union members and their insults. When white SLC member Gus Grabe attempted to get a black coworker to sign a union card, for example, the man responded, "You son-of-a-bitch, I will cut your God damn head off, if you say another word to me." When Grabe attempted to explain the various benefits the union had secured, the nonunion worker derisively dismissed him, claiming (not incorrectly) that such benefits had little to do with the union and more to do with the efforts of Judge Alschuler and the federal government.[27]

The mutual mistrust of white unionists and black nonunion workers quickly descended into violence.[28] One white employee recalled his horror at a group of black men who were discussing arming themselves for protection—"talking about guns and stuff." White and black employees "were afraid to work when they had their backs toward [each other], for fear of getting a knife jabbed into them."[29] Basic tasks became fraught with peril. One worker claimed that he and fellow union members were afraid of doing their job breaking cattle legs, since "non union men are working when our backs are turned to the gang . . . and we don't know when we are going to get it from the rear."[30] In one particularly gruesome case, a black nonunion man baited a white union organizer into a fight, then bashed him over the head with an iron pipe, knocking him unconscious. Despite the protestations of the union men in the work gang, the company refused to fire the offender, and he ultimately paid a fine of fifteen dollars. The union gang subsequently walked off the job, deriding "the attitude of the non-union men."[31] White workers increasingly viewed nonunion black workers as a dire economic, social, and even physical threat. For black workers, the union provided few benefits, and its members spent more time intimidating than organizing. As a result, workers of both races spent the weeks leading up to the riot in a state of violent agitation.

The explosion of Chicago's black population, the spread of African Americans into traditionally white neighborhoods, and fear of a rising racial consciousness among African Americans all contributed directly to the rise of racial violence. Chicago's workers were also implicated in the racial anger that would explode into violence in late July. The efforts of bosses to both reduce and browbeat their workforce, the anger of union leadership at employer obstinacy, and workplace conflicts between rank-and-file whites and black workers combined to create a toxic workplace atmosphere by July 1919. Despite its claims to peace and interracial co-operation, the CFL would need to muster all of its power to restrain its members during the orgy of violence to follow.

The Land of Lincoln was no stranger to racial violence. In fact, by the time the 1919 riot swept across Chicago, Illinois was already home to two of the most notorious race riots in American history. In August 1908, a mob of whites was thwarted in their attempt to lynch a pair of black men jailed for rape and murder in the state capitol of Springfield. In response, the mob turned its rage against the city's black community, burning most of the city's black neighborhood and lynching two black citizens.[32] Tensions over labor led to the bloody race riot that swept East St. Louis in July 1917, where white mobs roamed the streets for two days, brutally murdering black men and women with guns, clubs, stones, and knives. The death toll is not known, but is widely considered to be no less than forty and possibly more than two hundred. The riot's violence was so horrific that W. E. B. Du Bois led ten thousand people in a silent protest march through Manhattan.[33] Both the Springfield and East St. Louis riots were, in essence, mass lynchings. Whites in each city reacted violently to the swelling of the black population and the resulting conflicts over jobs, public space, and racial order.[34] In both cases, the black populace was terrorized by marauding bands of whites who sought either to expel them from the city or kill them outright, and in both cases the black population—despite sporadic attempts at self-defense—was largely powerless.

By contrast, Chicago's race riot was unique in both its scale and its character. The Chicago riot was not a mass lynching or a massacre, but a race war—a series of pitched battles between white and black Chicagoans for control of their city.[35] As a coroner's investigator would later state, members of both races were "leaders and aggressors" in the Chicago race riot. The evidence for this theory was clear: by the time the Illinois militia put down the riot, 38 people (23 black and 15 white) had been killed, 537 injured (342 black and 205 white), and more than 1,000 left homeless, making it easily the most severe of the estimated 25 racial conflicts of the so-called "Red Summer" of 1919. Even more revealing, out of the riot's 38 victims, none were women or girls; of the 537 injured, only 10 were female. Moreover, unlike the gruesome spectacles in Springfield and East St. Louis, the Chicago riot "was marked by no hangings or burnings" of black citizens. Both facts point to the Chicago riot as more of a war between armed groups of men than a massacre of defenseless civilians.[36]

The unique character of the riot made it a particular challenge to the city's labor movement. Though the CFL would succeed in restraining its members from participating in the worst of the violence, the riot's warlike character cast black and white Chicagoans in a position of mutual distrust. Unlike the riots at Springfield and East St. Louis, which served to reinforce existing structures of racial hegemony, the race war in Chicago opened entirely new gaps between white and black citizens. For those who could not avoid racial contact—workers in the stockyards, for instance—the riot was a period of almost unbearable tension, as members of both races feared for their lives. Its aftermath would leave Chicago's workers and unions struggling to keep solidarity alive amid an atmosphere of fear, resentment, and lingering violence, and would set the CFL's organizing drive on a path toward decline.

Black and white Chicagoans had been contesting the occupancy of public spaces for months, so it was grimly appropriate that the riot began at a beach on the city's South Side. Around four o'clock in the afternoon on July 27, a group of black beachgoers walked through the white section of the Twenty-Ninth Street beach and waded into the water. A confrontation ensued, with white and black bathers throwing rocks at one another. Meanwhile, a seventeen-year-old African American boy named Eugene Williams was swimming in the water and drifted past the "imaginary boundary" into the white section of the water. A group of whites hurled rocks at him. Within minutes, Williams went under and drowned.[37] An angry crowd of white and black beachgoers was quickly dispersed by police, but the die was cast. A mere two hours later, with rumors regarding Williams's death sweeping the Black Belt, an angry crowd of black citizens gathered at Twenty-Ninth Street. When police tried to break up the group, an infuriated black citizen named James Crawford fired a pistol at them. The police returned fire, killing him instantly. The Chicago race riot had begun.[38]

Almost immediately after the death of James Crawford, the city's Black Belt became the site of furious violence. Throughout the night of July 27, from nine o'clock until the early predawn hours, twenty-seven black residents were beaten, seven were stabbed, and four were shot.[39] The violence escalated on Monday, as white rioters used wagons to block the city's thoroughfares and then pulled black trolley riders into the streets and beat them. Any African Americans who dared pass through traditionally white districts did so at their peril; several were killed as they walked to work.[40]

By Tuesday, the riot had descended into race warfare, with white and black Chicagoans launching violent offensives against one another. Whites loaded themselves into so-called "death cars" and careened through the Black Belt, firing indiscriminately into houses and storefronts. White rioters also struck at African American workplaces. In retaliation for the death of a white rioter, a white mob stormed the Palmer House hotel and the downtown post office, both of which employed a large number of African Americans.[41] Thousands of African Americans fled the Black Belt. Some traveled to Milwaukee or other cities, while others slept in local police stations—refugees in their own city.[42]

Black self-defense became a defining feature of the Chicago riot. Black citizens defended themselves by constructing barricades and sniping back at the cars. Black mobs also took the offensive against whites. A pair of whites who worked in the Black Belt were set upon and murdered on their way home from work.[43] Befitting a people whose very homes were under attack, black self-defense often took on a community character. In addition to creating barricades and sniping posts, black undertakers refused to accept the bodies of white riot victims. Following a skirmish, a group of black men followed an ambulance carrying wounded whites to black-owned and -operated Provident Hospital and had to be restrained by police lest they break down the doors and kill the whites being treated inside. The residents of the Black Belt barricaded their streets, stopping all traffic south of North Avenue and east of Wentworth Avenue.[44]

The descent of the riot into race warfare placed the CFL in an agonizing position. From the beginning of the riot, union leaders recognized the dire threat that racial violence represented. The warfare that swept Chicago, conducted primarily between blue-collar workers, threatened to destroy the interracial organization the CFL had spent two years constructing. As a result, federation leaders raced to restrain their white members from participating in the violence and took great pains to remind black

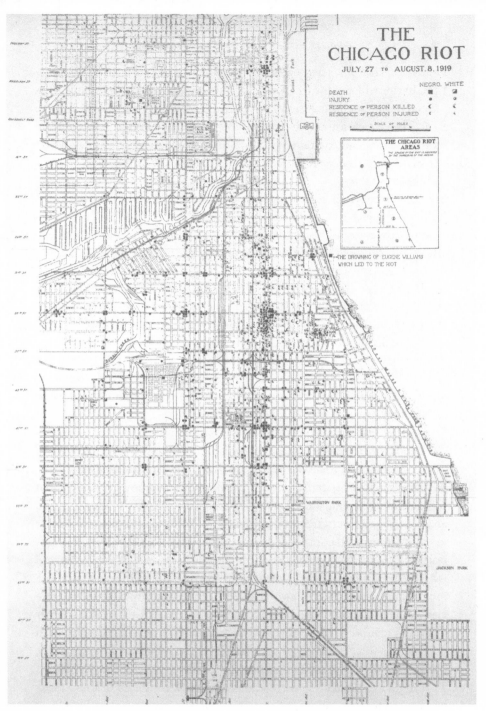

The Chicago Riot. This map, from a report on the race riot by the Chicago Commission on Race Relations, shows the location of deaths and injuries, as well as the residences of those killed or injured. The stockyards are at the center of the map; the worst of the riot's violence occurred nearby, in the Black Belt, and on thoroughfares leading to and from the stockyards. Chicago History Museum, ICHi-173838.

workers of the CFL's dedication to nonviolence and interracial cooperation. In the midst of the riot, the CFL published a lengthy broadside in its
official newspaper, the *New Majority*. Entitled "For White Union Men to
Read," the article argued that white workers had a duty not only to refrain
from violence, but to prevent it. That obligation fell most heavily "upon
the white men and women of organized labor," the editorial explained,
"not because they had anything to do with starting the present trouble,
but because of their advantageous position to help end it."[45] Seeking to
hold its tenuous coalition together, the SLC sent organizers into both
Packingtown and the Black Belt to restore trust and harmony between
white and black workers. Out of these meetings grew a confidence that the
union's message was being received. It was reported that white workers,
repulsed by the riot's violence, "expressed sympathy in many ways with
their Negro fellow-workers."[46] The union also managed to maintain unity
through financial aid. Adroitly recognizing that packing bosses might use
the riot to divide workers, the CFL offered a safe haven at its headquarters,
where workers—white and black—could receive a hot meal. The union's
soup kitchen not only brought in new streams of unorganized workers, it
also kept the men "out of the packers' bread line," where bosses peddled
antiunion propaganda to captive audiences.[47]

These efforts were largely successful: for the most part, SLC members
refrained from the riot's brutality.[48] Beyond the union's push for unity and
peace, geography provided the simplest explanation for union members'
lack of participation in the rioting. The SLC had an immense contingent
of Polish, Lithuanian, and Slovak workers, nearly all of whom lived south
and west of the stockyards in the Back of the Yards neighborhood—areas
in which interracial contact was rare. On the other hand, the Irish neighborhoods of Bridgeport and Canaryville, which lay east of the yards (and
which African Americans were forced to cross to get to work) saw the
most brutal violence of the riot. Indeed, while roughly one-third of the
clashes recorded by the CCRR occurred in the Black Belt itself, a greater
number (around 41 percent) took place along thoroughfares in the Irish
neighborhoods.[49] Blue-collar gangs, such as the infamous Ragen's Colts,
cheered by "vocal bystanders," initiated or escalated much of the violence.[50]
The frequent contact between whites and black residents of these areas
had caused tension before the riot; now, they became racial battlefields.

Indeed, black workers traveling to and from work were among the most
vulnerable. On Monday, July 28, a black stockyards worker named Henry
Goodman departed the yards and boarded a streetcar, which was stopped

by a white barricade. A mob surrounded the car, ordered its black passengers to disembark, and beat Goodman to death with bricks and stones. On the morning of Thursday, July 31, black butcher William Dozier was walking to work when a white mob began to chase him. Dozier fled into the yards, but the crowd overtook him, pelting him with stones and beating him with sticks and shovels. Bloodied, Dozier lay on the ground as a man named Joseph Carka split open his skull with a hammer. Another mob cornered a group of black stockyards workers as they left work; their lives were saved only when militia beat back the crowd.[51] The *Tribune* reported that stockyards police engaged in at least two "desperate revolver battles" with black men who were alleged to have killed a pair of white women and a white child.[52] Despite the absence of union members in the worst of the bloodshed, such acts of brutality near the stockyards inextricably linked work and violence—a grim harbinger for the CFL's efforts to create a racially harmonious atmosphere at the workplace.

By midweek, the riot had quieted significantly, thanks to the arrival of state militia on Wednesday, July 30, and a downpour the following day that broke the miserable heat that had characterized much of the week. Though the riot would not officially end until Sunday, August 3, governor Frank Lowden felt confident in declaring the situation to be "well in hand" by the morning of July 31.[53] There was only one serious incident after the arrival of the militia: on Saturday, August 2, a massive fire swept through a Lithuanian neighborhood west of the stockyards, destroying forty-nine buildings, causing a quarter-million dollars in damage, and leaving more than nine hundred people—the vast majority of them stockyards workers and their families—homeless. Whites immediately blamed African Americans for the fire, although it was speculated that white arsonists wearing blackface were responsible. In any event, the conflagration "enflamed the immigrant community against the Negroes and focused the racial conflict, hitherto generalized, in the stockyards," according to the CCRR.[54] The violence that overtook the stockyards district had now spread into a white community, augmenting feelings of racial resentment and threatening to explode into violence at the workplace. The CFL, fearful of a resumption of the riot, would have to work even harder to restore a sense of interracial unity to the yards.

The sheer brutality of the riot deepened divisions between white and black workers. Given the location of the violence in the stockyards district, the CFL's campaign—already beset by internal tensions and external predation—was hanging by a thread. The union moved quickly to frame the riot as the result of employer oppression, blaming the city's racial animus on "the enthusiastic idiots" who "imported" black labor into the city and "gleefully" murdered peaceful strikers. "The race trouble gripping Chicago," the *New Majority* argued, was merely "the whirlwind ... [coming] home to roost."[55] The CFL even accused the packers of deliberately inciting the race riot to halt the union's organizing campaign: "We had the Negroes ready to join in and it was then that the packers decided to array the races against each other." SLC secretary J. W. Johnstone publicly called for the prosecution of packing bosses for conspiracy to commit murder.[56] Set against the reckless greed of the packers was the CFL, which, in Johnstone's words, "knows no color line or sex, dismisses all creed and national distinctions and seeks to embrace the toiling masses from all four quarters of the globe in the high and noble purposes of ... unionism." If unionism were allowed to flourish—if, in Johnstone's words, "the toilers of both races in the stock yards and the great industries of Chicago were thoroughly organized"—then "serious race trouble would be impossible."[57]

But within the union's criticism of the packers was buried a kernel of resentment at black workers themselves, presaging the bitter conflict that would follow. In a hearing regarding the race riot before federal judge Samuel Alschuler, CFL president John Fitzpatrick accused the packers of creating "a situation among the colored people." But he also upbraided black "preachers and doctors and others" in the black community, claiming they were paid off by the packers to spread antiunion propaganda. Fitzpatrick also criticized black workers themselves, implying that they were clueless dupes all too easily led astray. "There is no friction between white non-union and colored non-union men," he claimed, with the exception that "the poor deluded colored non-union man will allow himself to be exploited by the packers to the detriment of his own fellow negroes, and to the great injury of the white worker too."[58] In a pamphlet edited by the communist organizer and writer Harrison George (in which statements from Fitzpatrick and Johnstone were reprinted), he argued that "the record of the colored unionist is good, where he has been unionized, but ... the great majority of Negroes have not assisted in the solidarity of labor by organizing."[59]

These words were born of both anger and fear, for the riot weakened the CFL in several crucial ways. First, the CFL experienced major financial losses. As the majority of stockyards workers remained at home for at least one day during the riot, the responsibility fell to the union to

Chicago Race Riots. The cover of a pamphlet edited by communist activist Harrison George—and containing statements from CFL leaders J. W. Johnstone and John Fitzpatrick—dramatizes the CFL's view of the riot as the product of racial resentment manufactured by the greed and mendacity of packing bosses. Special Collections, Daley Library, University of Illinois at Chicago.

support those who needed food or emergency assistance—a responsibility that became particularly important as the packers took the riot as an opportunity to break the power of the union and laid off a number of its members.[60] With numerous men discharged and others requiring emergency assistance, CFL locals found themselves laying out large sums of cash to support their members.[61] Second, the CFL suffered a major blow to its power as an organizing body. Seeking to prevent a resumption of violence in the stockyards district, Chicago police ordered the SLC to hold its meetings elsewhere. Without the advantage of a base of operations near the workplace, communication became nearly impossible. Many workers were unclear on when it was safe to return to work, and came back late only to find they had been replaced.[62] Combined with the fear and mutual distrust of white and black workers, such damage to the union's structure proved difficult to overcome. Third, and most critically, the riot widened the gap between white and black workers. The sheer terror of the riot itself created a venomous atmosphere of racial distrust that was carried into the workplace. Employers, seeking to cash in on the chaos of the riot, worked to recruit nonunion workers in great numbers. For the white union workers who were laid off, the continued "importation" of black nonunion labor was an open insult.[63]

This gap was most tragically pronounced in the union's attempt to control the formal reopening of the stockyards—an event that cemented the racial animus of the riot and finally doomed the CFL's attempts to organize black workers. Union officials and packing bosses alike feared a renewal of violence at the workplace. The CFL in particular was terrified by the prospect of white and black workers attacking one another on the shop floor. The brutality of the riot had already damaged CFL organizers' claims to interracial unity; if bloody racial strife emerged at the workplace, it would be nearly impossible to build a union of white and black workers. As a result, union leaders advised workers to remain home for much of the week. This call was poorly communicated and only intermittently heeded, resulting in much of the violence encountered by men traveling to and from work during the riot.[64]

With the militia in full control of the stockyards district, the packinghouses were ready to reopen. By Friday, August 1, the packers had formulated a plan for returning all employees to work: the stockyards would officially reopen on Monday, August 4, but police and state militiamen would be stationed within the yards to prevent any conflict from developing.[65] Union leaders were furious. The union viewed the use of armed guards, police, and militia as an open provocation, summoning bitter memories of repression during the Great Railroad Strike of 1877 and the Pullman strike of 1894. SLC organizer John Kikulski sneered at the militia, claiming that his men resented working "with a Boy Scout and a bayonet right behind them."[66] A *New Majority* editorial painted a darker picture. Demanding to know "what fiend could have devised a more diabolical plot?" the editors noted that meatpacking workers habitually worked with cleavers and "know how to use them." In the event of racial trouble, the editorial concluded that "machine guns will not be able to stop what will happen unless they mow down the workers, white and black."[67]

More importantly, it became clear almost immediately that the union workers' protests were racially charged. Union members circulated petitions "demanding that the packers decide once and for all between white or colored employes [sic]" and threatened to strike if black workers were not driven from the yards.[68] Rumors circulated of a general strike among the white workers if African Americans were permitted to re-enter the yards.[69] CFL officials scrambled to control the situation, announcing on Saturday, August 2, that "every effort is being made to allay racial prejudice" and pledging, in a joint statement with packinghouse owners, that "that no discrimination would be made against negroes when they returned to their jobs."[70] But even given these strident disavowals of prejudice, union leaders knew their position was precarious. J. W. Johnstone and John Kilulski grimly summed up the situation: "Five days of race riots have got some of our white workers alarmed and even inflamed [and] we do not know how much longer we can control them."[71] The protests were for naught. On Thursday, August 7 (the date had been pushed back due to the fire in the Lithuanian district), three thousand black workers were escorted into the yards by militia and police. As an added precaution, five hundred deputy sheriffs were stationed in the stockyards district as an "emergency constabulary."[72] The police and militia prevented outright violence, but by the end of the day, almost five thousand white SLC members had walked off the job in protest. Handbills were circulated in three different languages calling for a mass meeting to discuss a strike against the nonunion black workers.[73]

Perhaps more than any other single event, it was the CFL's handling of this wildcat strike that ultimately doomed the drive for interracial unionism. Because they had so vociferously opposed the deployment of militia and police, union leaders could not disavow the strike. At the same time,

Police officers watching packinghouse workers crossing train yards during a wildcat strike in August 1919. Though ostensibly protesting the presence of police and militia in the stockyards, such walkouts also reflected deep-seated resentments held by white CFL members against black workers. DN-0071240, Chicago Daily News negatives collection, Chicago History Museum.

it was clear that many union workers had trained their hatred not only on the guards, but on the black workers under their protection—thus undercutting the CFL's efforts to create a racially harmonious atmosphere in the yards. Without any other option, union leaders attempted to chart a middle course. They officially supported the strike, but downplayed its racial character, declaring that the walkout was not due to "the racial question" but to the presence of "an armed guard designed to protect non-union labor of whatever color at the expense of union men."[74] CFL leaders assumed that these reassurances would restore racial harmony to the stockyards, and hoped that black workers would join their white brethren in walking out to protest the militia.

This response proved disastrous for two reasons. First, it misapprehended the source of white workers' rage. The walkout of white union men was not merely a protest against armed guards. It was a clear expression of racial anger. Despite the strikers' claims of protest against an armed guard intended to protect strikebreakers "of whatever color," the white union men took particular umbrage at "the intention of the packers to disrupt the unions by the use of non-unionized *colored* labor."[75] These protests extended to black union workers as well. SLC president Martin Murphy "urged ... union white men not to leave their posts if working with union colored men," a clear indication that at least some of the strikers were protesting the presence of black workers, regardless of their union affiliation. Some of these protests were tinged with familiar prejudices regarding black workers' fitness for union membership. "While some of the negroes are union men, it is said they have not paid their dues for some time," the *Daily News* reported, concluding that the strikes were clearly a "double protest against the presence in the yards of military and police guards and the readmittance to the yards plants of colored workers."[76] The white unionists' anger was not merely against nonunion labor in general, but against the use of black nonunion workers specifically, and the presence of black workers more generally. CFL leaders, guided by a naïve belief in their ability to forge an interracial union, ignored the prejudices that underlay the wildcat strike.

Second, and more significantly, the CFL's response revealed that the union was blind to the needs of black workers. CFL leaders viewed the riot as an opportunity to rebuild the stockyards as a racially harmonious union shop, and assumed that black workers would follow them into the breach. But most black workers saw the presence of militia not as a union issue, but as a racial one. Black Chicagoans had just endured a week of unspeakable bloodshed. They had been beaten, stabbed, clubbed, and shot, forced to barricade their homes against the indiscriminate gunfire of "death cars," and fought pitched battles against marauding white gangs. Only the arrival of state militia finally halted the carnage. So, when the CFL endorsed a strike against the presence of militia in the yards—a strike marred by open appeals to antiblack hatred—the vast majority of black workers chose safety over solidarity and refused to walk off the job.[77]

The union's failed appeal to black workers was based on a narrow reading of the riot as essentially a conflict over labor and space, one that could be solved through interracial unionism. The words of mechanics union official Max Wegener are instructive. "We have heard reports that the whites will refuse to work when the negroes attempt to work," he said, but "the militia will do no good ... because, while troops may keep down riots, they can't make men work." Those workers could, on the other hand, "be reached through the unions."[78] Wegener's perspective reflects the broader view of CFL leadership: that unions and unions alone could promote interracial unity and workplace productivity. But this perspective was meaningless to black workers who had just endured a race riot. The two sides faced each other across a gulf of differences in historical experience. White union members responded to the presence of militia and police with a bitterness and terror born of hard-fought strikes brutally suppressed through the violent use of state power. But African Americans, whose own history was fraught with lynchings and massacres, viewed the troops as "offering protection from whites trying to deny them their right to earn a living."[79]

Indeed, black workers repeatedly expressed their desire for workplace protection in the wake of the riot. A conference of black citizens, including famed antilynching crusader Ida B. Wells-Barnett, convened on July 31 and demanded the deployment of more police to protect black laborers as they returned to work. Wells-Barnett recounted, with barely contained fury, the testimony of three black men set upon by a "mob of Polaks" and beaten "after colored workers had been promised protection if they returned to work."[80] In an editorial in the *Defender*, Robert Abbott noted with some skepticism the CFL's pledges that "not a single soldier or policeman would be required in that district to preserve order" and that the union "would see to it that the black workman would be protected by his white associates in the ranks of organized labor." While Abbott allowed that "it may be the part of wisdom for us to join with the white brother in the labor movement," he expressly repudiated the CFL's position that the riot was caused by employer manipulation of the races, arguing that unions must "remove from the mind of the white laboring man the notion that large employers of labor are using us as a big stick over their heads." Ultimately, Abbott's tepid overtures toward unionism reflected African Americans' hard-earned cynicism regarding the city's labor movement: "We confess that our experience with organized labor in this locality has not been reassuring. . . . If the leaders of the labor movement are anxious for our co-operation we stand ready to give it when we can be assured that we will not be deserted by our white brothers in a crisis."[81] For many black workers, that crisis was the reopening of the stockyards, and the CFL was found severely wanting.

The most damning indictment of the CFL strike was the response of the union's own black members. While the SLC claimed that some three thousand black members joined their white comrades in the strike, this argument is dubious at best.[82] In light of the union's protests against the police, "Colored" Local 651 broke with CFL leadership and published a blistering letter that rebuked white workers for "trying to prevent the re-employment of colored men in [the] packing houses" and lodged a "vigorous protest against this malicious attempt . . . [by] this unlawful element to prevent members of our race from returning to their places of employment." The letter's haymaker was a clear statement of support for the use of police and militia within the yards, and a direct repudiation of the CFL's opposition: Local 651 demanded "every means of protection that we as law-abiding citizens should receive, to the end that we can reach our places of work and not be menaced or intimidated by any group of people who are seeking to prevent our employment."[83] The letter gave the lie to CFL leadership's claim that the strikes were not primarily racial, and revealed the enormity of the rupture between white and black workers.

The CFL had made two major miscalculations. First, union leadership had assumed that their work of creating a racially harmonious union would insulate the workplace from racial violence. As a result, they were blindsided by white workers calling what was in effect a hate strike against their black counterparts. Second, and more critically, union leaders placed tremendous faith in their organizing and messaging efforts—and, as a result, felt confident that black workers would value class solidarity over protections against racial violence. This presumption placed African Americans, particularly union members, in the agonizing position of choosing between their union and their safety. In the end, they chose the latter, shattering the precarious alliance between white and black workers.[84] Ironically, it was an Armour superintendent, in an interview with Carl Sandburg for the *Chicago Daily News*, who expressed the CFL's blinkered perspective most astutely. The conflict was "not a race question at all," he explained, but "a labor union question" hinging on the fact that the SLC had exhausted its efforts "to get the negro into their membership, but they haven't got him."[85] The CFL had assumed that its pledges of protection would entice black workers to join. But by misapprehending the racial reality of the stockyards, the CFL alienated black workers and once more left itself vulnerable to the predation of the packers, whose successful deployment of militia served as a major defeat to the union. Though the physical and psychological damage of the Chicago race riot was severe, the CFL's response to the riot only increased tensions between the races and defeated its own efforts to create racial unity.

As the strike spread—the SLC estimated that some thirty-two thousand workers were out, though the packers claimed it was less than thirteen thousand—the union made one last-ditch effort to reassert its power.[86]

On Saturday, August 9, SLC officers J. W. Johnstone, John Kikulski, and Martin Murphy traveled to the offices of meatpacking tycoon J. Ogden Armour, who was in the midst of a meeting with the chief of police, the adjutant general of the militia, and other packing bosses. They claimed that since the union had "been on the firing line trying to prevent race rioting," they deserved a seat at the conference. After a humiliating wait of more than two hours, they were permitted to make a brief statement. Johnstone and Kikulski pleaded with Armour that all the workers of the stockyards district were underpaid, and that bringing them into a union shop "as fellow union men and women" would "hold the situation in hand" without the need for "machine guns or bayonets." They ended their statement by vowing that if the packers ignored their warnings, "the bloodshed that will follow will be greater than that [which] has occurred and we will be powerless to prevent it." Armour dismissed the trio—"contemptuously," in their words—and their proposal was ignored.[87] The union, trying for one last bit of leverage, ordered those on strike to remain out. Most of the men returned to work on Monday, August 11; roughly six hundred who worked for Armour and Morris discovered they had been fired. The union protested to Judge Alschuler, but he had no choice but to vindicate the employers. In walking out, the white unionists had broken the agreement's no-strike clause, and thus the employers were within their rights to discharge them.[88] The union's attempt to reopen the stockyards as a union shop had failed utterly.

The fault lines created by the race riot clearly damaged the relationship between Chicago's white and black workers. But the width and depth of the chasm that opened between them was not inevitable. CFL leaders' attempts to reopen the stockyards on their own terms, particularly their support of strikes against the use of armed guards and their utter misapprehension of the respective racial attitudes of white and black workers, bespoke a narrow understanding of racial conflict and undercut the union's claims to represent black and white workers equally. Packing bosses moved quickly to exacerbate these tensions, using police and militia to reassert their power and split workers along racial lines. With the union's interracial drive crumbling, more and more black workers fled the ranks of the union and instead pledged their fealty to paternalistic employers, who were all too eager to break the CFL along racial lines. With white unionists more determined than ever to organize their coworkers (and expel those who refused), and black workers more resistant than ever to the union appeal, the races drifted ever farther apart.

If the riot had augmented feelings of racial resentment among whites, it stoked stirrings of racial pride and consciousness among black Chicagoans, leading them to favor organizations that served their racial interests over those that served their class interests. The CFL's failed attempts to control the reopening of the stockyards, and the bitter response they provoked, made the African American community at large even less responsive to the union's appeal—a crippling blow, since the CFL's structure drew its strength from the links between community and workplace. Ultimately, black workers would take strength and pride in their own racial communities and largely abandon the CFL.

This self-reliance began during the riot itself, during which—despite the efforts of the SLC—African Americans relied on their neighbors, not their coworkers, for relief. A volunteer community in the city's predominantly black Second Ward distributed food baskets, while several black institutions, most notably the packer-subsidized Wabash Avenue YMCA and the Chicago Urban League, served thousands of black families.[89] Black community leaders championed such expressions of racial solidarity. At a meeting of Congregationalist ministers in September, black politician Oscar DePriest cited the riot as evidence that "patience is no longer a virtue; that [African Americans] are fighting back as any man should to defend his [manhood] and his home." T. Arnold Hill of the Chicago Urban League claimed the root of the problem was simple: white Chicagoans' perception that the city's black population "keeps getting out of line."[90] An editorial in the *Broad Ax* argued that "the old time darkey is dead" and that "the black citizen . . . must respect himself, and to do that his house must be protected from the mob and the bomb."[91] Perhaps most critically, the leaders made clear that African Americans comprised a distinct community "that is not seeking social contact with any race or person that bases such contact upon color and not character."[92] The riot's sharpening of racial tensions also provided the city's black community the occasion to join together under the banner of a new, racially independent consciousness.

Black Chicagoans were in the thick of the so-called "New Negro" movement. The feelings of the city's African Americans in the postriot period were most succinctly expressed by black World War I veteran Stanley B. Norvell. Just weeks after the riot ended, Norvell wrote a letter to Victor Lawson, the longtime editor of the *Chicago Daily News,* who had just been named to the newly formed Chicago Commission on Race Relations. In it, Norvell blames the riot on white racism—specifically, the fact that "sixty per cent of the male Negro population [of Chicago] is engaged in menial and servile occupations." But he also attributed the riot to a growing consciousness among the city's black population: "the gradual, and inevitable evolution—metamorphosis, if you please—of the Negro." Adopting the phrase of the day, Norvell claimed that "today we have with us a new Negro," and that "'Uncle Tom'... prototypes are almost as extinct as ... the dodo bird." Drawing on his own experiences in the military, Norvell attributed this awakening to the crucible of World War I, which gave African Americans "for the first time in their lives ... [insight] into the workings of governmental things of ... other countries, and ... brought us round to a sort of realization of how our government was made and is conducted." Norvell concluded that black Americans would not be satisfied until they were afforded the same rights as other citizens. "We ask not charity," he wrote, "but justice."[93]

Black Chicagoans' actions proved Norvell's words prophetic. A whole host of race-based organizations took root in the Black Belt. Seeking to countervail the influence of the Homeowners' Associations, a group of black citizens formed the Protective Circle of Chicago, seeking "to combat, through legal means, the lawlessness of the Kenwood and Hyde Park Property Owners' Association" and to "apprehend those persons who have bombed the homes ... of Negroes."[94] The riot certainly rallied African Americans to the group's cause. Their meeting in February 1920 drew more than three thousand black citizens. Under pressure from the black community, mayor William Hale Thompson approved a $25,000 appropriation dedicated to apprehending house bombers, as well as a $10,000 donation to the victims of the Tulsa race riot of 1921 via the Chicago Peace and Protective Association, another black community group.[95] By the late 1920s, the Whip was at the forefront of a "Don't Spend Your Money Where You Can't Work" campaign.[96]

Some of the city's black working class looked toward the politics of diaspora. In September 1919, Marcus Garvey visited the area and was greeted by throngs of black Chicagoans who braved a torrential downpour to hear him speak. Garvey established several chapters of his Universal Negro Improvement Association (UNIA) on the city's South Side. Though they were strongly opposed by the city's entrenched black elite—represented by the Defender and the local NAACP—these chapters reflected a growing racial consciousness among the city's African Americans. This was especially true among its working people, to whom Garveyism appealed most strongly.[97] From this group sprang a radical

If You are a Stranger in the City

If you want a job   If you want a place to live
If you are having trouble with your employer
If you want information or advice of any kind

CALL UPON

The CHICAGO LEAGUE ON URBAN CONDITIONS AMONG NEGROES

3719 South State Street

Telephone Douglas 9098   T. ARNOLD HILL, Executive Secretary

No charges—no fees. We want to help YOU

Urban League calling card. In the wake of the race riot and the CFL's bungled efforts to control the reopening of the stockyards, many black Chicagoans rejected unionism in favor of race-based organizations. This card advertises the Urban League's ability to fulfill many of the roles— such as job placement and adjudication of workplace disputes—that white workers would have entrusted to a union. Aldis Family papers, Special Collections, Daley Library, University of Illinois at Chicago.

fringe offshoot known as the Star Order of Ethiopia and Ethiopian Missionary to Abyssinia, better known as the Abyssinians, who concluded a parade in June 1920 by burning two American flags and shooting a black police officer and a white sailor who attempted to intervene.[98]

Though the UNIA represented a small segment of the black population (and the Abyssinians an even smaller one), a large number of the city's African Americans adopted increasingly nationalist rhetoric. In particular, many steadfastly denied any desire to mix with whites. In his letter, Stanley Norvell scoffed at white fears of "social equality." Calling this phenomenon "that ancient skeleton in the closet . . . whose bones are always brought out and rattled whenever the Negro question is discussed," he argued simply "considering the unsettled condition of the world at large, the white man of this country has a great deal more to be sensibly alarmed about than the coming of social equality."[99] Others agreed. At a conference at Olivet Baptist Church immediately after the riot, pastor J. K. Williams claimed that black Chicagoans wanted nothing more than "an equal economic and industrial chance with other races." But, he went on, "no self-respecting Negro wants what is commonly known as 'social equality,'" arguing that "sensible Negroes never make an attempt to 'mix' socially with white people, and don't want white people to 'mix' with them."[100] Black leaders aggressively denied accusations that they were pursuing "social equality" or racial mixing; on the contrary, African Americans were determined to preserve the sanctity and solidarity of their own community.

With a great number of black Chicagoans employed as industrial work-ers, it was inevitable that such sentiments would affect black perceptions of work and the labor movement. One particularly ugly incident is in-structive. In a work gang of 180 men, one black laborer, Harry Hawkins, represented the only nonunion worker. When his coworkers attempted to organize him, Hawkins responded, "To hell with that. I don't have to belong to the union, I got the company behind me." When the union workers pressed him, Hawkins became even more hostile: "Fuck that button . . . Fuck the union."[101] This latter comment nearly provoked a fistfight. Black union steward Frank Custer was summoned to try and keep the peace. Hawkins told Custer he had at one point been a member of the SLC, though he only joined "to keep down trouble" with his co-workers. Custer pleaded with Hawkins to return, but Hawkins refused, saying "the union was no good to me."[102]

Hawkins's recalcitrance sheds light on black workers' increasing dis-tance from the union. For one thing, Hawkins, like many African Ameri-cans in the stockyards, had come to resent foreigners, particularly recent immigrants from Southern and Eastern Europe. In recounting his story, Hawkins derisively referred to two of the union men as "Polaks," and recalled that they had intimidated him into joining the SLC and then assaulted him when he left.[103] Indeed, European immigrants were among the most energetic and enthusiastic supporters of the CFL campaign and represented a major source of labor competition for black workers. More importantly, their skin color entitled them to the benefits of white priv-ilege, while black Chicagoans, who served the nation both overseas and at home, faced discrimination and violence. The *Whip* was infuriated by the presence of African Americans on bread lines, claiming they had "out-stripped the foreigner in efficiency and endurance" during the war and should be offered more and better economic opportunities than "il-literate and semi-civilized" immigrants, who represented "the Scum of Europe."[104] Such conflicts widened the chasm between white and black workers. Given immigrants' steadfast support for the CFL, they inevitably came to color workplace culture as well.

The packers eagerly exploited these tensions. As contemporary observer Catherine Elizabeth Lewis noted, both the CFL and packing bosses "laid the responsibility for the race riot upon the other."[105] Faced with this choice, African Americans largely chose to follow their employers rather than the CFL. Stockyards bosses claimed they would reduce the size of their foreign workforce to create more jobs for black workers; they also publicized the fact that the CFL paid fifty dollars to white families whose homes were destroyed in the post-riot fire in the Lithuanian district, but nothing at all to black families who suffered the same fate.[106]

In Hawkins's case, these efforts proved successful. In response to the union appeal, Hawkins said simply: "I want to stay in the Stock Yards all my life." Hawkins felt the best way to secure that future was to remain nonunion: "I have got the company back of me and I don't have to go in. I have got the company [behind] me."[107] Many whites saw black reluctance to wear a union button as confirmation of their status as a "scab race" in league with employers. It is telling that several union men assumed that Harry Hawkins was a company "plant" employed only to undermine the union. As Frank Custer explained, "it seems to me that [bosses] have picked these men out simply because they are ignorant and low-minded, to start them agitating against the unions." Hawkins, he opined, started the trouble under the orders of packing bosses: "They got this man there not to get in the union."[108] Another black union organizer, Andrew Holmes, claimed that the union intended "to work harmoniously with other brothers, regardless of race, religion or politics," but claimed that some black workers, due to "narrowness or conceit or something," occasionally caused "an inconvenience to . . . [a large] number of men," and should be transferred away from union workers "for the good and harmony of the whole."[109]

These attitudes often resulted in unbridgeable gaps between the races. In the case of Hawkins, the white members of the work gang put down their tools, sent Hawkins to the superintendent's office, and refused to work until he either joined the union or was fired. Hawkins attempted to make peace by saying he might be open to rejoining the union. In response, his coworkers explained he needed to pay a year's worth of dues up-front—a ludicrous request. When Hawkins responded he couldn't do so, they replied, "We don't want you." A friend offered to pay the dues for him, but the whites still refused: "They didn't want me in," Hawkins later recalled, "didn't want the check, didn't want me in at all." The white workers, in his words, "wanted me off the place."[110] Such incidents reveal the rage of white union workers and their increasing desire to rid the workplace of black workers entirely, rather than bring them into the union as equals.

Though black workers turned against the CFL in the wake of the riot, they were not in any sense opposed to unionism in principle. Throughout World War I, independent black unions sprang up in several cities, including organizations in Chicago comprised of all-black plumbers, lathe operators, and electricians.[111] Quite simply, black workers desired organizations that could serve their racial interests as well as their class interests. But the CFL's ability to represent black interests was dubious at best, as evidenced by the antimilitia strike in the yards. Instead of working to make their actions match their rhetoric, CFL leaders excoriated black workers for their reticence, while CFL members threatened physical violence against those who would not join. This combination of black skepticism and union resentment only deepened divisions between the races.

A growing racial consciousness pushed Chicago's African Americans toward organizing on the basis of race, not class, and many explicitly rejected alliances with whites. Community leaders and rank-and-file workers both viewed fealty to employers as the best way to advance socially and economically, particularly given the mistakes committed by the CFL. As a result, the workplace conflicts that pushed black and white workers apart spread into the black community as a whole and created a nearly unbridgeable chasm between the races. As historian Catherine Elizabeth Lewis has concluded, "No issue was more irrevocably determined as a result of [the race riot] than the labor policy which was to prevail henceforth in the packinghouse establishments." With that policy decided largely by racial antagonism, the aftermath of the Chicago race riot bequeathed to the city a profound distrust between white and black workers—a distrust that, in the words of one contemporary observer, "brought to an abrupt end" black workers' participation in the CFL.[112]

The Chicago race riot of 1919 had a tremendous effect on the fortunes of the city's labor movement. The CFL, whose campaign to organize the stockyards had gathered significant momentum, was suddenly on the defensive, as the riot afforded employers an opportunity to exploit racial schisms for their own gain. Perhaps more significantly, the violence that engulfed Chicago in summer 1919 increased the reluctance of black Chicagoans to ally themselves with organized labor. From the shop floor to the street corner to the pulpit, African Americans turned away from the

CFL's vision of class solidarity and toward racially conscious organizing among themselves.

Chicago was certainly no stranger to racial violence, but the 1919 riot was larger than any previous conflict the city had witnessed. The riot itself was the culmination of years of strife between black and white Chicagoans, resulting from the explosion of the city's black population and resultant clashes over housing and jobs. Though Chicago's stockyards and the surrounding area were the site of racial clashes before the riot and racial violence during the riot, the CFL was largely successful in restraining its own members from participating in the worst of the brutality.

In the wake of the riot, Chicago's unions and employers grappled over control of the workplace. The CFL staged a series of strikes protesting the presence of police and militia in the stockyards, believing that black workers would follow them. But black workers, including union members, appreciated police protection in the wake of the violence of the riot. This miscalculation allowed packers to prey on racial divisions within the union, while the bitterness of these strikes pushed black workers from the CFL. This distance only increased throughout the summer and fall of 1919, as black and white workers clashed on the shop floor and the black community retreated from alliances with whites—particularly labor unions.

In a way, progressive unionism can be counted among the casualties of the Chicago race riot. Though the CFL continued organizing throughout 1919 and beyond—even taking a leadership role in the great steel strike of that winter—its power had been significantly sapped by the riot. Despite its best efforts, the federation was unable to convince black workers that their best interests lay with the union. CFL leaders' overestimation of their ability to marshal support among black workers, union and non-union alike, led to the disastrous strike at the stockyards, a tragic mistake that both exposed the federation's vulnerability to employer assaults and gave the lie to its claims to true interracial representation. With black workers and community leaders alike abandoning the union, the CFL and its members grew more vulnerable; nonunion black labor represented a ready-made strikebreaking force that could be deployed at the will of employers. As the 1920s dawned, the CFL would become embroiled in a pair of major strikes—the steel strike of 1919 and the stockyards strike of 1921—that would further expose the union's inability to attract black members and ultimately doom its organizing drive altogether.

6.

"BORING FROM WITHIN": RACE AND THE DECLINE OF THE CFL, 1919–1922

I n November 1920, the *New York American* published an article detailing the response of the American Federation of Labor to a steel strike of 1919–1920. "There was a feeling," the article explained, that the executive council "should deal emphatically with the attempts of radicals to bore from within" and shun the "radical doctrines" that might weaken the very foundations of organized labor. The "radicals" in question were John Fitzpatrick and William Z. Foster.[1] Fitzpatrick was head of one of the most diverse and powerful city locals in the nation, and was considered by some to be a successor to Samuel Gompers as president of the AFL. Foster was an organizer of such brilliance that he earned the respect of the bosses he battled. Yet as the 1920s dawned, they had been marginalized within their own federation.

Progressive unionism was intended as a response to the bitter defeats of the early twentieth century—a method for constructing a militant, interracial unionism that could defeat employers with the power of solidarity. The tragic irony of progressive unionism is that it was defeated by the same forces that had crippled labor in 1903, 1904, and 1905: internal dissension regarding black workers and disastrous failed strikes broken with the use of nonunion black labor. Between 1919 and 1922, the federation suffered a series of blows that shattered Fitzpatrick's dream of a militant interracial union. The same combination of structural inertia and rank-and-file animus that stalled the CFL's previous efforts reached a fever pitch. The defeats suffered by the CFL during this period ultimately forced the federation into a decade-long period of dormancy. Not until the arrival of industrial organizing under the aegis of the Committee for Industrial Organization in the 1930s would the CFL once again become a major factor in the city's labor movement.

Four major events accelerated the collapse of the CFL and its organizing drive. The first was a vicious internecine war within the SLC. Lasting nearly ten months, this bitter clash over control of the city's meatpacking workers pitted unionist against unionist, exposing significant rifts between the union's conservative base of skilled workers and its recently organized mass of unskilled workers, and culminated in the dissolution of the SLC amid accusations of fraud, embezzlement, and murder. The second blow to the CFL was the Great Steel Strike of 1919. Though most historians associate the strike with the mills of western Pennsylvania, the organizing of the nation's steelworkers was first proposed by William Z. Foster at a CFL meeting, and the organization of workers in the Chicago district was the movement's first priority. But the union's failed attempts to recruit black workers, its response to the use of black strikebreakers, and the repression of the strike by employers reflected both the ways in which the union was defeated and the ways in which it defeated itself.

A third blow was the disastrous stockyards strike of 1921–1922. As the Alschuler award expired and packing bosses sought to consolidate their control, the weakened AMCBW called a nationwide strike in late 1921. Although the union redoubled its efforts to recruit black workers, the strike followed a familiar script. As in 1904, black strikebreakers kept the yards running, to the fury of the white community; as in 1904, white workers engaged in mass actions, including violence, to retake their jobs; and as in 1904, employers proved far too powerful to overcome. Fourth, although it did not cause the downfall of the CFL, the collapse of the Labor Party served as a bellwether of the union's fortunes in the early 1920s. Though the party made a respectable showing in the mayoral election of 1919, it quickly fell into decline. Fearful of a divisive platform, party leaders failed in their attempts to appeal directly to ethnic and racial minorities, preferring to stake the party's success on esoteric issues such as tax reform, municipal ownership of utilities, and the rewriting of the state constitution. As a result, the Labor Party became a niche group without a niche and simply could not compete with the well-oiled machines of the two major parties. By 1924, the party was defunct.

Taken together, these defeats reveal the limits of the CFL's vision of progressive unionism. Despite their idealism and verve, Fitzpatrick and other CFL leaders were simply unable to create a union structure that could appeal to African Americans and withstand employer counteroffensives. As such, the CFL was essentially a militant union that lacked the tools for militancy. Divided in its leadership, limited in its membership, and assailed by employers, the federation receded into obscurity.

The Chicago race riot had placed the CFL in the untenable position of choosing between embracing the presence of militia at the stockyards and promoting a bitter hate strike against black workers. The aftermath of this decision was felt long after the militia had departed and the strike had ended. The spectacular brutality of the riot, and the response it had elicited from stockyards workers, disturbed a number of AMCBW leaders. To them, the strike was unacceptable—not because it was racially tinged, but because, as AMCBW local secretary Dennis Lane argued, it was "a strike called without [AMCBW] sanction and in direct violation of the [Alschuler] agreement."[2] The central issue with the wildcat strikes, then, was their spontaneous nature. Lane and other AMCBW leaders were skilled workers, inured to the predictability and conservatism of craft unionism; to them, the SLC's aggressive militancy was foolhardy and even dangerous.

In July 1919, as the race riots began, CFL official Dennis Lane created a new central council known as AMCBW District Council No. 9, claimed it was the rightful governing body of the stockyards workers, and demanded that all AMCBW locals resign from the SLC. This was a major breach of union norms. Not only had Lane committed the mortal sin of dual unionism, his organization was opposed to many of the guiding principles of the SLC—namely, democracy and diversity. In particular, Lane allied himself with skilled craft workers, who were overwhelmingly white and native-born, and stipulated that local unions would be limited to five votes within the council, regardless of their size. This latter proviso was a clear attempt to limit the power and influence of the unskilled locals, which tended to be large and ethnically diverse. Eight of the SLC locals, comprising thousands of workers, refused to join and were suspended from the AMCBW International as a result.[3]

Once more, the limits of federated unionism became tragically apparent. Despite the SLC's ability to unite various locals into a central coordinating committee, actual control of the locals still rested with the officers of their respective international unions, leaving the CFL powerless to stop Lane's insurgency. Lane took full advantage of this power structure. In September 1919, he appealed directly to Samuel Gompers and the AFL, arguing that despite the SLC's success in organizing the yards, its federated structure was incompatible with the AFL's long-standing policy of craft autonomy. Specifically, Lane argued that the local unions' affiliation with the SLC violated the AMCBW's rights as the exclusive representative of the city's meatpacking workers. Predictably, the AFL agreed. AFL official Frank Morrison sent a letter to Fitzpatrick ordering him to immediately suspend all organizing by the SLC.[4]

The skilled butchers' opposition was not merely in the area of organizing jurisdiction. Ethnic and racial prejudice also played a role. The SLC had focused much of its campaign on appealing to recent immigrants from southern and eastern Europe, and to African Americans. To white native-born craft unionists whose careers had been spent in whitewashed industries, these were dangerous portents. The wildcat strikes, and the aggressive organizing of the SLC more generally, were seen as reflections of the horde of unskilled men: unlettered, impulsive, and dangerous.[5] In their letter to the AFL, the skilled butchers made sure to note that "some of the organizers ... were carrying on an agitation which was not in harmony with the constitution of the Amalgamated Meat Cutters and Butcher Workmen." Specifically, the AMCBW named John Kikulski and John Riley. Kikulski was a local Polish-American organizer whose charisma and oration had made him legendary within his community. Riley, a black organizer sent directly from the AFL, had made tireless efforts to recruit African Americans into the SLC. Because of the SLC's avowed focus on recruiting both ethnic immigrants and African Americans, both men were considered invaluable to the organizing drive. But Morrison ordered Kikulski to Pennsylvania to assist in organizing steelworkers. "In regard to John Riley," Morrison coldly wrote, "you are requested to see that he ceases any activities among [the] Butcher Workmen."[6] Losing Kikulski and Riley, energetic organizers with close ties to the Polish and African American communities, respectively, was a blow that cannot be overstated. As a result of the AFL decision, the SLC's greatest asset—its tireless organizing—evaporated.

The SLC quickly withered under such direct assaults. Faced with little other choice, the SLC's leadership resigned in January 1920 and affiliated their locals with District Council No. 9. In February, a new charter was issued making District Council No. 9 the sole representative of the city's meatpacking workers; former SLC officers Martin Murphy and J. W. Johnstone were elected as president and secretary-treasurer.[7] Though the SLC had effectively been destroyed, the CFL leadership had compromised with Lane and other AMCBW members to maintain peace and stabilize its presence in the stockyards.

Then, suddenly, the situation exploded. On March 16, Kikulski hastily assembled a district council meeting, held a vote, and was elected president. Murphy and Johnstone howled in protest, but to no avail—thousands of Polish union members had pledged their fealty to Kikulski and recognized him, and only him, as the council's rightful leader. Once more, the shortcomings of federated unionism were laid bare. The SLC had no power to compel the locals to recognize Murphy and Johnstone, and was forced to submit to the results of the phony election or risk alienating thousands of Polish workers. In response, Johnstone dropped a bomb-shell: he accused Kikulski of embezzling funds from the CFL treasury. An investigation by the CFL's executive concluded that Kikulski had collected per-capita donations from five local unions to assist striking butchers in Detroit, and never delivered the money.[8]

The rift between the SLC and the district council widened into a chasm. Though the executive board had found Kikulski guilty of fraud and expelled him from the federation, the CFL, bound by the rules of union autonomy, had no power to enforce its decision. District Council No. 9 vociferously defended Kikulski's innocence and refused to respect the CFL's ruling. Federation meetings descended into shouting matches crowded with resolutions and counterresolutions regarding the guilt or innocence of Kikulski. Delegate Hans Pfeiffer read a unanimous decla-ration from the district council condemning the accusations as false and vowing that if the CFL continued "encourag[ing] disruption in the rank and file," the council would advise its locals to disaffiliate from the CFL entirely.[9] Kikulski claimed that Johnstone himself had committed fraud, but those charges were quickly found to be groundless.[10]

The situation finally descended into violence. Early on the morning of May 3, Johnstone was entering the SLC offices when several gunshots were fired in his direction. When police arrived, they declined to take Johnstone's statement and instead ransacked the SLC offices and arrested him on trumped-up charges of assault and carrying a concealed weapon. Johnstone claimed the charges were made by members of the district council before a friendly judge. In a grimly appropriate finale, the battle ended with blood being spilled. On May 17, Kikulski was shot and died a few days later. The district council railed against Johnstone, Murphy, and the SLC chiefs, claiming that they had murdered Kikulski to consolidate their power. Though the district council succeeded in having Johnstone arrested and charged with murder, there was insufficient evidence to secure a conviction and he was acquitted. The identity of Kikulski's murderer remains a mystery.[11]

Were it not so tragic, the war between the SLC and District Council No. 9 would be almost comical in its absurdity. Perhaps no fact better illustrated the irrationality of the conflict than the fact that by the end of the controversy the stockyards were governed by three separate bodies: the Stockyards Labor Council, District Council No. 9, and a Mechanical

Trades Council, not to mention independent local unions who refused to affiliate with any of the councils.[12] But although the battle was bizarre, its costs were very real, and they were borne primarily by stockyards workers. Without a centralized system for coordinating and controlling tasks such as organizing, grievances, and dues payments, Chicago's meatpacking unions quickly fell into disrepair.

The internecine war between the SLC and District Council No. 9 reveals the limits of federated unionism. Although the SLC made great strides in organizing the previously impregnable fortress of the stockyards, its ability to direct the organizing campaign was subject to the voluntary participation of local unions. Despite its admirable goals of democratic representation and interracial harmony, the SLC was bound by its obligation to respect local union sovereignty. The militancy and diversity that had propelled the rise of the SLC proved its undoing. By engaging in a strike involving a large force of unskilled workers of various ethnicities, the SLC triggered a series of both jurisdictional and racial fears on the part of old-line craft unionists, who moved to reassert their control over the union and limit the influence of unskilled workers. Willing but unable to fully dedicate itself to democracy and diversity, the SLC ultimately failed in its task to permanently remake stockyards unionism.

Though it did not involve the same level of infighting as the stockyards controversy, the failed steel strike of 1919–1920 was far more injurious to the CFL. Though most strongly associated with western Pennsylvania, the strike began in the Chicago district—an area that organizers felt was equally vital to the success of the membership drive. More importantly, the CFL was directly implicated in the attempt to build a strong, diverse movement among steel workers, lending the campaign financial and strategic support. Ultimately, however, the strike ended as so many of Chicago's labor wars had: with a racially divided workforce warring with itself as employers destroyed the strike with nonunion labor. Though the introduction of federal troops was decisive in breaking the strike, the structure of the campaign both reflected and provoked racial divisions among the workers, which undermined the strikers' strength and momentum and ultimately left them bitter and defeated.

The organization of the steel industry was a gargantuan undertaking. After crushing the Amalgamated Association of Iron, Steel, and Tin Workers nearly out of existence in the 1890s, the steel industry had become a bulwark of the open shop—a fact reflected in the notoriously dreadful conditions faced by steelworkers. In 1919, the average workweek in the mills was sixty-nine hours. Wages were below subsistence levels, a problem exacerbated by wartime inflation that saw the price of foodstuffs rise 52 percent between 1916 and 1918. As late as 1919, two-thirds of the children of black and foreign-born steelworkers in Gary, Indiana, had no milk, eggs, or fruit in their diet; a number suffered from malnutrition and even bone defects. The workers themselves at first appeared immune to organization. Perhaps no other industry better reflected the reconstitution of the American workforce than steelworkers, who were a staggeringly diverse group. Unfortunately, steel bosses easily exploited this diversity for their own benefit. Most of the unskilled workers were uneducated and had little experience with unions.[13] Buried within this polyglot group, however, was the seed of resistance. By 1919, immigrant workers had acclimated to American customs to the extent that they felt comfortable engaging in informal work protests such as slowdowns. As the Interchurch World Movement found in its investigation of the strike, the immigrant workers had "developed a frame of mind of more or less chronic rebellion."[14] With workers increasingly radicalized, the situation was ripe for action.

Though the organization of Chicago's stockyards was their first priority, the rebellion of rank-and-file steelworkers struck both Fitzpatrick and Foster as an opportunity too rich to ignore. On April 7, 1918, Foster submitted a resolution to the Chicago Federation of Labor claiming that "the organization of the vast armies of wage earners employed in the steel industries is vitally necessary to the further spread of industrial democracy in America." Foster, the CFL's delegate to that summer's AFL convention, proposed to ask Gompers and AFL leadership to sponsor a mass organizing campaign among the iron and steel industries. The meeting's minutes recount what must have been a dramatic moment:

> [Foster] told how he had constantly heard the cry raised on all sides that "it can't be done" but that he for one refused to allow himself to be placed in any such state of mind. He told how, from time to time, various trade unions had tried to organize their own particular trade, working in these large industries with no result, and how, one after the other, had failed because each tried to do the job separately, instead of all banding together as a whole, and that there would never again be presented such an opportunity as existed at the present time.[15]

That summer, Foster traveled to the AFL convention and made his proposal. Befitting the AFL's traditional adherence to craft unionism, the response was less than enthusiastic. The AFL agreed to form a committee of twenty-two unions to organize the workers, but limited the financial contribution of each local to one hundred dollars, totaling far less than the $250,000 Foster felt was necessary to begin the campaign. Undaunted, Foster pressed on, proudly boasting that the committee itself was his greatest asset, representing as it did workers in "the steel and iron industries from mine to finished product."[16] Fitzpatrick agreed, noting that the committee could develop and channel "the strength which is within ourselves" and direct it toward a unified campaign in the industry.[17]

Such enthusiasm appeared warranted. The committee, led by Foster and Fitzpatrick, drafted an extensive list of demands, including the eight-hour day, seniority rights, abolition of company unions, and, of course, recognition of the Amalgamated and its subsidiaries as the sole collective bargaining representative of the workers. Organizing began immediately, with a focus on the Chicago district. The early results were nothing short of stunning. In one day, 1,200 workers signed up at Joliet. More than 1,500 signed cards at Gary. At Indiana Harbor, more than 6,000 workers attended a mass rally, with many staying to sign cards. By December, an estimated 25,000 steelworkers were organized nationwide; by June 1919, the number had risen to 100,000.[18] The furor was undeniable; workers who left the meeting at Indiana Harbor and returned to work without signing union cards were met with "jeers and hoots" from their newly organized colleagues.[19]

Recent immigrants from southern and eastern Europe seemed particularly entranced by the union appeal. These immigrants were highly politicized and even radicalized prior to the committee's organizing efforts, making them prime targets for Fitzpatrick and Foster's vision of progressive unionism. Wartime propaganda that decried "autocracy" and "Kaiserism" was easily reconciled with the cries of eastern European nationalists. As such, the immigrants regularly agitated for workplace control. Months before the strike began, a group of workers in the Calumet district, dubbed "foreigners" by plant bosses, engaged in a wildcat strike to protest the dismissal of a coworker. On May 4, a communist rally in Gary garnered an audience of some ten thousand workers. Committee members adroitly tailored the campaign to attract the immigrant workers. Bulletins were printed in nearly a dozen languages, and the committee hired twenty-five full-time organizers who spoke the languages of the immigrants. As a result, when the organizing call went out, immigrant workers responded in droves.[20]

With the steel companies refusing even to meet with the committee, a strike vote was held on August 20, 1919, with 98 percent of the steelworkers voting in favor.[21] The ever-cautious Samuel Gompers pleaded with the committee to postpone the strike while he tried to organize a parley with President Woodrow Wilson and the steel companies. Though Wilson uttered some banalities about industrial peace, the meeting never materialized. Pressure mounted. The committee boasted it had organized 80 percent of the industry. Rank-and-file workers began agitating on their own, engaging in wildcat strikes in Ohio and Indiana. Finally, the committee could wait no longer. On September 22, 1919, an estimated 275,000 steelworkers walked off the job. Within days, the number would surpass 300,000. The response in the Chicago district was overwhelming. In Waukegan, at American Steel and Wire, nearly 90 percent struck. Fully 95 percent of the men at Inland Steel at Indiana Harbor were reported out. In Joliet, the union claimed 98 percent participation, though the company claimed it was closer to 75 percent.[22] The battle of the steel industry had begun with a major union offensive.

Despite the strike's strong beginning, issues lurked just beneath the surface. For one thing, the steel trust was as much an empire as it was an industry. Steel magnates controlled not only the plants in which their employees worked, but the cities in which they lived. A U.S. Steel official presided over the city council in Gary, for example. As a result, unionism was denounced not just from the foreman's office, but from the halls of city government and "from pulpits and newspapers."[23] Store owners refused to extend lines of credit to union members, while landlords evicted "troublemaking" boarders. City officials blatantly flouted the First Amendment, passing ordinances to prevent parades, marches, and even large meetings. Union organizers were refused service in hotels, restaurants, and saloons, and ordered home by police. Those who refused to go were jailed or beaten. Any employee who dared sign a union card was discharged and blacklisted from the industry.[24]

Internal issues plagued the union as well. Because Fitzpatrick and Foster had chosen to "bore from within" the AFL, the organizing drive carried the full weight of the AFL's history of neglect toward unskilled workers, particularly ethnic and racial minorities. The AFL had made efforts to organize unskilled steelworkers into federal labor unions in the early twentieth century, but they met with little success; by the time of the strike, most of the unskilled workers were entirely new to unionism. Ethnic and racial conflicts immediately plagued the strike. Employers played on the discrimination of native whites against southern and eastern European workers. Native-born workers, already distrustful of the unskilled immigrants, were assured that the walkout was a "hunkie strike." Immigrant strikers were told that the skilled native workers would sell them out at the first available opportunity and were reminded that as early as 1902, South Chicago residents had demanded a government investigation as to the presence of Hungarian and Croatian workers. An infamous broadside appeared in the *Pittsburgh Chronicle Telegram* in early October: Uncle Sam, yelling "The Strike Has Failed, Go Back to Work" in eight different languages.[25]

The AFL's insistence on union autonomy created still more problems. Because the strike was initiated and led by organizations of skilled, primarily native-born workers, and because the AFL insisted that authority over the drive rested with the union locals, it was difficult to constructively channel the enormous energy of the unskilled men. The supremacy of local autonomy made the coordination of organizing a nightmare. As a result, some districts were unduly aggressive—even engaging in wildcat strikes during the summer—while others were barely organized by the time the strike was called. As one Pittsburgh organizer complained, "The dam broke before this district was more than half worked."[26] Though the industry was desperate for a new form of militant mass unionism, John Fitzpatrick—no conservative himself—quashed such desires, explaining, "This is not a fight of I. W. W. 'ism, or the One Big Union, or Syndicalism or any other 'ism . . . this is a fight of trade unions of the country as they exist and as we know them."[27]

Unfortunately, unions as they existed in the steel industry had a long history of racial exclusion; ultimately, divisions between white and black workers would prove decisive in the defeat of the strike. The historical composition of the Amalgamated made it unattractive to African Americans. Because black workers had not entered the industry in large numbers until the wartime era, they lacked even the minor experience of the AFL's brief FLU drive in the early twentieth century. As a result, black workers—12 percent of total workers in the Chicago district, and as high as 20 percent in some areas—represented the balance of power in the battle between the union and the industry. Many of their interactions with white workers had been negative. In 1909, one white steelworker derided his black coworkers for being "filthy in their personal habits" and "coarse, vulgar and brutal in their acts and conversation." Working with such men, he claimed, was "repugnant to any man who wants to retain his self respect." A workplace that employed African Americans was "no place for a man with a white man's heart to be."[28]

Once the organizing campaign began, the mutual distrust of white unionists and the black community helped torpedo any possibility of cooperation. If anything, black workers faced discrimination even greater than that of the immigrant workers. Earnest efforts had been made as early as 1909 to rid Gary of African Americans; though the plans failed, black residents were isolated into ghettoes, where they paid up to 20 percent more than whites for equivalent housing. On the job, black workers faced constant discrimination. Foremen often favored recent immigrants, augmenting feelings of mutual resentment.[29] The organizing committee, recognizing the danger of such realities, did not entirely neglect black workers. They took great pains to include black speakers during the mass rallies that became a regular feature of the campaign's early stages. The day after the strike began, the committee held a mass meeting in Gary's East Side Park and asked black attorney Lewis Caldwell to speak. Claiming the crowd was "a sea of black and white hands and waving hats," Caldwell admonished the black workers in particular: "The worst crime of civilization has been . . . the pitting of the two races against each other in the industrial struggle."[30]

But for the most part, the committee did little to make union membership enticing for black workers. As in the CFL's campaign, structural failings made it difficult for the Amalgamated to convince black workers that union membership was preferable to strikebreaking. Black workers were fully cognizant of the fact that many AFL unions continued to bar black members by constitutional fiat. That number included several international unions on the committee, particularly the mechanical trades. As a result, black workers resented the committee's efforts as merely perfunctory. There was little evidence to dispute this notion. The Amalgamated Association had technically authorized the organization of unskilled workers as early as 1889, but few of its lodges were interested in opening their ranks to white immigrants, let alone African Americans. Because organizing power rested with union locals, the rigor with which the committee pursued black workers varied by district. As a result, the relationship between the union and the black community was at times practically dysfunctional. The Pittsburgh Urban League, for example, told the committee they would support the organizing campaign if the committee would employ black organizers and make a concerted effort to organize black workers. Though Foster was amenable to the idea, the committee refused, and gained itself a powerful enemy.[31] As the strike wore on, Foster grew increasingly frustrated with the limits of the Amalgamated's model. "The unions are themselves in no small part to blame" for "fanning the flames of race hatred," he later lamented.[32]

Amid a paranoid postwar atmosphere in which labor unions were routinely painted as "red" in the press, the Amalgamated was desperate to avoid any accusations of radicalism. As a result, it repeatedly stressed the conservative, "bread-and-butter" nature of the strike, emphasizing at every turn that the workers were fighting for basic rights, such as union recognition, lower hours, and higher wages—not a revolution. For black workers, whose economic and racial oppression were intimately connected, and whose employment was much more tenuous, such appeals rang hollow.[33]

As a result, African Americans viewed the strike as a way to advance their interests as a race, not as a compelling moment of working-class solidarity. Black workers "are in a race war," Foster astutely recognized, and "inasmuch as the steel strike resulted in more negroes being in the industry than was the case before," strikebreaking represented "victory" for many black workers.[34] This attitude was widely reflected in the black press, which generally opposed the strike—or, more accurately, generally supported black strikebreaking. The *Chicago Defender* vowed that African Americans had no "ambition to antagonize unionism," but also acknowledged that "we stand as the big stick between labor and capital . . . [and] insist that the federation[s] of labor give us a square deal." Decrying "'Jim Crow' attachments" and "separate organizations," the *Defender* argued, "a half a loaf in this particular instance is not better than no loaf at all."[35] Even the nominally progressive *Chicago Whip* chastised the strikers. The paper railed against the beatings and harassment faced by black workers who refused to join the union. "THE NEGRO CANNOT BE DRIVEN IN," an editorial screamed, "HE MUST BE MET THRU CONSTRUCTIVE REASONING AND HUMAN TREATMENT."[36] Black workers' skepticism regarding the campaign constituted a major problem for the committee's organizers.

That problem only grew as the strike spread. Despite Lewis Caldwell's vision of "a sea of black and white hands and waving hats" and the CFL's claim that the committee "eradicated the differences of race," black workers simply did not join the organizing campaign or the strike.[37] Even during the early stages of the strike, black workers were rarely spotted at meetings and rallies. At a mass meeting of six thousand workers in Gary on the first day of the strike, organizers "were concerned largely with the fact that very few Negroes were present" among the throng—particularly since black union member William Elliston was a featured speaker.[38] White unionists' racial attitudes exacerbated these issues. Many white workers responded with venom to African Americans' reticence to join the union. Foster himself denounced African American strikebreakers for "breaking down the White working man" and their leaders for being "violently opposed to . . . trade unions" and "look[ing] upon strike-breaking as a legitimate and effective means of negro advancement." An editorial in the CFL's newspaper patronizingly wondered "what Lincoln would think could he see to what use the freedom he died for was being put today" and opined that the Great Emancipator would be sickened at the sight of "Negroes . . . being used not only to forge chains of economic slavery . . . for themselves but for white workers as well."[39]

Though such editorials were stained with a host of racist assumptions, it was true that black workers did not heed the union call in significant numbers. African Americans composed roughly 13 percent of the workforce at the Homestead plant, yet only eight of the mill's 1,737 black workers signed a union card, and only one of those struck. In Clairton, six of the three hundred black workers joined the union and struck, but went back to work after just two weeks. Not a single one of the 344 black workers at Duquesne went on strike.[40] Without the cooperation of black steelworkers, the campaign was practically doomed before it began. Black workers represented the balance of power in the strike, but the union's exclusionary history, coupled with its failure to organize black workers in large numbers, combined to swing that balance toward the employers.

Employers sensed the racial division of the workforce and introduced massive numbers of strikebreakers almost immediately. Most estimates place the total number of strikebreakers used at between 30,000 and 40,000, with perhaps as many as 10,000 used in the Chicago district alone. The employers' tactics were stunningly brutal. In his memoir of the strike, Foster reprinted a letter from a black strikebreaker named Eugene Steward. A native of South Carolina, Steward sought work in Baltimore, where a labor agent recruited him to work in Philadelphia for four dollars a day. He and other African Americans were loaded onto a train, which was then locked, and driven to Monessen, Pennsylvania. When Steward realized a strike was on, he attempted to escape the mill, but was captured and told he would be shot if he attempted to leave again.[41]

In reality, however this story was far from representative. Few African Americans were being "imported," and few were being duped into strikebreaking. The ease with which employers were able to recruit black workers, particularly black Chicagoans, as strikebreakers reveals the extent to which the CFL had failed to recruit African Americans. The Interchurch World Movement reported that far from the naïve victims portrayed by Eugene Steward, "the great numbers of negroes who flowed into the Chicago and Pittsburgh plants were conscious of strike breaking." In fact, black Chicagoans, fully cognizant of the situation, volunteered for work in significant numbers—to the point that supply exceeded demand, and five hundred black workers were sent to steel mills in Cleveland to fill struck jobs there.[42]

Due to the steel unions' long-standing policies of racial exclusion, strikebreaking afforded many black workers a heretofore unavailable opportunity. The strikebreakers were welcomed into the mills by the employers, and offered lodging and meals.[43] Indeed, the bitter and violent reaction of white strikers to the strikebreakers transformed the position of the *Defender* from one of neutrality to one of vocal support for strikebreaking. Referring to Gary as the "New Mecca," the *Defender* dubbed the strike a boon "for those of the Race . . . who have been looking for a place to establish homes where they might find a cordial welcome, plenty of employment, with an opportunity to enjoy the fruits of their labor and the pursuit of happiness in their own way." The newspaper's tone reflected the pride and excitement black workers felt about their new opportunity: "Our men played quite a part in the steel strike," the paper boasted. Encouraging the continuation of strikebreaking, the paper concluded that "the strike gave members of the Race an opportunity to obtain positions which they had never before held," resulting in "steel officials . . . look[ing] with particular favor upon Colored employe[e]s."[44] Black workers had never before been welcome in the steel industry or its unions. Without a stake in the organizing drive or the strike, they now viewed strikebreaking as an opportunity for economic advancement.

Indeed, simple economics played a major role in black reticence to join the strike. During World War I, thousands of black southerners, encouraged by steel trust labor agents, hopped aboard the Illinois Central and traveled from Mississippi and Louisiana to Chicago, where workers could not only find a good job, but escape southern racial apartheid and make a life in the so-called "Land of Hope." Even the exhausting, miserable, and relentlessly dangerous life of the unskilled steel worker was preferable to sharecropping. As Bruce Nelson has found, many black workers entered the steel industry *before* the strike—that is, they applied for work not merely to temporarily fill the spots of striking union men, but to make a lasting career. At Gary Works alone, the number of black employees rose from 407 in 1916 to 1,072 in 1917 and 1,295 in 1918. By the end of the war, black workers made up 11.4 percent of the steel workforce in Illinois and 14.2 percent in Indiana. The relatively high pay of steel work meant that jobs were jealously guarded. This was particularly true given black workers' low social and occupational status, which made them vulnerable to mass discharges during the postwar recession of 1919. A Division of Negro Economics report estimated that more than 90 percent of black World War I veterans had not yet found work by April of that year; another estimate held that as many as ten thousand black Chicagoans were unemployed. For black workers facing such conditions, the prospect of risking one's job by joining a union must have seemed ludicrous.[45]

The steel companies recognized the potential of the strikebreakers to foment discontent—not only by their undermining of the strike, but by the implied racial insult of their very presence. Bosses paraded black strikebreakers past union pickets whenever possible; the Interchurch World Movement noted that "in Gary the negroes were marched ostentatiously through the streets."[46] The *New Majority* furiously reported that enticements like liquor, women, and movies were "held out as bait" to "lure … colored scabs," who were also "encourage[d] to shoot craps" and then tell their friends of their exploits "to tempt others in."[47] Such acts eroded the morale of the strikers, but they also fomented hatred and resentment against the strikebreakers, who were increasingly seen as a mass of invaders. Company officials eagerly spread such feelings, responding to any accusations of strikebreaking, provocation, or violence by saying "niggers did it."[48]

White strikers grew increasingly agitated about the presence of the strikebreakers, and began to take drastic steps against them. In South Chicago, a group of a thousand union pickets stationed itself at every rail station of the Illinois Central, seeking to chase away a group of thirty black strikebreakers. The strikers, alerted by union railroad workers, even went so far as to grease the tracks, so that the trainload of strikebreakers could not stop at its intended destination.[49] Such resentment and racial animus was not limited to the rank and file. In October, the committee summoned a group of two hundred delegates of various local unions to Chicago for a conference. Among the resolutions passed was one lamenting the fact that "75 per cent of the labor going on in the mills at present is being done by Negro labor," but that "95 per cent of the Negroes have never worked in steel mills before."[50] The presence of the black strikebreakers was both a racial insult and an insult to the workers' sense of pride in their work. The solution, "if a great racial feeling is to be averted," was for the black strikebreakers to be expelled. The feelings of the strikers were so intense that Illinois governor Frank Lowden intervened, asking that the steel companies stop the hiring of black strikebreakers at Joliet. Lowden agreed with union leaders that "if this practice is continued it may lead to serious race trouble."[51]

Inevitably, "serious race trouble" occurred. On the night of October 4, a black strikebreaker was pulled out of a streetcar in Gary and beaten. The episode remains controversial. According to union representatives, a group of strikers was walking home from an outdoor meeting when, in Foster's words, they "fell foul of some homeward bound scabs."[52] A scuffle ensued, with a few dozen people being arrested and one black strikebreaker, pulled from a streetcar, suffering minor injuries. But the press immediately sensationalized the event; the virulently antiunion *Chicago Tribune* described it as "a pitched battle between 5,000 strikers and several hundred policemen and special deputy sheriffs."[53] Foster and other unionists were stunned at reports of "the hospitals . . . full of wounded" and "the city . . . running in blood."[54] Whatever the reality of the situation, the incident was sufficient pretext for Indiana governor James Goodrich to summon federal troops to occupy the city. Army regulars under the command of General Leonard Wood soon arrived and placed the city under martial law, forbidding any public meeting by union members.[55]

The Gary incident poisoned public opinion against the strikers and allowed the press to inflame hysteria that the strike was a Bolshevik plot. The nationalist propaganda of the war, and the unprecedented wave of militant strikes (including the Seattle general strike and the Boston police strike) that galvanized the nation in 1919 created widespread paranoia about subversion and revolution. The presence of large numbers of immigrants in the strike only served to corroborate this assumption. Union leaders feebly replied that steel bosses had hired the immigrants in the first place, but to no avail. The charges of radicalism became more vociferous when reporters discovered Foster's syndicalist past and publicized quotes from his youth regarding plans to foment revolution by "boring from within the labor movement."[56]

With Gary under martial law, the strike quickly collapsed in the Chicago district. Small groups of strikers began to trickle back into work, a number that swelled as the committee's meager strike fund was exhausted and a brutally cold winter set in. By November, all of the mills in the district save Waukegan and Joliet were running at 50 percent of capacity or greater, with some as high as 85 percent. Although the committee estimated more than a hundred thousand men were still out in mid-December, committee leadership could no longer continue, and the strike officially ended on January 7, 1920. Though some small groups of men remained on strike, they were striking in name only; in reality, they had been blacklisted and would never be welcomed back to their old jobs.[57]

The defeat of the steel strikers was a grave blow to the CFL. Fitzpatrick and Foster had hoped to bring to the industry the same democratic spirit that, however briefly, had made the SLC a major power in the city's labor movement. But the steel union's history of discrimination, the AFL's insistence on local control, the mutual distrust of white and black workers, and the determined counteroffensive of the steel companies combined to crush the committee's efforts. Foster resigned from the committee in January 1920; it was formally dissolved that summer. Though a new committee was formed, it was purely perfunctory. The union had been utterly defeated. Though twenty strikers had been killed in conflicts with police and mill guards (most of them in the Pittsburgh district), they won not a single concession. A study by the Department of Labor found that the twelve-hour day was just as prevalent in 1920 as it had been in 1910.[58] The defeat chased unionism from the industry entirely. Unions would make no headway in steel until 1935. The racial legacy of the strike was equally bitter. The tragic irony of black strikebreaking is that African American workers derived little tangible economic benefit from their loyalty to employers. According to Bruce Nelson, 73.6 percent of black steelworkers were employed in unskilled positions in 1910. Despite the central importance of African Americans in breaking the 1919 strike, their position barely changed. Two decades later, in 1930, the percentage of unskilled black workers stood at 73.5 percent.[59]

As in the meatpacking industry, the union's problem was one of necessary and sufficient conditions. Though the strike was lost due to black strikebreakers, their presence and importance was in turn due to the long-standing policies of the AFL, the structural failures of the committee, and the racial attitudes of rank-and-file workers. The solution to the AFL's problems lay not in excoriating black workers, but in correcting its own myopia. For evidence, one need look no further than the story of a black machinist in the Youngstown district who walked off the job with his white comrades, stayed out to the bitter end, and still was not admitted to the machinists' union.[60]

The first industry to be tackled by the CFL—meatpacking—was also the site of its final major defeat. In 1921, Chicago packers slashed wages, built a strike reserve force, and openly provoked the weakened AMCBW into calling a nationwide strike. The strike would follow a familiar and tragic pattern. The union, unable to recruit black workers in significant numbers, was left vulnerable to the race-baiting counteroffensive of employers. The introduction of black strikebreakers added a volatile element to the strike, and despite the unified (and violent) response of the white community, the strike was soon defeated, leaving the already weakened stockyards organizations shattered.

By the early 1920s, the CFL was ill-prepared to defend itself against an employer onslaught in the meatpacking industry. The postwar depression and resultant labor surplus created a crisis of employment for stockyards workers. Though the union had used the looming expiration of the Alschuler award in summer 1919 to initiate a new campaign to secure 100 percent unionization of the yards, it had failed. The explosion of racial violence during the summer of 1919 derailed the campaign and added a volatile racial element to the union's activities. Meanwhile, internal strife between the SLC and AMCBW diverted the time, energy, and resources of the leaders of both unions away from the campaign.[61] By the time of the strike, the SLC had reached its lowest ebb.

Central to this weakness was the continuing issue of race. Employers had used racial tensions to break strikes in the past, but in the World War I period, the CFL's efforts to organize black workers, flawed as they may have been, served as a bulwark against open race-baiting by employers. With the horrors of the race riot, the defeat of the steel strike, and the collapse of the SLC into civil war, the packers confidently used race to help provoke a strike. The packers had chosen their battlefield well. By 1921, membership in the all-black Local 651 was down to 112, with only forty-nine members in good standing. Agents of the company began openly hiring black workers as a strike reserve force. Not only did the packers choose not to conceal this information; they directed their spies on the killing floors to spread the word.[62]

The packers also used their contacts with the black community to foment discord. The mysterious R. E. Parker—editor of the *Chicago Advocate* and founder and head of the American Unity Labor Union and Colored Welfare Club (AULU)—reappeared on the scene. White workers claimed that Parker was recruiting black southerners to work in the stockyards in case of a strike. Others speculated that the packers had paid Parker to incite a race war and thus justify the intervention of federal troops, who could be used to destroy the union once and for all. Most galling to the SLC was an open letter from Parker to the city's packers. The letter claimed that "six thousands of colored laborers" belonged to the AULU, and claimed that every one of them would "accept 20 per cent reduction of wages on skilled labor and 10 per cent reduction on unskilled labor as you have agreed to give." Parker was careful to note that he had "no affiliation with the American Federation or the Amalgamated Meat Cutters' Union," and pledged that his men would not join any strike called by the AMCBW. Parker ended his letter with a stinging critique of the CFL: "We believe we are better off by not being in the white union as they have always been unfair to colored laborers."[63] Parker's claim to six thousand members is highly dubious; Lane also mocked Parker's intention to "offset" a mass stockyards rally with a meeting of his own, noting that an interracial crowd of thousands attended the stockyards march, while Parker's counterprotest garnered a mere one hundred.[64] Regardless of the actual strength of the AULU, the CFL's reaction to Parker suggests that he posed a significant threat to the union's power. One labor leader referred to the publication of Parker's open letter in several city dailies as an act "either . . . [of] idiotic ignorance or . . . criminal intent to help stir up a new race warfare." Another worker, mindful of the lessons of Gary, called it a "deliberate attempt to incite riot so that soldiers, machine guns, mounted police and all the other instruments of terror may be turned loose in the streets."[65]

The blows the federation had suffered in the race riot and the steel strike had taught its leaders a harsh lesson. As the packers attempted to appeal to black workers in anticipation of a strike, so too did the CFL. The union's primary tool in defending itself against possible race-baiting was the mass meeting. The feeling predominated among CFL leaders that if the benefits of unionism were simply and directly explained to black workers, they would flock to the union in droves. During the summer of 1921, a series of nightly meetings consisting of "a continuous program of music and short, snappy speeches" was held at the Pekin Theater on the South Side. Led by A. K. Foote, secretary of Local 651, the meetings sought to counteract the efforts of bosses, preachers, politicians, and antiunion newspapers to paint unions as "disorderly outlaw bodies that are prejudiced against [black workers]."[66] In September, an estimated 25,000 union members attended a mass rally; union leaders proudly noted that "I. H. Bratton, colored, president of Local 651 of the Butcher Workmen—the

Negro local—was enthusiastically received as a speaker by the 2,000 or more members of his race who were in the throng," though the number of black attendees was likely exaggerated.[67]

Unfortunately for the CFL, the meetings had diminishing returns. A week after the September meeting, an assembly intended to rally the black stockyards workers drew a mixed-race crowd of less than a thousand. In October, the union boasted of an "overflow meeting" of black stockyards workers held at Forresters' Hall, but the meeting was held in conjunction with the Pullman porters and it is impossible to know how many workers attended solely in support of the AMCBW.[68] The most productive of the meetings, held at Unity Hall in December, was attended by a mere six hundred workers, though once more the numbers were inflated by the presence of members of the Pullman porters, waiters, and musicians unions. The CFL appealed to the stockyards workers with a prestigious set of speakers—John Fitzpatrick; black former alderman Oscar DePriest; and Irene Goins, president of the Federation of Colored Women's Clubs and a member of Woman's Trade Union League—who stumped for the union and its potential to uplift the black community. Fitzpatrick even attempted to heal the rift caused by the waiters' strike of 1903, explaining that the so-called "betrayal" of black waiters was the doing of bosses, not the union. Most importantly, the union made concrete promises to solicit the advice and approval of black community leaders, to strengthen Local 651, and to create a "central council of Negro unions" to better organize and coordinate black members.[69]

But even this meeting was largely ineffectual. Though the idea of the council seemed progressive on its face, it revealed the impotence of the CFL's federated structure in the face of racial tension. In reality, the council served merely as another form of so-called "Jim Crow unionism." The CFL chartered the black labor council and secured a meeting space for it, but black interest in joining segregated federal unions remained so low that the council had little to do. The organizers the CFL hired to support the council were not worth the salary they were paid. Though they managed to convince perhaps a hundred black workers to sign union cards, they spent much of their time unsuccessfully attempting to convince potential strikebreakers to reconsider. The council soon abandoned the stockyards for the more fruitful organizing ground of the hotel and restaurant industry.[70]

Despite the union's best efforts at awakening black support, the bloody racial history of unionism in Chicago, coupled with the lingering distrust engendered by the race riot, caused most black workers to keep the CFL at arm's length. As contemporary observer Catherine Elizabeth Lewis noted, the CFL's policy toward African American workers on the eve of the 1921–22 strike was essentially identical to its iteration during the World War I–era organizing drive: first, the employment of "a few Negro organizers to tell Negroes the advantages of trade unionism," and second, the practice "of proclaiming 'brotherhood'" while organizing African Americans into all-black federal unions.[71] If race was to be a deciding factor in the strike, the CFL was already at a disadvantage.

Whatever the strength of Parker's organization or the effect of the CFL's efforts to organize black workers, pure arithmetic held that the packers had chosen the right time and place to battle the union. War-time inflation had caused cost of living in Back of the Yards and other blue-collar neighborhoods to skyrocket, with one estimate claiming it was as high as $1,850 per year; an unskilled stockyards worker making the average salary of $22 per week would fall short of that amount by more than seven hundred dollars. Unemployment among African Americans was even higher than that of whites. During 1920 alone, more than five thousand African Americans applied for employment through the Urban League; only 608 found jobs.[72]

Perhaps most critically, with the war over, the federal government was no longer in the labor mediation business. The Alschuler award—savior of the stockyards workers—was set to expire on September 15, 1921. Sensing an opportunity, the packers announced plans for drastic wage cuts in February. Though weakened and divided, especially in Chicago, the AMCBW had no choice but to fight back. On March 10, a strike vote was held at a mass conference in Omaha, and passed with more than 99 percent support. Anticipating the immensity of the fight to come, smaller packing companies began laying off employees immediately. By the expiration date of the Alschuler award, both sides were in a state of high agitation. When the packers increased their proposed wage cut from 12.5 percent to 15 percent, the union formulated a list of demands and pleaded with the packers for negotiation. They refused. The die was cast: on December 5, 1921, the stockyards strike officially began.[73]

The response, as in other strikes, was immediate: forty-five thousand men walked out nationwide, an estimated twenty-five thousand in Chicago alone. But it quickly became clear that the packers were fighting from a position of strength. On the first day of the strike, a group of two hundred police was deployed in the stockyards. The packers met union boasts regarding the number of strikers with calm rebuttals that the strike was having no effect on production. The packers announced that advertisements requesting strikebreakers had already run in newspapers in both Chicago and Kansas City, and coldly stated that none of the strikers would be permitted to return to their jobs. If the packing bosses seemed unruffled by the prospect of a lengthy siege, the union appeared disorganized and ill-prepared. Crucial segments of the workforce—namely, the firemen and engineers who ensured smooth transit of goods into and out of the yards—did not walk out. More damningly, the same problem had plagued the union during the 1904 strike, and CFL leadership had done nothing to correct it during the intervening years. Fearful of backing a losing cause, even the fire-breathing teamsters refused to walk out in support of the embattled AMCBW.[74]

In spite of the workers' isolation, or quite possibly because of it, the strike became a community affair. Crowds constantly filled the streets in an endless, raucous protest. A judge issued an injunction prohibiting picketing in the stockyards district, an order the strikers completely ignored. When mounted police arrived to clear the strikers out of Davis Square Park, they felt the rage of Packingtown. For days, the strikers engaged in riots against an army of more than a thousand police. Men hurled bricks and stones, while women flung pepper and paprika into the eyes of police and their horses. Motorcycle-mounted police were knocked from their vehicles "and strikers tore pickets from fences with which to club them."[75] Several reports even claimed that snipers stationed in upper-story windows were firing down at the police.[76]

But the solidarity of the white community went largely for naught, as the packers moved quickly to replace the striking workers. As before, the packers made use of black strikebreakers, augmenting the volatile racial atmosphere of the strike. Unlike the 1904 strike, however—in which the packers brought strikebreakers into the yards under cover of darkness—the packers' strength allowed their recruitment of strikebreakers in the 1921 strike to be outright brazen. Morris and Company opened an employment office in the heart of the Black Belt, infuriating strikers and widening the gap between white and black workers. Their rage only increased when it was revealed that the packers were again lodging black strikebreakers in the yards, leading to another outbreak of smallpox among the replacement workers and familiar recriminations of the strikebreakers' immoral and degenerate behavior. Most importantly, unlike previous conflicts, the strikebreakers were almost exclusively black. In one major plant, the proportion of black employees rose from 25 percent to 33 percent in the span of a few weeks; another firm saw its black employment double, from a sixth to a third. Many plants ran at only 25 percent capacity, but the sight of black strikebreakers marching into the yards to do "white" jobs substantially weakened the resolve of the strikers. Though the violence of the strike never reached the brutal fever pitch of the 1904 strike, the mob soon turned its fury on the strikebreakers, pulling African Americans off of streetcars and beating them. At least one black strikebreaker was stoned to death during a riot.[77]

White rage did little to sway the packers or the strikebreakers. The most damaging fact of the strike was that most black stockyards employees, unmoved by the union's recruiting drive, refused to strike. Indeed, the packers' efforts to win the fealty of black workers were richly rewarded, as black community leaders openly urged workers to remain on the job. The Sunday before the beginning of the strike, black ministers throughout the city included antiunion messages from the packers in their sermons and urged their parishioners to ignore the strike call.[78] In October, the Wabash Avenue YMCA opened its membership drive with a dinner funded by the packers. Speakers included Harvey Ellerd of Armour, who spoke on "The Y. M. C. A. as an Expression of Good Will Between Employer and Employe[e]," and George Merritt, president of the Armour Efficiency Club, whose speech was entitled "Why the Industrial Workers Support the Y. M. C. A."[79] The packers had deployed such paternalistic tactics for years, but the dire economic conditions of 1921 meant that for African Americans, a choice between striking and strikebreaking was essentially a choice between unemployment and employment. As a result, black workers abandoned even their tenuous support for the CFL and stayed at work.

The strategic paternalism of the packers made the decision simple. There was perhaps no better evidence of the effect of such largesse than the actions of the Chicago Urban League. Though nominally neutral in industrial disputes, and sometimes even prounion, the league—facing the prospect of thousands of unemployed black Chicagoans—had little choice but to support employers during the strike. Just as critically, the league was dependent on contributions from local black elites, nearly all of whom opposed the strike, as well as from the stockyards firms themselves. Ultimately, the league supplied nearly five hundred strikebreakers to the packers. After the strike was over, the league's industrial secretary openly boasted of replacing the striking workers, claiming that black employees had managed to regain skilled jobs previously lost to white workers.[80]

The black press also overwhelmingly supported the strikebreakers. The *Defender* so vociferously supported strikebreaking that it refused to use the term "strikebreaker," claiming that nonunion black workers who remained at work in the yards were simply desperate men in need of an opportunity: "The prospect of a job in these times of near-starvation looks good to [any] idle worker, black or white," the paper argued, lamenting that "such opportunities only come to the black worker on occasions like this."[81] Black politician and editor Roscoe Simmons claimed to be an "ardent believer in unionism," but excoriated the AFL for its discriminatory policies, and also decried the use of the term "scab," claiming that it could not fairly be applied to black workers "because so many union doors are closed against [them]."[82] More importantly, the *Defender* took aim directly at the CFL. The editorial railed against Jim Crow unionism, arguing that "the doors have not been sufficiently opened to bring about complete racial unification" and demanding that black workers be accepted "unreservedly into every trades union."[83] The very presence of black strikebreakers, of course, made the prospect of a successful interracial union bleaker than ever. Nonetheless, the *Defender* scoffed at the CFL's mass-meeting strategy, citing its neglect of black workers during the wartime period: "Unions cannot expect to close the working door in his face in peaceful times and expect his co-operation in troublesome times."[84] Desperate to salvage the CFL's relationship with the black community, John Fitzpatrick met with Robert Abbott in November "to secure co-operation in the labor movement" from the influential *Defender* editor. The meeting was for naught. In an editorial recounting the meeting, Abbott railed against the persistence of "Jim Crow labor unions" and refused to support the CFL "as long as its house was dirty."[85]

Even the progressive *Chicago Whip* found it impossible to support the CFL. "The majority of our workers are outside the pale of unionism," an editorial claimed, "not because they want to be but because ... they have been barred from linking their fortunes with them." With no stake in the success of unionism, the paper argued, black workers turned to self-preservation: "WE MUST LIVE, AND IF WE CANNOT GET A WHOLE LOAF WE WILL TAKE THE PART OF THE LOAF WE CAN GET." Though the editor lamented the low wages that resulted from black strikebreaking, he claimed, "this is a situation for which the unions are entirely responsible."

If the white unionist "wants . . . full power in the economic world," he concluded, "he must take his black fellow workman as a partner."[86]

With the participation of black strikebreakers, the strike soon became a desperate proposition. The strikers, their strike fund quickly exhausted, struggled to provide food and coal for their families during the brutal Chicago winter. Within a matter of mere weeks, the strike appeared hopeless. By January, the CFL was openly soliciting donations of coats and other winter clothes at its meetings. The strike was officially called off on January 31, although by that time only a small number of the workers were still on strike. With their victory secured, the packers moved to consolidate their power and annihilate the union once and for all. Dozens of union activists were summarily fired and blacklisted. The eight-hour day, enjoyed by stockyards workers as a result of the Alschuler award, was abandoned in favor of the ten-hour day. As in steel, Chicago's meat industry would not see a union presence of any significance until the mid-1930s.[87]

Much as the steel strike had done, the stockyards strike of 1921–22 left a bitter racial legacy in its wake. The defeat of the strike helped drive black and white workers even further apart; more than ever, white workers resented black workers as a "scab race."[88] In this way, the strike represented the final blow to the CFL's already tattered hopes for an interracial union. Though black workers had made tremendous inroads into the meatpacking industry—after the strike, they constituted fully 30 percent of the stockyards labor force—they fared little better. The packers' victory had taught them the value of a permanent strike insurance force of black labor. While African Americans retained stockyards jobs in larger numbers, the vast majority remained consigned to the lowest-paying and most dangerous jobs. A 1926 survey of one large plant reported that less than 40 percent of the white employees but nearly 70 percent of black employees were paid the unskilled "common labor rate" of forty-five cents. These unskilled workers labored under truly offensive conditions. At both Swift and Armour, management forbade black workers from handling any finished products, claiming that white customers would be repulsed by African Americans touching their food.[89]

The defeat in the stockyards was a crippling blow to the CFL. Not only did it constitute the union's second resounding loss in a major industry in the span of two years, but the packers had deliberately provoked racial conflict in hopes of dividing and defeating the union. The fact that this plan was an unqualified success is a sad testament to the degree to which the CFL failed in its stated mission to attract black workers. Despite the union's efforts to win the loyalty of African Americans, their class appeal failed in part because black workers were more responsive to the needs of their race, and because the class appeal of the packers—the guarantee of employment—was far more persuasive. Without the support of black workers, the CFL added another defeat to its ledger.

The disintegration of the Labor Party represented the final defeat for Fitzpatrick's vision of progressive unionism. Despite the party's respectable showing during the mayoral election of 1919, it quickly collapsed and finally was abandoned by its architect. Though not nearly as dramatic as the civil war of the SLC or the strikes in steel and meatpacking, the death of the Labor Party is similarly instructive. Fitzpatrick had envisioned a true people's party beholden not to moneyed interests but to workers. But as with his failed attempts to organize the meat and steel industries, the structure of the organization proved an obstacle. By organizing the party along local union lines, the CFL tied the party to a diverse and often competing set of ethnic political interests inflamed by the nationalism of the World War I era. In seeking to appeal to this coalition while avoiding accusations of radicalism, party officials seemed determined to steer a torturous middle course. The party took virtually no role in the CFL's major crisis points—the race riot, the steel strike, and the meatpacking strike—despite the fact that each represented an opportunity to transform working-class militancy into electoral power.[90]

Such a philosophy resulted in disaster for the party. Instead of forming a militant political coalition, the party's insistence on local trade union control alienated moderates, while its relatively conservative program failed to attract more militant unionists. The latter problem was exacerbated by the AFL's Non-Partisan Political Campaign, which was launched just as the party was gaining momentum. The Non-Partisan Campaign adopted several of the Labor Party's planks—public ownership of utilities, recognition of the rights to organize and bargain collectively, democratic governance of industry—while deriding the efficacy of a third party, simultaneously co-opting the party's influence and undermining its authority. Moreover, the Non-Partisan Campaign was legitimated by the imprimatur of the AFL, making it far more attractive to unionists who doubted the strength of the Labor Party. The party's activities consisted primarily of electing delegates to the state's woefully underattended constitutional convention. In other words, the Labor Party was founded with the hope of effecting massive change in the American political system, but its leaders chose to affect that change through plodding, staid means. As a result, the party's 1920 convention was sparsely attended and its coffers nearly empty. The party's official newspaper, the *New Majority*, was running a deficit of nearly $2,000 every month. The party's 1920 campaign was a disaster: the total number of votes cast for hundreds of Labor Party candidates nationwide was less than twelve thousand. Fitzpatrick, making a run for the U.S. Senate, gained only 0.5 percent of the vote.[91]

The specter of racial division also reared its ugly head once more. Despite its efforts, the Labor Party was unable to connect with the city's vital ethnic communities, in part because the militant cadre of the union consisted largely of recent immigrants who were not registered to vote and thus took little interest in the party's activities. But even those eligible to vote had already been bought off by the major political parties. Lacking contacts with ward captains, the union could not attract a large number of ethnic voters. African Americans in particular were wedded to the city's Republican machine. Just as black workers would not pass up the packers' promise of employment for the union's appeal to class solidarity, neither would they abandon the patronage of Bill Thompson in favor of the Labor Party's limp pledges to amend the state's constitution. Despite the avowed antiracism of the Labor Party platform and its promises to recruit African American voters, the party largely failed in these attempts. In 1920, for example, the *Defender* reported that black editor Hugh Nanton would be traveling to the party's convention in Schenectady, New York, but could not resist pointing out that "Nanton . . . has the distinction of being the only one of our people represented."[92]

Despite these setbacks, Fitzpatrick insisted on moving forward with the founding of a national labor party in 1920. The result was the Farmer-Labor Party, a tenuous alliance of workers, farmers, and intellectuals. The new party nominated a number of U.S. Senate candidates for the 1920 election and selected a little-known Utah attorney named Parley Christensen as a presidential candidate. Their aims were modest—it was expected that Christensen could carry a half-dozen states, and three of the senatorial candidates had a strong chance of election. Instead, the campaign was an abject disaster. Christensen gained only 1 percent of the popular vote (compared to the 3.5 percent earned by socialist Eugene V. Debs, who conducted his campaign from federal prison) and did not carry a single state. None of the senatorial candidates were elected. The Illinois results were particularly discouraging: Christensen's presidential campaign received fewer votes statewide than John Fitzpatrick's 1919 mayoral campaign had earned in Chicago alone.[93]

Beset by structural flaws, preyed upon by the AFL, ignored by African Americans, and rapidly losing strength, the Farmer-Labor Party was in disarray. Desperate to salvage the party, Fitzpatrick called for a convention in 1923, at which he planned to reorganize the party along the British Labour Party model. But the party's structure proved problematic once more. The party's power rested with its member unions, and many of those unions had abandoned the party due to pressure from the AFL and the party's lack of electoral success. As a result, the party was forced to forge alliances with nonlabor groups, many of whom had different priorities than Fitzpatrick's narrow trade-union political agenda. A large contingent of communists attended the 1923 convention, for example, and attempted to wrest control of the party from Fitzpatrick. When Fitzpatrick attempted to limit their power, he was voted down, and the communists formed the short-lived Federated Farmer-Labor Party. Fitzpatrick marched his delegation out of the conference in disgust. In Chicago, the party was losing strength as well. Christensen's embarrassing showing in the party's home state of Illinois signaled its irrelevance. In May 1924, Fitzpatrick officially counseled the CFL to embrace the AFL's non-partisan position.[94] The Labor Party was dead.

The Labor Party suffered the same fate as the CFL drives in meatpacking and steel. Weakened by a flawed structure, the party made few inroads among African Americans and lacked the funds and organizational energy to seriously threaten the status quo. The predation of the AFL and the internal flaws of the party only served to accelerate its demise. The quiet death of the Labor Party signaled the full defeat of John Fitzpatrick's vision of progressive unionism. Despite his best efforts, the CFL entered the 1920s much as it had entered the 1910s: divided, weakened, and lacking direction.

Fitzpatrick's noble vision died with the Labor Party. The CFL had made a valiant effort to "bore from within"—to reform existing union structures and create a dynamic, democratic unionism based on a militant, diverse membership, a sense of interracial solidarity, and an independent labor politics. But the CFL was defeated at every stage. Old-line trade unionists resented Fitzpatrick's efforts to recruit African Americans and recent immigrants, as well as his militant posture regarding employers. The union's inability to effectively appeal to black workers led directly to its defeat in major strikes in steel and meatpacking. Finally, the Labor Party's schizophrenic nature—functioning both as a political party and a representative of union locals—rendered it ineffective and futile.

James Barrett has noted that "Chicago's militant labor movement . . . did not simply fall apart; it was attacked and destroyed."[95] Certainly one cannot underestimate the active role employers played in the destruction of progressive unionism. Their carefully cultivated alliances with black community leaders, their paternalistic attitude toward black workers, and their successful use of race-baiting tactics to defeat strikes in steel and meatpacking dealt severe blows to the CFL's ability to build a truly interracial organization. With that said, the true legacy of progressive unionism is its inability to recognize the degree to which African Americans' identity was tied to their race and not their class. Confident that the union appeal would succeed within the black community if only it were properly delivered, Fitzpatrick and the CFL, as historian James Grossman has argued, woefully underestimated the degree to which African Americans' response to the union call would be "shaped by the overwhelming reality of racial discrimination as part of a historical experience."[96] Without such an understanding, the CFL's efforts to organize an interracial union would remain merely a dream.

CONCLUSION: THE PAST, PRESENT, AND FUTURE OF INTERRACIAL UNIONISM

I t goes without saying that the story of unionism in Chicago did not end with the collapse of the 1921 meatpacking strike. But it is equally undeniable that the city's labor movement reached its lowest ebb during the 1920s. Eagerly attempting to exploit labor's weakness, employers instituted the so-called American Plan, a sweeping ideology of reform that reached a number of major industries after the war. Though its specifics differed by industry and even company, the general idea was to destroy trade unions and replace them with paternalistic corporate welfare schemes. For the packers, such plans took many forms. Chief among them was the employee representation plan, known to workers as the company union. Ostensibly a tool for shared democratic governance, company unions were in reality nothing more than a perfunctory nod toward union values. Bosses often targeted specific employees to receive the benefits of the company's largesse, rewarding loyal (i.e., nonunion) workers with plum appointments.[1] In meatpacking, these efforts went beyond company unions. By the early 1920s, both Armour and Swift would add a variety of programs meant to ensure worker loyalty: company recreation outings, plant beautification programs, internal publications, English education and Americanization programs for immigrants, and stock purchases. Taken together, these programs served to normalize the relations of production while maintaining a divided workforce through preferential distribution of benefits.[2]

As it had in the previous decade, the specter of race continued to loom over the industry. The Great Migration continued apace, and packing bosses welcomed increasing numbers of African Americans into their workforce as a "strike insurance" force. The packers also stepped up their attempts to sow racial discord. Superintendents promoted black workers into more skilled positions than ever before, threatening the traditional racial privilege of white workers. For African Americans, such advancement was an enormous boon, carrying as it did not only higher wages but seniority and prestige both on and off the shop floor. But such promotions were cynical attempts by the packers to cleave racial pride from labor solidarity.[3] Company unions assiduously cultivated black leaders, further distancing African Americans from Chicago's unions.[4] The same pattern persisted in the city's other major industries, including steel. Such efforts helped subvert loyalties to racial or ethnic cohorts and (in particular) coworkers in favor of loyalty to the employer.[5] For African Americans, primary beneficiaries of the failed SLC strikes and the American Plan, burgeoning nationalism and racial pride ensured that such loyalty was never absolute. But it is difficult to argue that the 1920s represented the consummation of black workers' estrangement from Chicago's unions.

How, then, can one account for the resounding success of Chicago's labor movement in the late 1930s? Given the failures of the CFL in meatpacking and steel, it is instructive to examine the efforts of the Committee for Industrial Organization/Congress of Industrial Organizations (CIO) in the Depression decade. Much like the SLC, the CIO saw the city's ballooning black population—which doubled during the 1920s, bringing the total number of black Chicagoans to 300,000 by 1930—as an opportunity for a new kind of muscular, interracial unionism.[6] Like the SLC, it received critical assistance from federal intervention: in this case, the National Industrial Recovery Act and its famous Section 7(a), which guaranteed American workers the right to organize.[7] Unlike the SLC, the CIO faced a city devastated by economic trauma. In white ethnic neighborhoods, unemployed workers organized councils to feed families using reclaimed bread and meat stolen from the stockyards. In the Black Belt, the situation was even more dire, as African Americans were "last hired, first fired" from any job in the city, and relied increasingly on the meager funds of the NAACP and Urban League for relief.[8]

But where the SLC created a fairly traditional union draped in the clothing of innovation and interracial solidarity, the CIO adopted those elements as central to its identity. Where the SLC used a federated structure to avoid questions of craft autonomy, the CIO simply organized all workers along industrial lines. Where the SLC employed neighborhood locals to reinforce ethnic and racial bonds through union solidarity, the CIO took pains to create such bonds itself, creating local Youth Councils and organizing through churches, fraternal organizations, and saloons.[9] Where the SLC declaimed Foster's radical heritage, particularly during the steel strike, the CIO enthusiastically embraced Communist Party members as organizers, deploying them throughout Packingtown and the Black Belt. Where the SLC gestured clumsily toward political independence, the CIO embraced the Democratic Party, weaving together political and union loyalty at the very moment the party was consolidating its electoral dominance over the city.[10] In short, the CIO created something that was more akin to "a social movement," as Rick Halpern has dubbed it, than merely a union. Or, as Lizabeth Cohen put it, the CIO was built around a "culture of unity" that "permeated all . . . union activities in Chicago on and off the shop floor."[11]

Perhaps nowhere was this pervasive sense of purpose more evident than in the CIO's treatment of race. The CIO made interracial organizing a central goal of its campaign, but unlike the CFL, it pursued that goal with genuine zeal. The CIO's organizers made antiracist appeals to black workers, which were backed by burgeoning alliances with black churches, politicians, and middle-class leaders.[12] The CIO also aggressively campaigned for its black members. CIO national director John Brophy declared that "behind every lynching is the figure of the labor exploiter . . . the man or corporation who would deny labor its fundamental rights."[13] The organization backed such rhetoric with hard work on the shop floor. Packinghouse Workers Organizing Committee (PWOC) militated against the tagging of black workers' time cards and the segregation of departments, and named a black meatpacker as its first assistant national director.[14] Meanwhile, the Steelworkers Organizing Committee (SWOC) placed black workers on bargaining and grievance committees and refused to meet in hotels or halls with color bars.[15] Unlike the SLC, the CIO viewed civil rights and racial justice as a central part of its mission, and thus, unlike the SLC, the CIO birthed unions filled with, and led by, activist black members.[16] By World War II, the city's major industries were largely organized, with black and white workers standing together.

But one must avoid the temptation to view the success of the CIO solely as a condemnation of the CFL. Organizers and leaders of the CIO were the beneficiaries of any number of external factors—the largesse of a generally prolabor New Deal government, a massive national upsurge in labor activity that crossed lines of industry and geography, and a widespread embrace of radical organizers that would have been unthinkable during the post-World War I Red Scare. And yet most of the CFL's most grievous failures—its unwillingness to buck traditional union structures, its naiveté and paternalism regarding black workers' loyalties, its inability to make inroads in the black community, and its tragic misapprehension of critical situations such as the race riot—were self-inflicted. Given African Americans' enthusiastic embrace of the CIO less than two decades after the death of the Stockyards Labor Council suggests that its failure was by no means inevitable. Though historical conditions were certainly different during the time of Fitzpatrick's drive for progressive unionism, it is difficult not to wonder what might have been.

The drama and turbulence of the 1930s represent a constant source of interest to historians, but in many ways the CFL's failed campaign has just as much to teach us. By accommodating traditional union ideas regarding craft autonomy, the CFL inadvertently reinforced existing patterns of segregation and helped provoke antipathy and even violence. This book has examined the ways in which that failure both produced, and was the product of, the complex interplay of union structures and interpersonal shop-floor relations. Unlike the CIO, which used the language of civil rights to build a genuinely interracial union movement, or openly and brutally racist unions, such as those in the railroad and building trades, the CFL stands athwart a strange middle ground. Though the CFL's leaders were progressive by any conceivable standard of their day, they were unable to conceive of racial justice outside of the paradigm of class struggle. As a result, their efforts toward interracial unionism, however well-intentioned, were blundering and ultimately self-defeating. Examining such unions—those that possess progressive ideas but are thwarted by a lack of will or skill, or by historical contingency—expands our understanding of how race and class intersect and blurs the boundary between interracial solidarity and bitter exclusion that so often defines scholarship of race and the labor movement.[17]

The CFL's failure also holds lessons for today. Organized labor has once more reached a low ebb. Unions in higher education, the public sector, and the service industry are the movement's strongest hope for the near future, but the specter of racial conflict has once more reared its ugly head. With memberships consisting largely of women and people of color, these unions are increasingly assailed as bastions of sloth, greed, and entitlement. Meanwhile, many activists, grappling with the results of the 2016 election, have become embroiled in self-defeating arguments that pit "identity politics" against "class politics," implying that protections for marginalized people are in some way incompatible with expanded social welfare programs and more equitable distribution of wealth. If workers are to endure this trying period, let alone to flourish as they once did, it is incumbent upon them to learn the lessons of the past. The failures of the SLC prove that any social movement cannot make compromises with the mistakes of the past by accommodating traditional structures or abiding antiquated ideas. Instead, it must embrace people of all walks of life—seeking not only tolerance but justice.

NOTES

BIBLIOGRAPHY

INDEX

NOTES

INTRODUCTION: RACE AND AMERICAN LABOR HISTORY

1. Chicago Commission on Race Relations (hereafter CCRR), *Negro in Chicago*, 1.

2. Sandburg, *Chicago Race Riots*, 3.

3. Tuttle, *Race Riot*, viii.

4. CCRR, *Negro in Chicago*, 424.

5. Foner, *Organized Labor*; Spero and Harris, *Black Worker*, 463.

6. Herbst, *Meat-Packing Industry*, xviii–xix.

7. Fogel, *Meat Industry*, 31.

8. General treatments of labor that discuss race include Gutman, *Work, Culture, and Society*; and Montgomery, *House of Labor*. For more focused discussions of race, see Dickerson, *Out of the Crucible*; Meier and Rudwick, *Black Detroit*; Nelson, *Divided We Stand*; and Cohen, *Making a New Deal*.

9. Barrett, *Work and Community*; Barrett, "Racial and Ethnic Fragmentation," 288.

10. Tuttle, *Race Riot*, 153.

11. Grossman, *Land of Hope*, 241; Grossman, "White Man's Union," 83–105.

12. Street, "Working in the Yards," 179; Street, "Logic and Limits," 659–81; Street, "Swift Difference," 15–50; Halpern, *Down on the Killing Floor*; Horowitz, *"Negro and White."*

13. McCartin, "Industrial Unionism," 701–10; Brody, "Old Labor History," 111–26; Brody, "Reconciling the Old," 1–18; Kimeldorf, "Bringing Unions Back In," 91–103; Kazin, "Union-Centered History," 104–27.

14. McCartin, "Industrial Unionism," 708.

15. Hill, "Problem of Race," 192; see also Painter, "New Labor History," 367–70; Roediger, "Race and the Working-Class," 127–43.

16. Tuttle, *Race Riot*; Barrett, *Work and Community*; Horowitz, *"Negro and White."*

17. Hill, "Problem of Race," 190; see also Painter, "New Labor History."

18. Letwin, *Challenge of Interracial Unionism*, 6.

1. "A DEEP, DARK PLOT": RACE IN THE CHICAGO
LABOR MOVEMENT, 1894–1905

1. "Foolish Colored Men," *Chicago Daily Tribune* (25 August 1903), 6.

2. Delegates, for example, could not be suspended or even censured by the Federation, but only by their locals. Constitution of the Chicago Federation of Labor (1896), Chicago History Museum; Bigham, "Chicago Federation of Labor," 12–16.

3. CFL Constitution. For a discussion of race and the AFL, see chapter 3.

4. Merriam, *Chicago*, 11; Henri, *Black Migration*, 51, 83.

5. Bigham, "Chicago Federation of Labor," 21–22, 40; Hutton, "Negro Worker," 18–19; Taft, *A. F. of L.*, 311–13; see also Whatley, "African-American Strikebreaking," 525–58; Schneirov, *Labor and Urban Politics*, 236–328; Henri, *Black Migration*, 153; Spero and Harris, *Black Worker*, 53.

6. Barrett, "Racial and Ethnic Fragmentation," 289.

7. Feldman, *Racial Factors*, 32; Cohen, *Racketeer's Progress*, 107–8; Roediger, *Wages of Whiteness*, 178; see also Spero and Harris, *Black Worker*, 18–35; Foner, *Organized Labor*, 82–107; Tobias, "Black Strike-Breakers," 3.

8. Letter from Ben F. Ricketts, *Mixer and Server* 12, no. 5 (May 15 1903): 46–48; Josephson, *Union House, Union Bar*, 54.

9. "Kohlsaat Waiters' Strike," *Chicago Daily News* (5 May 1903), 1; "Strike Epidemic On," *Chicago Daily News* (6 May 1903), 2; "Waiters on Strike Now," *Chicago Daily Tribune* (6 May 1903), 3; Letter from Ben F. Ricketts, *Mixer and Server* 12, no. 6 (15 June 1903); 45; Josephson, *Union House, Union Bar*, 54; Cohen, *Racketeer's Progress*, 107–8.

10. Josephson, *Union House, Union Bar*, 55.

11. "Waiters on Strike Now," *Chicago Daily Tribune* (6 May 1903), 3; "Bakers Push Up Prices," *Chicago Daily Tribune* (8 May 1903), 3; "Peace Fails at Deering," *Chicago Daily Tribune* (9 May 1903), 3; Letter from Ben F. Ricketts, *Mixer and Server* 12, no. 6 (15 June 1903): 45; Cohen, *Racketeer's Progress*, 107–8.

12. "Fear a Labor Crisis," *Chicago Daily News* (21 May 1903), 1–2; "Labor Crisis is Near," *Chicago Daily News* (23 May 1903), 1–2; "Decide to Deny Labor's Demands," *Chicago Daily Tribune* (23 May 1903), 1; "To Oppose the Union," *Chicago Daily News* (28 May 1903), 2; "Waiters' Demand Held Exorbitant," *Chicago Daily Tribune* (29 May 1903), 3; "Big Clash Impending," *Chicago Daily News* (1 June 1903), 3.

13. "Big Clash Impending," *Chicago Daily News* (1 June 1903), 3; "Shut Out the Diners," *Chicago Daily News* (4 June 1903), 1–2; "Waiters Tie Up Two Big Hotels," *Chicago Daily Tribune* (5 June 1903), 1; "Chicago Waiters' Strike," *New York Times* (5 June 1903), 1.

14. "The End of a Strike," editorial, *Chicago Daily News* (22 June 1903), 4; "The Restaurant Workers," *Chicago Daily News* (25 August 1903), 6.

15. "The Chicago Strike," *New York Times* (14 June 1903), 6; "Chicago's Famine Peril," *New York Times* (28 May 1903), 1; see also "Chicago Hotels are Paralyzed by Strike," *New York Times* (13 June 1903), 1; "An Unjust Strike," *Chicago Daily Tribune* (13 June 1903), 12; "Waiters' Strike Nears a Finish," *Chicago Daily Tribune* (17 June 1903), 3.

16. "An Unjust Strike," *Chicago Daily Tribune* (13 June 1903), 12; "Chicago's Famine Peril," *New York Times* (28 May 1903), 1; see also "Waiters Falter; One Leader Out," *Chicago Daily Tribune* (16 June 1903), 1; "Waiters' Strike Nears a Finish," *Chicago Daily Tribune* (17 June 1903), 3.

17. "Banded to Wage War on Tipping," *Chicago Daily Tribune* (8 June 1903), 2.

18. "Waiters Falter; One Leader Out," *Chicago Daily Tribune* (16 June 1903), 1.

19. Ibid., see also "An Unjust Strike," *Chicago Daily Tribune* (13 June 1903), 12; "Waiters' Strike Nears a Finish," *Chicago Daily Tribune* (17 June 1903), 3.

20. "Laundry Strike is Ended at Last; Peace in Hotels," *Chicago Daily Tribune* (6 June 1903), 1; "Union Censure Waiters' Course," *Chicago Daily Tribune* (15 June 1903), 1; "Food Servers Yield," *Chicago Daily News* (17 June 1903), 1–2; "Hitch in Peace Plan," *Chicago Daily News* (18 June 1903), 1–2; "Waiters Give In; Will Arbitrate," *Chicago Daily Tribune* (18 June 1903), 2; "Still Try for Peace," *Chicago Daily News* (19 June 1903), 2; "Waiters Open War Anew," *Chicago Daily Tribune* (19 June 1903), 1; "Striking Employes [*sic*] Capitulate," *Chicago Eagle* (20 June 1903), 8.

21. "Waiters at Work; Strike is Ended," *Chicago Daily Tribune* (20 June 1903), 3; "Big Strike is Ended," *Chicago Daily News* (20 June 1903), 2; "Kohlsaat War Ends," *Chicago Daily News* (26 June 1903), 1–2; see also "The End of a Strike," editorial, *Chicago Daily News* (21 June 1903), 4.

22. "Waiters Attack Terms of Peace," *Chicago Daily Tribune* (21 June 1903), 6.

23. Letter from B. F. Ricketts, *Mixer and Server* 20, no. 9 (15 September 1903): 40; see also "Waiters May Quit Again," *Chicago Daily Tribune* (23 August 1903), 2; "Cafes Prepared to Fight Strike," *Chicago Daily Tribune* (24 August 1903), 1; Josephson, *Union House, Union Bar*, 54–56.

24. "Waiters Told to Work," *Chicago Daily Tribune* (9 July 1903), 5.

25. "Waiters Renew War," *Chicago Daily News* (8 July 1903), 1–2; "Another Chicago Waiters' Strike," *New York Times* (9 July 1903), 12; "Waiters May Quit Again," *Chicago Daily Tribune* (23 August 1903), 2; "Cafes Prepared to Fight Strike," *Chicago Daily Tribune* (24 August 1903), 1; Letter from B.

F. Ricketts, *Mixer and Server* 12, no. 9 (15 September 1903): 40; Josephson, *Union House, Union Bar*, 54.

26. "Waiters Told to Work," *Chicago Daily Tribune* (9 July 1903), 5; "Cloak-makers in War," *Chicago Daily News* (9 July 1903), 1–2.

27. "Foolish Colored Men," *Chicago Daily Tribune* (25 August 1903), 6.

28. "Waiters Renew War," *Chicago Daily News* (8 July 1903), 1–2; see also "Threatened Waiters' Strike," *Chicago Daily Tribune* (24 August 1903), 6; see also "Foolish Colored Men," *Chicago Daily Tribune* (25 August 1903), 6.

29. "Waiters Beaten; Negroes to Go," *Chicago Daily Tribune* (27 August 1903), 5.

30. "Go After More Cafes," *Chicago Daily News* (24 August 1903), 1–2; "Queer Mix-Up in Cafe," *Chicago Daily News* (25 August 1903), 1–2; "Ends Colored Help," *Chicago Daily News*, 2; see also "Waiters Beaten; Negroes to Go," *Chicago Daily Tribune* (27 August 1903), 5; "Strike Epidemic On," *Chicago Daily News* (6 May 1903), 2.

31. "Waiters Beaten; Negroes to Go," *Chicago Daily Tribune* (27 August 1903), 5; see also "Seek to End Strike," *Chicago Daily News* (26 August 1905), 2; "To Control Strikes," *Chicago Daily News* (1 September 1903), 4; Josephson, *Union House, Union Bar*, 55.

32. Report of President Robert A. Callahan, *Proceedings of Twelfth General Convention*, Hotel and Restaurant Employees' International Alliance and Bartenders' International League of America (1904), 10; Josephson, *Union House, Union Bar*, 55.

33. "Unions Draw Color Line," *Chicago Daily Tribune* (25 September 1903), 2.

34. Ibid.; Report of President Robert A. Callahan, *Proceedings of Twelfth General Convention*, Hotel and Restaurant Employes' International Alliance and Bartenders' International League of America (1904), 10; "Cracker Makers Sue for Peace," *Chicago Daily Tribune* (5 October 1903), 3; Josephson, *Union House, Union Bar*, 54–56.

35. Chicago Federation of Labor Minutes, 2 June 1905, 2–3; Chicago Federation of Labor Minutes, 10 June 1905, 13–14; Minutes of Chicago Federation of Labor Grievance Committee Meeting, 15 September 1905, 2; *Proceedings of Twelfth General Convention*, Hotel and Restaurant Employes' International Alliance and Bartenders' International League of America (1904). 55, 77.

36. See L. W. Washington, "The Afro-American Waiters of Chicago," *Broad Ax* (23 July 1904), 1.

37. CCRR, *Negro in Chicago*, 426; see also Andrew Holmes, "Labor Organizer Says Race Must Spurn Charity," *Chicago Whip* (14 February 1920), 1, 5; Tuttle, *Race Riot*, 108–56; Meyers, "Policing of Labor Disputes," 500.

38. Jablonsky, *Pride in the Jungle*, 10; see also "What Packingtown is Striking Against," *Chicago Socialist* (30 July 1904), 2; "Chicago Union Stock Yards," *Chicago Eagle* (6 August 1904), 7.

39. Barrett, *Work and Community*, 28–31, 36–63; Slayton, *Back of the Yards*, 87; Halpern, *Killing Floor*, 23–30; Brody, *Butcher Workmen*, 33–40; Meyers, *Labor Disputes*, 500–501.

40. "Army at Yards is Out," *Chicago Daily News* (12 July 1904), 1–2; "Packing House Strike Involves 45,000 Men," *New York Times* (13 July 1904), 1; A. M. Simons, "The Packingtown Strike," *Chicago Socialist* (6 August 1904), 1; "Packing Strikers State Their Case," *Chicago Socialist*, 3; "Federation Endorses Strike," *Chicago Eagle* (13 August 1904), 8; Simons, "The Battle of the Meat Makers," *Chicago Socialist* (27 August 1904), 1; "Past Year in Review," *Broad Ax* (31 December 1904), 7; Thompson, "Packing Industry" 98; Street, "Working in the Yards," 186; Pacyga, *Polish Immigrants*, 175; Commons, "Labor Conditions," 245–47; Brody, *Butcher Workmen*, 51; Herbst, *Meat-Packing Industry*, 23; Clark, "Labor and Capital," 90–118; Meyers, "Labor Disputes," 502–3. Though daring, the effort to impose a standard wage scale on a major industry was not a new idea; the butchers were carrying on a tradition begun by Pennsylvania coal miners as early as the 1850s. See Montgomery, "Strikes in Nineteenth Century," 81–104.

41. "Votes Aid for Strike," *Chicago Daily News* (13 July 1904), 1–2; "The Strike in the Packing Industry," *Chicago Daily News* (13 July 1904), 6; "Strife Attends Packers' Strike," *Chicago Daily Tribune* (13 July 1904), 1; "Packing House Strike Involves 45,000 Men," *New York Times* (13 July 1904), 1; "The Packing House Strike," *Chicago Socialist* (23 July 1904), 1; "The Strike Situation," *Chicago Socialist* (30 July 1904), 1; "Labor Notes," *Chicago Socialist* (13 August 1904), 1; "The Packingtown Strike," *Chicago Socialist* (20 August 1904), 1.

42. Spero and Harris, *Black Worker*, 264–65; Brody, *Butcher Workmen*, 41; Clark, "Labor and Capital," 27.

43. "Strife Attends Packers' Strike," *Chicago Daily Tribune* (13 July 1904), 1; "Packers Stand Firm," *Chicago Daily News* (15 July 1904), 1–2; "Strike Hangs on Packers' Action," *Chicago Daily Tribune* (20 July 1904), 1; Clark, "Labor and Capital," 128.

44. "Midnight Riot at Stockyards," *Chicago Daily Tribune* (24 July 1904), 2; "Peace Hope is Revived," *Chicago Daily News* (16 July 1904), 1–2; "All Plead for Peace," *Chicago Daily News* (19 July 1904), 1–2; "Midnight Riot at Stockyards," *Chicago Daily Tribune* (24 July 1904), 2; "Drivers' Council Against Strike," *Chicago Daily Tribune* (25 July 1904), 1; "Workers: Strike Breakers in Big Storage Rooms Have Good Dinner After Hard Work of

Day," *Chicago Daily Tribune* (1 August 1904), 4; Spero and Harris, *Black Worker*, 265–67; Street, "Working in the Yards," 215–16; Fogel, *Meat Industry*, 26–27; Pacyga, *Polish Immigrants*, 177; Henri, *Black Migration*, 151–52; Lewis, "Trade Union Policies," 20–22; Meyers, "Labor Disputes," 517–19.

45. "Strife Attends Packers' Strike," *Chicago Daily Tribune* (13 July 1904), 1.

46. Neither Packers Nor Strikers Will Yield," *New York Times* (16 July 1904), 1; "Strike May Involve Chicago Railroads," *New York Times* (29 July 1904), 1; "Strike Adds to Deaths," *Chicago Daily Tribune* (29 August 1904), 3; "Race Hatred Cannot Displace Class Struggle," *Chicago Socialist* (8 October 1904), 1; Harry Rosenberg, "On the Packing Industry and the Stockyards," (c. 1907), Mary McDowell Settlement Records, Chicago History Museum, Part 1, Box 3, 11; Spero and Harris, *Black Worker*, 265–67; Pacyga, *Polish Immigrants*, 177. See also L. W. Washington, "The Afro-American Waiters of Chicago," *Broad Ax* (23 July 1904), 1.

47. "Strife Attends Packers' Strike," *Chicago Daily Tribune* (13 July 1904), 1; "Keeping Order at the Stockyards," editorial, *Chicago Daily News* (16 July 1904), 6; "All Plead for Peace," *Chicago Daily News* (19 July 1904), 1–2; "Strike Hangs on Packers' Action," *Chicago Daily Tribune* (20 July 1904), 1; "Midnight Riot at Stockyards," *Chicago Daily Tribune* (24 July 1904), 2; "Workers: Strike Breakers in Big Storage Rooms Have Good Dinner after Hard Work of Day," *Chicago Daily Tribune* (1 August 1904), 4; "Packers See Early Settlement of Strike," *New York Times* (14 July 1904), 2; *Chicago Eagle* (27 August 1904), 2; Henri, *Black Migration*, 151–2; Fogel, *Meat Industry*, 20–22; Herbst, *Meat-Packing Industry*, 25–27; Meyers, "Labor Disputes," 520–22.

48. Rosenberg, "Packing Industry," 12; Meyers, "Labor Disputes," 521; Norwood, *Strikebreaking and Intimidation*, 80, 91–93; see also Hall, "Sanitary Condition," *Broad Ax* (31 December 1904), 5; Letter to the editor, *Broad Ax* (13 May 1905), 2.

49. "Workers: Strike Breakers in Big Storage Rooms Have Good Dinner after Hard Work of Day," *Chicago Daily Tribune* (1 August 1904), 4.

50. A. M. Simons, "The Battle of the Meat Makers," *Chicago Socialist* (27 August 1904), 1; Norwood, *Strikebreaking and Intimidation*, 80, 91–93.

51. "Workers: Strike Breakers in Big Storage Rooms Have Good Dinner after Hard Work of Day," *Chicago Daily Tribune* (1 August 1904), 4; "Make Merry in 'Yards,'" *Chicago Daily Tribune* (14 August 1904), 3; A. M. Simons, "The Battle of the Meat Makers," *Chicago Socialist* (27 August 1904), 1; Herbst, *Meat-Packing Industry*, 25–27; Clark, "Labor and Capital," 130–32; Henri, *Black Migration*, 151–52; Drake and Cayton, *Black Metropolis*, 55–56; see also "The Packingtown Strike," *Chicago Socialist* (20 August 1904), 1.

52. "Workers: Strike Breakers in Big Storage Rooms Have Good Dinner after Hard Work of Day," *Chicago Daily Tribune* (1 August 1904), 4; "Make Merry in 'Yards,'" *Chicago Daily Tribune* (14 August 1904), 3.

53. Ibid.; A. M. Simons, "The Battle of the Meat Makers," *Chicago Socialist* (27 August 1904), 1; Herbst, *Slaughtering and Meat-Packing*, 25–27; Clark, "Labor and Capital," 130–32; Meyers, "Labor Disputes," 520–22; Norwood, *Strikebreaking and Intimidation*, 80, 91–93.

54. A. M. Simons, "The Battle of the Meat Makers," *Chicago Socialist* (27 August 1904), 1; Clark, "Labor and Capital," 130–32; see also Norwood, *Strikebreaking and Intimidation*, 103–4. Recognizing the explosive danger that racism posed to the success of the strike, CFL leadership attempted to convince Booker T. Washington to visit the city and entreat black workers to refrain from strikebreaking, but he refused; it is unclear whether Washington refused the CFL's request because of a previous engagement or because of his probusiness ideology and general opposition to labor unions, particularly vis-à-vis black workers. See Spero and Harris, *Black Worker*, 267; Herbst, *Slaughtering and Meat-Packing*, 25–27.

55. Spero and Harris, *Black Worker*, 265–67; Street, "Working in the Yards," 215–16; Fogel, *Meat Industry*, 26–27; Pacyga, *Polish Immigrants*, 177; Henri, *Black Migration*, 151–52; Lewis, "Negro Worker," 20–22.

56. "Strike Hangs on Packers' Action," *Chicago Daily Tribune* (20 July 1904), 1; Spero and Harris, *Black Worker*, 265–67; Street, "Working in the Yards," 215–16; Fogel, *Meat Industry*, 26–27; Pacyga, *Polish Immigrants*, 177; Henri, *Black Migration*, 151–52; Lewis, "Negro Worker," 20–22.

57. "Strikers Guard Men Who Desert," *Chicago Daily Tribune* (31 July 1904), 1; Neither Packers Nor Strikers Will Yield," *New York Times* (16 July 1904), 1; Henri, *Black Migration*, 151–2.

58. Henri, *Black Migration*, 151–2.

59. "Strikers Have Stocks of Food," *Chicago Daily Tribune* (24 July 1904), 2; see also "The Union Button," *Chicago Socialist* (30 July 1904), 3; "Tighten Tension of the Strike," *Chicago Daily Tribune* (8 August 1904), 1; Resolution No. 1, CFL Minutes, 7 August 1904, 9–11; "Strikers of Many Races," *Chicago Daily Tribune* (31 July 1904), 2.

60. Grossman, *Land of Hope*, 218–19; Herbst, *Slaughtering and Meat-Packing*, xviii; Brody, *Butcher Workmen*, 40; Barrett, *Work and Community*, 137–42.

61. A. M. Simons, "The Packingtown Strike," *Chicago Socialist* (6 August 1904), 1; Brody, *Butcher Workmen*, 40; Barrett, *Work and Community*, 64–117, 138–42; Slayton, *Back of the Yards*, 8–9; Pacyga, *Polish Immigrants*, 8–9, 43–81; Smith, "Limitations of Racial Democracy," 29; Drake and Cayton, *Black Metropolis*, 46–57.

62. Spero and Harris, *Black Worker*, 265–67. John R. Commons claimed that pay for the black strikebreakers was $2.25 per day. See Commons, "Labor Conditions," 247.

63. "What Packingtown Is Striking Against," *Chicago Socialist* (30 July 1904), 2; "Workers: Strike Breakers in Big Storage Rooms Have Good Dinner after Hard Work of Day," *Chicago Daily Tribune* (1 August 1904), 4; "Make Merry in 'Yards,'" *Chicago Daily Tribune* (14 August 1904), 3; "The Packingtown Strike," *Chicago Socialist* (20 August 1904), 1; Pacyga, *Polish Immigrants*, 177; Herbst, *Slaughtering and Meat-Packing*, 25–27; Meyers, "Labor Disputes," 500–501; Norwood, *Strikebreaking and Intimidation*, 80, 91–93; see also "Famine at the Yards," *Chicago Daily News* (26 July 1904), 1–2. The room-and-board arrangement was not fully satisfactory, and in fact helped cause the 31 July walkout of the black strikebreakers. A leader of the aggrieved men claimed that "some of the men asked the company to pay us in cash and were told that, as we had no need for money as long as we were housed and fed by the company, the demand was unreasonable." See "Strikers Guard Men Who Desert," *Chicago Daily Tribune* (31 July 1904), 1; Henri, *Black Migration*, 151–52.

64. A. M. Simons, "The Packingtown Strike," *Chicago Socialist* (6 August 1904), 1; A. M. Simons, "The Battle of the Meat Makers," *Chicago Socialist* (27 August 1904), 1; Grossman, *Land of Hope*, 218–19; Herbst, *Slaughtering and Meat-Packing*, xviii; Brody, *Butcher Workmen*, 40; Barrett, *Work and Community*, 137–42.

65. "Strike Rioters Injure Four," *Chicago Daily Tribune* (16 July 1904), 2; "Put a Stop to Rioting," *Chicago Daily Tribune* (19 July 1904), 2; "Workers Stoned by Mob of 5,000," *Chicago Daily Tribune* (22 July 1904), 1; "Fight and Riot Near the Yards," *Chicago Daily Tribune* (27 July 1904), 2; "Riots in Streets after Nightfall Involve Drivers," *Chicago Daily Tribune* (10 August 1904), 1; "Senator Ben Tillman," *Broad Ax* (15 October 1904), 1.

66. "Fight and Riot near the Yards," *Chicago Daily Tribune* (27 July 1904), 2.

67. "Riots at Yards; Seven Men Hurt," *Chicago Daily Tribune* (18 July 1904), 1; "Small Riot Marks Final Day," *Chicago Daily Tribune* (21 July 1904), 2; "Fight and Riot near the Yards," *Chicago Daily Tribune* (27 July 1904), 2; "First Murder in Rioting at Yards," *Chicago Daily Tribune* (21 August 1904), 1; "Seizes Weapons of the Workers," *Chicago Daily Tribune* (13 August 1904), 3; "Attack Workers; Women Leading," *Chicago Daily Tribune* (14 August 1904), 3; "Rioters' Victim Is Dead," *New York Times* (28 July 1904), 5; "Meat Riots in Chicago," *New York Times* (13 August 1904), 12.

68. "Negroes Slash White Striker," *Chicago Daily Tribune* (9 August 1904), 5; Norwood, *Strikebreaking and Intimidation*, 89–90.

69. "Labor Wars Bitter," *Chicago Daily Tribune* (1 April 1904), 1; "Policemen Fire on the Strikers," *Chicago Daily Tribune* (15 July 1904), 1; "Girl Mobbed by 1,000," *Chicago Daily Tribune* (23 July 1904), 1; "Keep the Peace," *Chicago Daily Tribune* (25 July 1904), 6; "Mob Vents Its Fury," *Chicago Daily Tribune* (25 July 1904), 1; "More Nonunion Men Beaten," *Chicago Daily Tribune* (5 August 1904), 3; "Strike Battle in Chicago" and "Strikers Battle with Police," *Chicago Eagle* (6 August 1904), 8; "Students Beaten by Pickets," *Chicago Daily Tribune* (17 August 1904), 3; "Mob of 4,000 Men Charges Police," *Chicago Daily Tribune* (19 August 1904), 1; "Charge a Downtown Mob," *Chicago Daily Tribune* (27 August 1904), 3; "Fatal Riot in Chicago," *Chicago Eagle* (27 August 1904), 8; Meyers, "Labor Disputes," 533–36.

70. "Negro Non-Unionist Kills Meat Striker," *New York Times* (27 July 1904), 1; "Fight and Riot near the Yards," *Chicago Daily Tribune* (27 July 1904), 2.

71. "Girl Mobbed by 1,000," *Chicago Daily Tribune* (23 July 1904), 1.

72. "Negro Non-Unionist Kills Meat Striker," *New York Times* (27 July 1904), 1.

73. "Strike Is Ended; Men Surrender," *Chicago Daily Tribune* (9 September 1904), 1.

74. "Claim Victory over Strikers," *Chicago Daily Tribune* (2 August 1904), 2; "Says Strike Is at End," *Chicago Daily News* (2 August 1904), 1–2; "Strikers Learn Packers' Secret," *Chicago Daily Tribune* (6 August 1904), 1; "Nonunion Men Secure," *Chicago Daily News* (18 August 1904), 1–2; "Recognize No Strike," *Chicago Daily News* (25 August 1904), 1–2; "Packers Again Say No," *Chicago Daily News* (26 August 1904), 1–2; "Plan Fight on Unions," *Chicago Daily News* (30 August 1904), 1–2; "Unions Still for War," *Chicago Daily News* (30 August 1904), 3; "Shun All Meat, Says Donnelly," *Chicago Daily Tribune* (3 September 1904), 3; "Men Will Vote on Ending Strike," *Chicago Daily Tribune* (5 September 1904), 1; "Yards Unions Ballot," *Chicago Daily News* (6 September 1904), 1–2; "Bolt Strike at Yards," *Chicago Daily News* (5 September 1904), 2; "Reign of Chaos in Meat Strike," *Chicago Daily Tribune* (8 September 1904), 3; "Strike Is Ended; Men Surrender," *Chicago Daily Tribune* (9 September 1904), 1; "All to Ask for Work," *Chicago Daily News* (9 September 1904), 1–2; "Past Year in Review," *Broad Ax* (31 December 1904), 7; Clark, "Labor and Capital," 136; Halpern, *Killing Floor*, 34–38; Street, "Working in the Yards," 186; Commons, "Labor Conditions," 222; Brody, *Butcher Workmen*, 55–58; Barrett, *Work and Community*, 179–80; Meyers, "Labor Disputes," 525–30.

75. "Suddenly Stop Hiring," *Chicago Daily News* (3 August 1904), 1–2; Clark, "Labor and Capital," 139–41; Brody, *Butcher Workmen*, 58–69; Barrett, *Work and Community*, 179–81; Meyers, "Labor Disputes," 532–33; "Terrible Conditions in Stock Yards," *Chicago Socialist* (24 June 1905), 6.

76. "Shots Fired at Yards," *Chicago Daily News* (3 August 1904), 2; "Bricks and Rocks Fly," *Chicago Daily News* (9 August 1904), 1–2; "Strikers Chase Colored Men," *Chicago Daily News* (1 September 1904), 1; "Strikers Rush to Resume Work," *Chicago Daily Tribune* (11 September 1904), 4; *Chicago Eagle* (17 September 1904), 1; *Broad Ax* (17 September 1904), 4; Herbst, *Slaughtering and Meat-Packing*, 27.

77. Spero and Harris, *Black Worker*, 153; Clark, "Labor and Capital," 27; Fogel, *Meat Industry*, 23; Meyers, "Labor Disputes," 518–19; Halpern and Horowitz, *Meatpackers*, 27.

78. Herbst, *Meat-Packing Industry*, viii–xix, 24–25; Lewis, "Negro Worker," 20–21; Tuttle, *Race Riot*, 114–17; see also Coit, "Discourse of Racial Violence," 63.

79. "More Rioting near the Yards," *Chicago Daily Tribune* (14 September 1904), 4.

80. "Stockyards Strike Has Echo," *Chicago Daily Tribune* (20 May 1905), 2.

81. "Girls Safeguard Strike Breakers," *Chicago Daily Tribune* (17 March 1905), 5; "Teamsters Open Great Struggle," *Chicago Daily Tribune* (7 April 1905), 5.

82. "Teamsters Open Great Struggle," *Chicago Daily Tribune* (7 April 1905), 5; "Fierce Class War Raging," *Chicago Socialist* (15 April 1905), 1; "Drivers Line Up for Labor War," *Chicago Daily Tribune* (27 April 1905), 1; "Gigantic Strike Is in Full Swing," *Chicago Daily Tribune* (28 April 1905), 1; Witwer, *Corruption and Reform*, 28; Witwer, "Race Relations," 514–15; see also "Reaping the Whirlwind," *Chicago Eagle* (25 July 1903), 4.

83. CFL Minutes, 26 March 1905, 1–3; CFL Minutes, 2 April 1905, 2–3; CFL Minutes, 2 April 1905, 2–3; "Teamsters' Strike Spreads," *Chicago Eagle* (6 May 1905), 7; Witwer, *Corruption and Reform*, 29–30; Witwer, "Race Relations," 505. The local unions' affiliation with the international teamsters afforded them a tremendous amount of influence in the industry, to the point that teamster locals briefly joined with employer representatives to form a de facto arbitration board that governed disputes within the city. See Commons, "Teamsters of Chicago," 42.

84. "Strike Must End, Say Team Owners," *Chicago Daily Tribune* (13 May 1905), 1; Spero and Harris, *Black Worker*, 132; Fitch, *Solidarity for Sale*, 126.

85. Editorial, *Magazine of the International Brotherhood of Teamsters* (June 1905), 14; see also "Rioters Fight in the Streets," *Chicago Daily Tribune* (29

April 1905), 3; "Rain of Missiles Batters Drivers," *Chicago Daily Tribune* (4 May 1905), 3; "Twelfth Victim of Strike Dead," *Chicago Daily Tribune* (11 June 1905), 5.

86. "Capitalist Despotism in Chicago," *Chicago Socialist* (13 May 1905), 1; "A Dastardly Crime," *Chicago Socialist* (13 May 1905), 1; "D. E. Tobias, "Black Strike-Breakers," *Chicago Socialist*, 3; Fitch, *Solidarity for Sale*, 126; Witwer, "Race Relations," 520.

87. "Sheriff Takes Command Today with 500 Men," *Chicago Inter Ocean* (6 May 1905), 1–2. "Team Owners Propose New Project to Settle Strike," *Chicago Daily Tribune* (6 May 1905), 2; "Capitalist Despotism in Chicago," *Chicago Socialist* (13 May 1905), 1.

88. Report of Special Committee, CFL Minutes, 7 May 1905, 7; see also untitled editorial, *Broad Ax* (27 May 1905), 1.

89. "Dastardly Deception," *Chicago Socialist* (20 May 1905), 1; "The Employers Association of Chicago," *Broad Ax* (9 July 1904), 1.

90. "Black Drivers Have Fun," *Chicago Daily Tribune* (8 May 1905), 2; "The Race Issue in the Strike," *Chicago Daily Tribune* (13 May 1905), 8; Fitch, *Solidarity for Sale*, 127; see also George C. Hall, "The Health or the Sanitary Condition of the Negro in Chicago," *Broad Ax* (31 December 1904), 5; "Colored Men," *Broad Ax* (6 May 1905), 1; "A Dastardly Crime," *Chicago Socialist* (13 May 1905), 1.

91. Powers, "Chicago's Strike Ordeal," *World's Work* 10, no. 3 (July 1905): 6383.

92. Ibid., 6383–84.

93. "Class War Still Rages," *Chicago Socialist* (22 April 1905), 1; "Curry Slugged in Eye," *Chicago Daily Tribune* (3 May 1905), 2; "Lack of Police Bar to Business," *Chicago Daily Tribune* (4 May 1905), 3; "Big Strike Has Small Beginning," *Chicago Daily Tribune* (20 May 1905), 2; "Union Men Ready for Grand Jury," *Chicago Daily Tribune* (1 June 1905), 40; Fitch, *Solidarity for Sale*, 126–28; Meyers, "Labor Disputes," 593–98.

94. CFL Minutes, 7 May 1905, 14, 17; Meyers, "Labor Disputes," 572–73, 598–600; Witwer, "Race Relations," 517–18.

95. William Mailly, "Inside Story of Great Strike," *Socialist* (6 May 1905), 8.

96. "Union Men Ready for Grand Jury," *Chicago Daily Tribune* (1 June 1905), 40; "Rifle-Armed Drivers Man Chicago Wagons," *New York Times* (2 May 1905), 2; Meyers, "Labor Disputes," 593–96; Witwer, "Race Relations," 517–18.

97. Curry Slugged in Eye," *Chicago Daily Tribune* (3 May 1905), 2.

98. "Strike to Continue," *Chicago Socialist* (29 April 1905), 1; "Capitalist

Despotism in Chicago," *Chicago Socialist* (13 May 1905), 1; see also Fitch, *Solidarity for Sale*, 127.

99. "Rioters Fight in the Streets," *Chicago Daily Tribune* (29 April 1905), 3; "Rain of Missiles Batters Drivers," *Chicago Daily Tribune* (4 May 1905), 3; "Twelfth Victim of Strike Dead," *Chicago Daily Tribune* (11 June 1905), 5; see also "War Tactics in Strike Violence," *Chicago Daily Tribune* (28 April 1905), 2; Witwer, "Race Relations," 520.

100. "Strike Breaker Kills Boy," *Chicago Daily Tribune* (17 May 1905), 1; "Held as Boy's Slayers," *Chicago Daily Tribune* (19 May 1905), 2; "Held as Slayers of Carlson," *Chicago Daily Tribune* (25 May 1905), 2; "2 Men Fatally Shot in a Chicago Riot," *New York Times* (7 May 1905), 1; "Race Rioting in Chicago," *Broad Ax* (27 May 1905), 1; "More Bloodshed in Chicago," *New York Times* (11 June 1905), 1; Fitch, *Solidarity for Sale*, 120–27; Meyers, "Labor Disputes," 576–77.

101. "Strike Rioters Block Streets," *Chicago Daily Tribune* (8 April 1905), 1; "New Missiles for Strikers," *New York Times* (9 April 1905), 4; "Violence Ends the Day," *Chicago Daily Tribune* (15 April 1905), 3; "Acid as Strike Weapon," *New York Times* (22 April 1905), 8; "Drivers Line Up for Labor War," *Chicago Daily Tribune* (27 April 1905), 1; "War Tactics in Strike Violence," *Chicago Daily Tribune* (28 April 1905), 2; "Shoots to Kill Bogus Deputies," *Chicago Daily Tribune* (7 May 1905), 2; Commons, "Teamsters of Chicago," 64; Fitch, *Solidarity for Sale*, 120; Meyers, "Labor Disputes," 576–77, 581–86.

102. "Go on Strike in School," *Chicago Daily Tribune* (11 May 1905), 4; "Striking Pupils Picket School," *Chicago Daily Tribune* (12 May 1905), 2; "Strike of Pupils Grows," *Chicago Daily Tribune* (13 May 1905), 2; *Chicago Eagle* (13 May 1905), 1; "Blow for School Strike," *Chicago Daily Tribune* (18 May 1905), 2; "The School Strike," *Chicago Socialist* (20 May 1905), 1; *Chicago Eagle* (20 May 1905), 4; "Put Down the School Strikes," *Chicago Eagle* (27 May 1905), 4; Tuttle, *Race Riot*, 120–23; Norwood, *Strikebreaking and Intimidation*, 102; Cohen, *Racketeer's Progress*, 111–18; Meyers, "Labor Disputes," 575; Katzman and Tuttle, "Chicago Strike," 116–17, 120–21.

103. "Fines Paid by Pupils' Parents," *Chicago Daily Tribune* (19 May 1905), 2; "Boy 'Strikers' Pay the Penalty," *Chicago Daily Tribune* (20 May 1905), 2; "Negro Attacked; Shoots to Kill," *Chicago Daily Tribune* (21 May 1905), 2; "Two Men Killed in Race Rioting," *Chicago Daily Tribune* (22 May 1905), 1; "War on School Strikes," *Chicago Daily Tribune* (23 May 1905), 2; "Law to End School Strike," *New York Times* (16 May 1905), 1; CFL Minutes, 12 May 1905, 12–13; Tuttle, *Race Riot*, 120–23; Cohen, *Racketeer's Progress*, 111–18.

104. "Negro Attacked; Shoots to Kill," *Chicago Daily Tribune* (21 May 1905), 2; "Two Men Killed in Race Rioting," *Chicago Daily Tribune* (22 May

1905), 1; "Killed in Chicago Riots; Strike May Spread," *New York Times* (22 May 1905), 1.

105. "Milk Wagon Men Strike," *Chicago Daily Tribune* (4 May 1905), 3.

106. "Negro Protest against Race Prejudice in Strike," *Chicago Daily Tribune* (10 May 1905), 2; *Broad Ax* (13 May 1905), 4; Cohen, *Racketeer's Progress*, 141–42.

107. "War Tactics in Strike Violence," *Chicago Daily Tribune* (28 April 1905), 2; "Shoot and Slug in Strike Riot," *Chicago Daily Tribune* (2 May 1905), 2; "Wreck Wagons; Destroy Goods," *Chicago Daily Tribune* (5 May 1905), 3; "Shoots to Kill Bogus Deputies," *Chicago Daily Tribune* (7 May 1905), 2; "Grand Jury to Indict Rioters," *Chicago Daily Tribune* (23 May 1905), 2; "Twelfth Victim of Strike Dead," *Chicago Daily Tribune* (11 June 1905), 5; "2 Men Fatally Shot in a Chicago Riot," *New York Times* (7 May 1905), 1; "Race Rioting in Chicago," *Broad Ax* (27 May 1905), 1; "Whose Race War Is It?," *Broad Ax* (27 May 1905), 1; Fitch, *Solidarity for Sale*, 120–27; Norwood, *Strikebreaking and Intimidation*, 100–101.

108. "Strike Breaker Kills Boy," *Chicago Daily Tribune* (17 May 1905), 1; "Held as Boy's Slayers," *Chicago Daily Tribune* (19 May 1905), 2; "Held as Slayers of Carlson," *Chicago Daily Tribune* (25 May 1905), 2; "Striker Shot a Boy," *New York Times* (17 May 1905), 2; "Crimes, Murder," *Broad Ax* (20 May 1905), 1; "Slaying the Children," *Chicago Socialist* (20 May 1905), 1; Untitled editorial, *Broad Ax* (27 May 1905), 2; D. E. Tobias, "Black Strike-Breakers," *Chicago Socialist* (27 May 1905), 6; Fitch, *Solidarity for Sale*, 127; Meyers, "Labor Disputes," 586–87; "The Chicago Strike," in Katzman and Tuttle, 116–17; see also "The Teamsters' Strike," *Broad Ax* (3 June 1905), 1; Witwer, "Race Relations," 518–19.

109. "Reflections on the Great Teamsters' Strike," letter to the editor, *Broad Ax* (13 May 1905), 2; "2 Men Fatally Shot in a Chicago Riot," *New York Times* (7 May 1905), 1; "Shoots to Kill Bogus Deputies," *Chicago Daily Tribune* (7 May 1905), 2; "Grand Jury to Indict Rioters," *Chicago Daily Tribune* (23 May 1905), 2; see also Katzman and Tuttle, "Chicago Strike," 116–17.

110. "Fierce Class War Raging," *Chicago Socialist* (15 April 1905), 1; "Capitalist Despotism in Chicago," *Chicago Socialist* (13 May 1905), 1; "The Real Strike-Breakers," *Chicago Socialist* (27 May 1905), 1; Meyers, "Labor Disputes," 605–13.

111. "Gigantic Strike Is in Full Swing," *Chicago Daily Tribune* (28 April 1905), 1; "Strike Victim Is Near Death," *Chicago Daily Tribune* (28 April 1905), 2; Witwer, *Corruption and Reform*, 36; "Chief O'Neill and the Colored Policemen," *Broad Ax* (17 June 1905), 1; "Policeman Kills a Boy," *Chicago Daily Tribune* (30 June 1905), 5; Meyers, "Labor Disputes," 606–27. Such

venomous racial feelings seemed to take hold of the entire city, particularly in the context of work. In a plant in Franklin Park, nearly fifty employees struck to protest the hiring of black workers hired as extra help (not as strike-breakers), stoned the black workers during their dinner break, and physically threatened a deputy sheriff who attempted to intervene. See "Race Hatred Causes Strike," *Chicago Daily Tribune* (9 June 1905), 3.

112. "Cease to Support Striking Drivers," *Chicago Daily Tribune* (27 May 1905), 1; "Bullets Rain in Riots," *Chicago Daily Tribune* (4 June 1905), 2; "Policeman Kills a Boy," *Chicago Daily Tribune* (30 June 1905), 5.

113. "More Strikes for Today," *Chicago Daily Tribune* (5 May 1905), 2; "City Gets More Police," *Chicago Daily Tribune* (4 May 1905), 2.

114. "Cease to Support Striking Drivers," *Chicago Daily Tribune* (27 May 1905), 1; "In Guise of Deputies Attack Strikebreakers," *New York Times* (8 May 1905), 5; see also "Sheriff Thomas E. Bartlett . . ." *Broad Ax* (13 May 1905), 1; "Race Rioting in Chicago," *Broad Ax* (27 May 1905), 1; "Whose Race War Is It?," *Broad Ax* (27 May 1905), 1; Witwer, "Race Relations," 516–17.

115. Report of Executive Board, CFL Minutes, 3 February 1907, 5–7; see also "Cease to Support Striking Drivers," *Chicago Daily Tribune* (27 May 1905), 1.

116. "Strike Riot in Chicago," *New York Times* (14 April 1905), 1; "Strike Rioters Make Big Raid," *Chicago Daily Tribune* (30 April 1905), 3; "Twelve Labor Heads Indicted in Chicago," *New York Times* (30 April 1905), 1; "Annoy the Women Buyers," *Chicago Daily Tribune* (2 May 1905), 3; "Curry Slugged in Eye," *Chicago Daily Tribune* (3 May 1905), 2; "One Killed, 150 Hurt in Chicago Rioting," *New York Times* (3 May 1905), 1; Untitled editorial, *New York Times* (13 May 1905), 8; "Big Strike Has Small Beginning," *Chicago Daily Tribune* (20 May 1905), 2; "Frank Curry Is Slugged," *Chicago Daily Tribune* (4 August 1905), 5; Witwer, *Corruption and Reform*, 36; Meyers, "Labor Disputes," 570–73, 581–86.

117. "Chicago Streets Scene of Many Strike Riots," *New York Times* (4 May 1905), 1.

118. "Wreck Wagons; Destroy Goods," *Chicago Daily Tribune* (5 May 1905), 3; "The Race Issue in the Strike," *Chicago Daily Tribune* (13 May 1905), 8; "Crimes, Murder," *Broad Ax* (20 May 1905), 1; "Porter is Fined for Running," *Chicago Daily Tribune* (9 June 1905), 3; Katzman and Tuttle, *Plain Folk*, 116; Witwer, "Race Relations," 515–16.

119. "One Killed, 150 Hurt in Chicago Rioting," *New York Times* (3 May 1905), 1; "Strikers Try to Lynch a Negro in Chicago," *New York Times* (19 June 1905), 7.

120. "Torch Is Applied as Riot Weapon," *Chicago Daily Tribune* (6 May 1905), 3.

121. "The Race Issue in the Strike," *Chicago Daily Tribune* (13 May 1905), 8; see also "Chicago Tie-Up Break; More Victims of Riot," *New York Times* (9 May 1905), 5; Katzman and Tuttle, *Plain Folk*, 116; Witwer, "Race Relations," 515–16.

122. "Sluggers Quiet; More Teams Move," *Chicago Daily Tribune* (9 May 1905), 1.

123. "Stone Thrower Shot and Killed," *Chicago Daily Tribune* (9 May 1905), 2.

124. "Mayor Proclaims a Strike Inquiry," *Chicago Daily Tribune* (7 May 1905), 1; "'Judas' Charge Made and Denied," *Chicago Daily Tribune* (7 May 1905), 2.

125. "Twelve Labor Heads Indicted in Chicago," *New York Times* (30 April 1905), 1; "Mayor Proclaims a Strike Inquiry," *Chicago Daily Tribune* (7 May 1905), 1; "'Judas' Charge Made and Denied," *Chicago Daily Tribune* (7 May 1905), 2; "Five Union Men Held for a Strike Killing," *New York Times* (15 May 1905), 2; "Union Officers Involved," *Chicago Eagle* (20 May 1905), 7; "Tell of Bribery behind Strikes," *Chicago Daily Tribune* (2 June 1905), 1; "The Teamsters' Strike," *Broad Ax* (3 June 1905), 1; "Says $50,000 Was Price of Peace in Chicago," *New York Times* (3 June 1905), 2; "Strikers' Price Fixed at $50,000," *Chicago Daily Tribune* (3 June 1905), 1; "Drivers Resent New Strike Levy," *Chicago Daily Tribune* (3 July 1905), 5; "Take Strike Control Out of Shea's Hands," *New York Times* (28 May 1905), 5; "Shea under Arrest for Strike Conspiracy," *New York Times* (6 June 1905), 6; Witwer, *Corruption and Reform*, 30–37; Commons, "Teamsters of Chicago," 64; Katzman and Tuttle, *Plain Folk*, 116; Meyers, "Labor Disputes," 562–73, 589–92, 636–37; Witwer, "Race Relations," 525.

126. Report of Special Committee, CFL Minutes, 7 May 1905, 7; "Chicago Strike Broken," *New York Times* (21 July 1905), 1; "The Sinister Strike Ended," *Chicago Daily Tribune* (22 July 1905), 6; "Strikers Unable to Regain Jobs," *Chicago Daily Tribune* (23 July 1905), 8; "Strike Changes into a Lockout," *Chicago Daily Tribune* (25 July 1905), 3; "The Teamsters Surrender," *Chicago Socialist* (29 July 1905), 1; "Union Men Taken Back," *Chicago Daily Tribune* (1 August 1905), 2; CFL Minutes, 4 February 1906, 17–18; Witwer, *Corruption and Reform*, 29–36; Witwer, "Race Relations," 525; Tuttle, *Race Riot*, 120–23; Cohen, *Racketeer's Progress*, 108.

127. "Mob Attacks 16 Wagons," *Chicago Daily Tribune* (27 July 1905), 1; see also "Union Teamsters Resume Rioting," *Chicago Daily Tribune* (9 August 1905), 4; "Frank Curry Is Slugged," *Chicago Daily Tribune* (4 August 1905),

5. Curry not only procured strikebreakers, he also took part in a number of street brawls with strikers. See Norwood, *Strikebreaking and Intimidation*, 97–100.

128. Bigham, "Chicago Federation," 14.

129. Ibid.; Witwer, *Corruption and Reform*, 29–30.

130. Tuttle, *Race Riot*, 120–23; Cohen, *Racketeer's Progress*, 108–18. David Witwer has argued that the 1905 strike did not necessarily foreclose the possibility of interracial unionism in team driving. Though he acknowledges that "it was a bargain frequently violated at the local level by white union members," he argues that teamsters "redoubled their efforts to organize African Americans" by offering "equal wages and fair treatment" to black workers "in return for loyal membership" in the union. See Witwer, "Race Relations," 508.

131. "Negro Protest against Race Prejudice in Strike," *Chicago Daily Tribune* (10 May 1905), 2; see also "Jolt for the Negro Race," *Chicago Daily Tribune* (19 August 1905), 3; Cohen, *Racketeer's Progress*, 141–42.

2. "EVERY NEGRO CAN MAKE A FIGHT": RACE AND THE CFL CAMPAIGN, 1916–1921

1. Walsh, *Over the Top*, 95; CFL Minutes, 17 February 1918, 15–18; Herbst, *Meat-Packing Industry*, 37–39; Clark, "Labor and Capital," 163; Barrett, *William Z. Foster*, 81–82; McCartin, *Labor's Great War*, 83.

2. Clark, "Labor and Capital," 12–15; 107; Jablonsky, *Pride in the Jungle*, 10; Street, "Working in the Yards," 257; Halpern, *Killing Floor*, 10–12; Federal Trade Commission, *Report*, Part 1, 105–59; Federal Trade Commission, *Report*, Part 3, 189–277; Federal Trade Commission, *Report*, Part 5, 17–45.

3. CFL Minutes, 2 December 1917, 4–5.

4. Street, "The Swift Difference," 19–20; Barrett, *Work and Community*, 58, 119; 154–61; Halpern, *Killing Floor*, 9–10, 14–21.

5. Watkins, *Labor Problems*, 31–32; CFL Minutes, 16 December 1917, 44–46; see also Sinclair, *The Jungle*.

6. Cohen, *Making a New Deal*, 3–4; Keiser, "John Fitzpatrick," 34; CFL Minutes, 2 December 1917, 4–5.

7. Street, "Working in the Yards," 257; Lewis, "Negro Worker," 24; see also CCRR, *Negro in Chicago*, 357.

8. Barrett, *Work and Community*, 58; Barrett and Roediger, "Inbetween Peoples," 16.

9. Watkins, *Labor Problems*, 30.

10. CFL Minutes, 2 December 1917, 4–5; Reports of Organizations, CFL Minutes, 21 May 1916, 13; see also Cohen, *Making a New Deal*, 24; Barrett,

Work and Community, 44–47, 54–58. For a deeper explanation of work and the experience of Americanization, see Jacobson, *Whiteness*; Roediger, *Working toward Whiteness*; Guglielmo, *White on Arrival*.

11. CCRR, *Negro in Chicago*, 80–86; Smith, "Limitations of Racial Democracy," 6–7; Henri, *Black Migration*, 51–52; Arnesen, *Black Protest*, 2–4; Grossman, *Land of Hope*, 16–29; Barrett, *Work and Community*, 48–54; "Reasons Why Negro Is Leaving South," *Butcher Workman* 3, no. 7 (July 1917), 5.

12. "Reasons Why Negro Is Leaving South," *Butcher Workman* 3, no. 7 (July 1917), 5.

13. Grossman, *Land of Hope*, 98–122.

14. Henri, *Black Migration*, 51–52.

15. CCRR, *Negro in Chicago*, 358; Henri, *Black Migration*, 51–54; Arnesen, *Black Protest*, 1; Dubofsky, *Industrialism*, 131; Joseph A. Hill, "Recent Northward Migration of the Negro," *Monthly Labor Review* 18, no. 3 (March 1924): 1.

16. Tuttle, *Race Riot*, 76.

17. Michaeli, *Defender*, xii; "Northern Drive to Start," *Chicago Defender* (10 February 1916), 3; "The Exodus," *Chicago Defender* (2 September 1916), 1; "Farewell, Dixie Land," *Chicago Defender* (7 October 1916), 12; Smith, "Limitations of Racial Democracy," 10.

18. Emmet J. Scott, "Letters of Negro Migrants," 298, 337; Smith, "Limitations of Racial Democracy," 8–10; Tuttle, *Race Riot*, 76; CCRR, *Negro in Chicago*, 87–92.

19. Estelle Hill Scott, *Occupational Changes among Negroes*, 7; DOL, *The Negro at Work*, 68; CCRR, *Negro in Chicago*, 2, 79, 602; Chicago Urban League, introduction *to First Annual Report*, 4; Grossman, *Land of Hope*, 4; Merriam, *Chicago*, 11; Smith, "Limitations of Racial Democracy," 6; Pacyga, *Polish Immigrants*, 212–13.

20. Joseph A. Hill, "Recent Northward Migration of the Negro," *Monthly Labor Review* 18, no. 3 (March 1924): 11; CCRR, *Negro in Chicago*, 357–59; Barrett, *William Z. Foster*, 79; Foner, *Organized Labor*, 131–35.

21. "2,000 Southern Negroes Arrive in Last 2 Days," *Chicago Daily Tribune* (4 March 1917), 1; see also Tuttle, *Race Riot*, 89; Smith, "Limitations of Racial Democracy," 8; Coit, "Racial Violence," 60–61; Grossman, *Land of Hope*, 69–74.

22. Resolution No. 160, *Proceedings of the American Federation of Labor* [hereafter *AFL Proceedings*] (1893), 56; Resolution No. 160, *AFL Proceedings* (1897), 78; Resolution No. 160, *AFL Proceedings* (1910), 237; Resolution No. 120, *AFL Proceedings* (1919), 228; see also Resolution No. 120, *AFL Proceedings* (1918), 130–31; Resolution No. 37, *AFL Proceedings* (1920), 272;

"Samuel Gompers, President of the American Federation of Labor," *Broad Ax* (3 December 1910), 3; Mandel, "Samuel Gompers," 34; Lewis, "Negro Worker," 84; Taft, *A. F. of L.*, 313–14.

23. *AFL Proceedings* (1882), 17–18; Supplementary resolution, *AFL Proceedings* (1881), 4; *AFL Proceedings* (1881), 20; *AFL Proceedings* (1886), 7, 17; Resolution No. 20, *AFL Proceedings* (1887); *AFL Proceedings* (1889), 15; *AFL Proceedings* (1893), 13; Report of President Samuel Gompers, *AFL Proceedings* (1894), 12; *AFL Proceedings* (1900), 27; Resolutions No. 9 and 11, *AFL Proceedings* (1905), 86–87; Report of Committee on Resolutions, *AFL Proceedings* (1905), 192; Resolution No. 37, *AFL Proceedings* (1907), 109, 314; Report of Committee on President's Report, *AFL Proceedings* (1912), 344–45; Report of Executive Council, *AFL Proceedings* (1915), 396–97; *AFL Proceedings* (1917), 118; Report of Executive Council, *AFL Proceedings* (1917), 386.

24. *AFL Proceedings* (1910), 237; ibid.; William Z. Foster, *The Great Steel Strike and Its Lessons* (New York: B. W. Huebsch, 1920), 209.

25. Foster, *Steel Strike*, 209; Mandel, *Samuel Gompers*, 43–46, 60; Resolution No. 48, *AFL Proceedings* (1920), 276–77.

26. Brecher, *Strike!*, 1, 237–38; Keiser, "John Fitzpatrick," 23; Cohen, *Making a New Deal*, 3.

27. Hutton, "Negro Worker," 18–19; Taft, *A. F. of L.*, 311–13; see also Henri, *Black Migration*, 153; Spero and Harris, *Black Worker*, 53; see also letter from Eugene Kincale Jones and Fred R. Moore to American Federation of Labor, dated 6 June 1918, *AFL Proceedings* (1918), 198–99.

28. Letter from Eugene Kincale Jones and Fred R. Moore to American Federation of Labor, dated 6 June 1918, *AFL Proceedings* (1918), 198–99.

29. *AFL Proceedings* (1890), 31.

30. *AFL Proceedings* (1891), 12; Report of Committee on President's Report, *AFL Proceedings* (1891), 39–40; Mandel, *Samuel Gompers*, 34–37, 51. The AFL would encounter similar issues among blacksmiths and a number of railway trades. See Mandel, *Samuel Gompers*, 38–39; Arnesen, *Brotherhoods of Color*; Taillon, *Good, Reliable, White Men*.

31. Report of Committee on Organization, *AFL Proceedings* (1918), 351–52; Resolution No. 101, *AFL Proceedings* (1919), 223; "'No Discrimination,' Says Gompers," *Chicago Defender* (21 June 1919), 2; Foner, *Organized Labor*, 153–55; see also letter from Eugene Kincale Jones and Fred R. Moore to American Federation of Labor, dated 6 June 1918, *AFL Proceedings* (1918), 198–99.

32. "Undertaker Daniel Jackson ..." *Chicago Defender* (26 November 1910), 1; see also *IFL Proceedings* (1919), 132–37.

33. "Undertaker Daniel Jackson…" *Chicago Defender* (26 November 1910), 1; "Come Now, Lord Gompers!" *Chicago Defender* (23 February 1918); *Chicago Defender*, Box 6, Folder 45, Fitzpatrick Papers, Chicago History Museum; see also untitled editorial, *Chicago Defender* (19 February 1916), 8; "Gompers Addresses Longshoremen," *Chicago Defender*, 1.

34. CCRR, *Negro in Chicago*, 424–26; Grossman, *Land of Hope*, 217; see also Andrew Holmes, "Labor Organizer Says Race Must Spurn Charity," *Chicago Whip* (14 February 1920), 1, 5; Tuttle, *Race Riot*, 108–56; Meyers, "Labor Disputes," 500.

35. Untitled editorial, *Chicago Defender* (27 May 1911), 4.

36. Andrew Holmes, "Why Colored Workers Are Generally Anti-Union," *Chicago Whip* (28 February 1920), 1, 6.

37. "Readjustment of Labor," *Chicago Defender* (23 March 1918), 16.

38. M. O. Bousfield, "Union Labor and the Race," *Chicago Defender* (4 May 1918), 16.

39. CCRR, *Negro in Chicago*, 428–29; see also Fogel, *Meat Industry*, 31; Smith, "Limitations of Racial Democracy," 31–32; Herbst, *Meat-Packing Industry*, 60–61; Schneider, *"We Return Fighting,"* 155; Tuttle, *Race Riot*, 145; Spero and Harris, *Black Worker*, 462; Foner, *Organized Labor*, 127.

40. Keiser, "John Fitzpatrick," iii–iv; see also Shapiro, "Hand and Brain," 69–70.

41. Madden's secretary was accused of embezzling funds and destroying incriminating documents. Fitzpatrick's election occurred only after it was discovered that Madden's thugs had tampered with union ballot boxes. A group of members walked out of the election meeting, convened at another hall, and elected Fitzpatrick as the federation's rightful president. See Bigham, "Chicago Federation of Labor," 14–16.

42. Keiser, "John Fitzpatrick," 1–27; McKillen, *Chicago Labor*, 46–47.

43. Barrett, *William Z. Foster*, 68–77; Barrett, "Revolution and Personal Crisis," 465–82; Street, "Working in the Yards," 260; Bart, *Working-Class Unity*, 5.

44. Bart, *Working-Class Unity*, 5.

45. Keiser, "John Fitzpatrick," 20; Bart, *Working-Class Unity*, 5, 25.

46. Clark, "Labor and Capital," 145–74; Bigham, "Chicago Federation of Labor," 46; Bart, *Working-Class Unity*, 7.

47. "A Brief History of Organization in Chicago Stock Yards by the A. M. C. & B. W. of N. A.," *Butcher Workman* 5, no. 11 (November 1919), 1-2; Clark, "Labor and Capital," 148–50; Keiser, "John Fitzpatrick," 28; Barrett, *William Z. Foster*, 78–79; Grossman, *Land of Hope*, 211; Herbst, *Meat-Packing Industry*, 29–30; Pacyga, *Polish Immigrants*, 8–9, 183.

48. *CFL Minutes*, 15 July 1917, 15; *CFL Minutes*, 5 August 1917, 17–18; Barrett, *William Z. Foster*, 77–78; Keiser, "John Fitzpatrick," 25–27; Bigham, "Chicago Federation of Labor," 46–48; Bart, *Working-Class Unity*, 7–12; McCartin, *Labor's Great War*, 82; Street, "Working in the Yards," 258.

49. Ibid.; *CFL Minutes*, 19 August 1917, 5; Resolution No. 23, *Proceedings of the 34th Annual Convention of the Illinois State Federation of Labor*, 1916, 256; Grossman, *Land of Hope*, 211; Brody, *Butcher Workmen*, 76.

50. Ibid.; Barrett and Roediger, "Inbetween Peoples," 24–25.

51. CFL Minutes, 17 November 1918, 12–16; Strouthous, *U.S. Labor*, 9–10.

52. Ibid.; "Independent Labor Party Platform," 17 November 1918, John Fitzpatrick Papers, Box 7, Folder 51, Chicago History Museum; Letter, Fitzpatrick to officers and members of affiliated unions, 20 November 1918, John Fitzpatrick Papers, Box 7, Folder 51, Chicago History Museum; Letter, Ed Nockels to officers and members of affiliated unions, 11 December 1918, John Fitzpatrick Papers, Box 7, Folder 52, Chicago History Museum; "Chicago for the Workers," undated pamphlet, c. February 1919, John Fitzpatrick Papers, Box 8, Folder 56, Chicago History Museum; "Labor Gang Sharpening Their Bills," *Chicago Eagle* (21 December 1918), 1; "County Labor Party is Now a Reality," *New Majority* 1, no. 1 (4 January 1919), 1); "Federation of Labor Proposes John Fitzpatrick for Mayor," *Chicago Eagle* (18 January 1919), 1. Though it makes up only a minor portion of this project, the Cook County Labor Party is a fascinating story that deserves further scholarly treatment. For examinations of the party itself, see Simonson, "Labor Party of Cook County"; Horowitz, "Failure of Independent Political Action; Dolnick, "Role of Labor." For discussions of the CCLP as part of national politics, see Fine, *Labor and Farmer Parties*, 377–80; Sell, "A.F. of L.," 66–94; Shapiro, 69–145; Bigham, "Chicago Federation of Labor," 132–39; Bart, *Working-Class Unity*, 23–24; Keiser, "John Fitzpatrick," 106–54.

53. Resolution No. 41, *Proceedings of the 36th Annual Convention of the Illinois State Federation of Labor* (1918), 134–54; McKillen, *Chicago Labor*, 87–89.

54. "Fitzpatrick Gains Another Vote," *Chicago Eagle* (22 March 1919), 2.

55. "Labor Takes Stand on Big City Issues," *New Majority* 1, no. 1 (4 January 1919), 7; Platform of the Labor Party of Illinois, *Proceedings of the 37th Annual Convention of the Illinois State Federation of Labor*, 1919, 39–42.

56. "Fitzpatrick Gains Another Vote," *Chicago Eagle* (22 March 1919), 2.

57. CCRR, *Negro in Chicago*, 361; Herbst, *Meat-Packing Industry*, 28; Spero and Harris, *Black Worker*, 269.

58. Report of President John H. Walker, *Proceedings of the 35th Annual Convention of the Illinois State Federation of Labor*, 1917, 42–43; Zieger, *For*

Jobs and Freedom, 82; Keiser, "John Fitzpatrick," 166; Clark, "Labor and Capital," 151; Herbst, *Meat-Packing Industry*, 28; see also CCRR, *Negro in Chicago*, 647.

59. CCRR, *Negro in Chicago*, 428–29.

60. CFL Minutes, 19 August 1917, 5; Grossman, *Land of Hope*, 209–19; Foner, *Organized Labor*, 163–64.

61. CCRR, *Negro in Chicago*, 387–90, 428–29.

62. CFL Minutes, 21 October 1917, 18, 23–24; Barrett, "Racial and Ethnic Fragmentation," 294.

63. CFL, 4 December 1921, 12.

64. Ibid., CFL Minutes, 5 January 1919, 13–14; "New Angle in Yards Inquiry Taken Up Today," *Chicago Daily Tribune* (25 February 1918), 13; Mark Solomon, *The Cry Was Unity: Communists and African-Americans, 1917–36* (Jackson: University Press of Mississippi, 1998), 44–45; Barrett, *William Z. Foster*, 80; Barrett, *Work and Community*, 204–7; Herbst, *Meat-Packing Industry*, 36–40.

65. "Co-Operative Store for Colored Folks," *New Majority* 2, no. 5 (2 August 1919), 10; John Riley, "Police Protection in the Yards," *Chicago Whip* (25 July 1919), 3; Notes from meetings with local ministers, c. August 1920, John Fitzpatrick Papers, Box 25, Chicago History Museum.

66. John Riley, "Police Protection in the Yards," *Chicago Whip* (25 July 1919), 3.

67. Andrew Holmes, "Colored Labor Being Sought by Stock Yards Labor Council," *Chicago Whip* (31 January 1920), 8.

68. G. W. Reed, "The Negro's Great Opportunity as I See It," *Butcher Workman* 5, no. 5 (May 1919), 4.

69. Resolution No. 17, Proceedings of the Convention of the Labor Party of the United States of America (1919), John Fitzpatrick Papers, Chicago History Museum.

70. CFL Minutes, 2 September 1917, 13–14; Bigham, "Chicago Federation of Labor," 49.

71. Lewis, "Negro Worker," 24.

72. Chicago Federation of Labor Minutes, 2 December 1917, 3–4.

73. Ibid.; Report of Stockyards Labor Council, CFL Minutes, 4 November 1917, 21–22; Report of Stockyards Labor Council, CFL Minutes, 18 November 1917, 4–6; Bigham, "Chicago Federation of Labor," 49; Herbst, *Meat-Packing Industry*, 29.

74. Barrett, *Work and Community*, 195–96.

75. Testimony of John Kikulski, untitled hearing, Records of the Federal Mediation and Conciliation Service, Record Group 280: Dispute Case

Files [hereafter "FMCS"], Box 46, 1127–28; Melvyn Dubofsky, "Abortive Reform: The Wilson Administration and Organized Labor, 1913–1920," in *Work, Community, and Power: The Experience of Labor in Europe and America, 1900–1925*, ed. James E. Cronin and Carmen Sirianni (Philadelphia: Temple University Press, 1983), 211–12; Grossman, *Land of Hope*, 211; Street, "Swift Difference," 22; Herbst, *Meat-Packing Industry*, 29. Estimates of SLC membership, as well as the timing of various milestones of the campaign, remain somewhat vague, in part due to the high turnover of stockyards employment. SLC members who lost their jobs remained on the membership rolls, but because they paid no dues, they were no longer considered "members in good standing"; this accounting problem would later prove a bellwether of the CFL's failure to maintain a consistent cadre of black members. John Keiser claims that the SLC hit the forty thousand–member mark before the end of 1917, but this appears unlikely. The most reliable source is SLC organizer John Kikulski, who estimated membership at around twenty-four thousand during a federal hearing. In some ways, the percentage number is more significant—high proportional membership would insulate the SLC from strikebreaking—and that indisputably reached past 90 percent in many departments. For membership estimates, see Herbst, *Meat-Packing Industry*, 29; CFL Minutes, 2 December 1917, 6–7; CFL Minutes, 16 December 1917, 45–46; CFL Minutes, 20 January 1918, 7–9; Keiser, "John Fitzpatrick," 39. For disparities in black membership, see chapter 3.

76. Foster, 210–12; CCRR, *Negro in Chicago*, 413; John H. Riley, "Suppression of Free Speech on the South Side of Chicago," c. July 1920, John Fitzpatrick Papers, Box 25, Chicago History Museum; Signed agreement between Stockyards Labor Council and President's Mediation Commission, c. June 1919, John Fitzpatrick Papers, Box 8, Folder 60, Chicago History Museum; Grossman, *Land of Hope*, 212; Herbst, *Meat-Packing Industry*, 41; Horowitz, "Political Action," 39–41; Coit, "Racial Violence," 75; Barrett, *William Z. Foster*, 80.

77. Report of Stockyards Labor Council, CFL Minutes, 18 November 1917, 4–6.

78. Report of Stockyards Labor Council, CFL Minutes, 4 November 1917, 21–22; Report of Stockyards Labor Council, CFL Minutes, 18 November 1917, 4–6; Bigham, "Chicago Federation of Labor," 49.

79. CFL Minutes, 2 December 1917, 7–8; see also Clark, "Labor and Capital," 153–62; Grossman, *Land of Hope*, 211; Barrett, *William Z. Foster*, 80–81.

80. CFL Minutes, 6 January 1918, 18–21; CFL Minutes, 20 January 1918, 2–3; Walsh, *Over the Top*, 80–81; McCartin, *Labor's Great War*, 82–83.

81. Appendix to Stock Yards Wage Award, reprinted in CFL Minutes, 7 April 1918, 14b–14d; see also CFL Minutes, 3 February 1918, 6–11.

82. Ibid.; CFL Minutes, 17 February 1918, 15–18.

83. CFL Minutes, 3 February 1918, 10–11; CFL Minutes, 17 February 1918, 15–18.

84. Predictably, this point of view was not without controversy. The commission was so rent by internal dissension that it issued three separate reports, each authored and signed by a different segment. The report signed by Walsh, authored by attorney Basil Manly, was the most progressive of these. See Commission on Industrial Relations, *Final Report*.

85. CFL Minutes, 3 March 1918, 22–24; CFL Minutes, 17 March 1918, 23–24; Conner, *National War Labor Board*, 52–53; Herbst, *Meat-Packing Industry*, 37–39.

86. CFL Minutes, 17 February 1918, 15–18.

87. Clark, "Labor and Capital," 163; see also CFL Minutes, 17 February 1918, 15–18; Barrett, *William Z. Foster*, 81–82; McCartin, *Labor's Great War*, 83.

88. CFL Minutes, 17 February 1918, 15–18.

89. Ibid.; see also Clark, "Labor and Capital," 163; Barrett, *William Z. Foster*, 81–82; McCartin, *Labor's Great War*, 83; Herbst, *Meat-Packing Industry*, 37–39.

90. "Arbitration of Wages and Hours of Labor in the Packing House Industry," 19–22 February 1918, Samuel Alschuler Papers, Chicago History Museum, Box 1, 1293–1302, 1683–85; Clark, "Labor and Capital," 163; McCartin, *Labor's Great War*, 83; Barrett, *William Z. Foster*, 81–82; Conner, *National War Labor Board*, 52–53.

91. Walsh, *Over the Top*, 32; CFL Minutes, 3 March 1918, 22–24; CFL Minutes, 17 March 1918, 23–24; Clark, "Labor and Capital," 162–70; McCartin, *Labor's Great War*, 83; Barrett, *William Z. Foster*, 81–82; Conner, *National War Labor Board*, 52–53.

92. Walsh, *Over the Top*, 32–33, 95; Herbst, *Meat-Packing Industry*, 40.

93. Ibid.

94. Stock Yards Wage Award and Appendix to Stock Yards Wage Award, reprinted in CFL Minutes, 7 April 1918, 14–14d; see also Walsh, *Over the Top*, 107–20; "Eight Hour Day and More Adequate Wages for Workers in Yards," "Judge Alschuler Award," *Butcher Workman* 4, no. 4 (April 1918), 1; "Award an Inspiration for Freedom, Justice and Democracy," ibid., 1; "Complete Transcript of Judge Alschuler's Findings," ibid., 1–2; McCartin, *Labor's Great War*, 83; Brody, *Butcher Workmen*, 80–100; Herbst, *Meat-Packing Industry*, 39–40; Street, "Swift Difference," 22; Keiser, "John Fitzpatrick," 39–41; Clark, "Labor and Capital," 166–70; Barrett, *William Z. Foster*, 82; Conner, *National War Labor Board*, 52–53.

95. CFL Minutes, 16 June 1918, 9–10; see also CFL Minutes, 19 May 1918, 15; Dubofsky, "Abortive Reform," 211–12; Bigham, "Chicago Federation of Labor," 50–52; Brody, *Butcher Workmen*, 82; Grossman, *Land of Hope*, 211.

96. "Giant Stockyards Union Celebration," *New Majority* 2, no. 2 (12 July 1919), 1; "Chicago Campaign Nets Big Results," *Butcher Workman* 5, no. 7 (July 1919), 1, 3.

97. Ibid.; see also CFL Minutes, 3 August 1919, 19–20; John Riley, "Big Parade by Stockyards Workers Features Big Drive for Members," *Chicago Whip* (19 July 1919), 2, 7; "Black and White Workers Are Fighting the Same Battle Say Labor Chiefs," *Chicago Whip* (15 August 1919), 3; Grossman, *Land of Hope*, 208–12; Grossman, "White Man's Union," 87; Herbst, *Meat-Packing Industry*, 41; Horowitz, 39–41; Coit, "Racial Violence," 99–100; Strouthous, *Political Action*, 63. Despite the turnout, the parade was not entirely a success; in many ways it reflected the declining fortunes of the CFL, particularly in regard to black workers. For more, see chapter 5.

98. *AFL Proceedings* (1891), 15; Report of President Samuel Gompers, *AFL Proceedings* (1895), 15–16; *AFL Proceedings* (1896), 21–22; *AFL Proceedings* (1906), 31–35; Report of Committee on President's Report, *AFL Proceedings* (1906), 183–204; Resolution No. 148, *AFL Proceedings* (1913), 246–47; Report of Committee on Resolutions, *AFL Proceedings*, 314–15; *AFL Proceedings* (1920), 74–81.

99. Untitled editorial, *New Majority* 1, no. 1 (4 January 1919), 6; see also Memo from Labor Party of Cook County, 10 February 1919, John Fitzpatrick Papers, Box 8, Folder 56, Chicago History Museum; Letter from Labor Party Campaign Committee, 17 February 1919, John Fitzpatrick Papers, Box 8, Folder 56, Chicago History Museum; Shapiro, "Hand and Brain," 94–95; Horowitz, "Political Action," 26.

100. Memo from Labor Party of Cook County, 10 February 1919, John Fitzpatrick Papers, Box 8, Folder 56, Chicago History Museum.

101. "Challenges Roscoe Simmons in Debate," *Chicago Defender* (10 April 1920), 18; see also "County Labor Party Is Now a Reality," *New Majority* 1, no. 1 (4 January 1919), 1–2; "Candidates of the Labor Party for Alderman," *New Majority* 1, no. 11 (15 March 1919), 18; Gosnell, *Negro Politicians*, 15–19, 39–50; Simonson, "Labor Party," 11–21; Strickland, *Chicago Urban League*, 60; CCRR, *Negro in Chicago*, 591; Merriam, *Chicago*, 144–46; Tuttle, *Race Riot*, 184–207.

102. Resolution No. 41, *Proceedings of the 36th Annual Convention of the Illinois State Federation of Labor*, 1918, 134–54; see also Resolution Nos. 71 and 76, *Proceedings of the 36th Annual Convention of the Illinois State Federation of*

Labor, 1918, 317–19; *Proceedings of the 37th Annual Convention of the Illinois State Federation of Labor*, 1919, 42; Dolnick, "Role of Labor," 5; Fine, *Labor and Farmer*, 397; Horowitz, "Political Action," 3, 31–33; Simonson, "Labor Party," 22, 74–82; Shapiro, "Hand and Brain," 92–113; Street, "Working in the Yards," 272.

103. Dolnick, "Role of Labor," 5; Fine, *Labor and Farmer*, 397; Horowitz, "Political Action," 3, 31–33; Simonson, "Labor Party," 74.

104. Horowitz, "Political Action," 32–33; Simonson, "Labor Party," 81–82; Street, "Working in the Yards," 272.

3. "DEMORALIZED BY ITS OWN WEAKNESSES": THE STRUCTURAL LIMITS OF FEDERATED UNIONISM, 1916–1921

1. Resolution passed by District Council No. 9, Amalgamated Meat Cutters & Butcher Workmen of North America, reprinted in I. H. Bratton, "Colored Workers Should Join Movement," *Butcher Workman* 6, no. 8 (August 1920), 12; Letter, Forrester B. Washington to John Fitzpatrick, 25 January 1919, John Fitzpatrick Papers, Box 25, Chicago History Museum; see also Fogel, *Meat Industry*, 31; Spero and Harris, *Black Worker*, 270–71; Grossman, *Land of Hope*, 210; Henri, *Black Migration*, 152; Sandburg, *Chicago Race Riots*, 53; Tuttle, *Race Riot*, 142; Barrett, *William Z. Foster*, 80.

2. Grossman, *Land of Hope*, 219–20; Cohen, *Making a New Deal*, 45–46; Fogel, *Meat Industry*, 30; Street, "Working in the Yards," 260; Lewis, "Negro Worker," 26–33; Bigham, "Chicago Federation of Labor," 48–49.

3. Grossman, *Land of Hope*, 221; Foster, *Steel Strike*, 210–11; Zieger, *For Jobs and Freedom*, 84; see also Andrew Holmes, "Labor Organizer Says Race Must Spurn Charity," *Chicago Whip* (14 February 1920), 1, 5; Holmes, "Why Colored Workers Are Generally Anti-Union," *Chicago Whip* (28 February 1920), 1, 6.

4. Foster, *Steel Strike*, 209; Spero and Harris, *Black Worker*, 88; see also Cohen, *Racketeer's Progress*, 141–42.

5. Mandel, "Samuel Gompers," 57. Report of President Samuel Gompers, *AFL Proceedings* (1900), 22–23; *American Federationist* (April 1901), 118–20; Taft, *A. F. of L.*, 312; Hutton, "Labor Unions in Chicago," 20. For the AFL's response to industrial unionism, see Resolution No. 102, *AFL Proceedings* (1904), 133, 175–76; *AFL Proceedings* (1920); Mandel, "Samuel Gompers," 44–45; Brecher, *Strike!*, 116; Keiser, "John Fitzpatrick," 23; Cohen, *Making a New Deal*, 3.

6. Report of President Samuel Gompers, *AFL Proceedings* (1897), 15–16; see also *AFL Proceedings* (1887), 10.

7. Report of President Samuel Gompers, *AFL Proceedings* (1900), 22–23;

Report of Committee on President's Report, *AFL Proceedings* (1900), 112; Report of Committee on Law, *AFL Proceedings* (1900), 129.

8. Ibid.; see also Spero and Harris, *Black Worker*, 95; Report of President Samuel Gompers, *AFL Proceedings* (1897), 15–16; *AFL Proceedings* (1887), 10.

9. Spero and Harris, *Black Worker*, 91–93; Tuttle, *Race Riot*, 144; see also Report of President Samuel Gompers, *AFL Proceedings* (1900), 22–23.

10. Report of President Samuel Gompers, *AFL Proceedings* (1900), 22–23.

11. *American Federationist* (April 1901), 118–20; Taft, *A. F. of L.*, 312; Hutton, "Labor Unions in Chicago," 20; Herbst, *Meat-Packing Industry*, 31; Clark, "Labor and Capital," 151; Spero and Harris, *Black Worker*, 269–70.

12. Grossman, *Land of Hope*, 216; Northrup, *Organized Labor*, 8–9; Spero and Harris, *Black Worker*, 95–98, 102–4; see also Report of President Samuel Gompers, *AFL Proceedings* (1900), 22–23; Report of Committee on President's Report, *AFL Proceedings* (1900), 112; Report of Committee on Law, *AFL Proceedings* (1900), 129.

13. Ibid.

14. Spero and Harris, *Black Worker*, 102–4, 269–70; Herbst, *Meat-Packing Industry*, 31; Clark, "Labor and Capital," 151; Foner, "Organized Labor," 169; Report of Committee on President's Report, *AFL Proceedings* (1900), 112.

15. Untitled editorial, *Chicago Defender* (27 May 1911), 4.

16. Street, "Working in the Yards," 260.

17. "A Brief History of Organization in Chicago Stock Yards by the A. M. C. & B. W. of N. A.," *Butcher Workman* 5, no. 11 (November 1919), 1–2; Street, "Working in the Yards," 260; Cohen, *Making a New Deal*, 45–46.

18. Cohen, *Making a New Deal*, 45–46; Street, "Working in the Yards," 260; Grossman, *Land of Hope*, 219–20; Lewis, "Negro Worker," 26; Bigham, "Chicago Federation of Labor," 48–49.

19. CFL Minutes, 2 December 1917, 11; Street, "Working in the Yards," 273–79; McKillen, *Chicago Labor*, 86.

20. "Arbitration of Wages and Hours of Labor in the Packing House Industry," 19–22 February 1918, Samuel Alschuler Papers, Box 1, Chicago History Museum, 1771.

21. Testimony of Dennis Lane, "Violation of Agreement by Employes [*sic*]," Hearings before Judge Samuel Alschuler, 20 June 1919, FMCS, Box 42, 65–66.

22. Ibid., 69; see also Testimony of William Bremer, Hearings before Judge Samuel Alschuler, 20 June 1919, FMCS, Box 42, 194, 214–15; Testimony of Robert Bedford, Hearings before Judge Samuel Alschuler, 20 June 1919, FMCS, Box 42, 220–29; Testimony of William Ghee, Hearings before

Judge Samuel Alschuler, 20 June 1919, FMCS, Box 42, 249–58; Testimony of Frank Guzior, Hearings before Judge Samuel Alschuler, 20 June 1919, FMCS, Box 42, 304–6; Testimony of Gus Grabe, Hearings before Judge Samuel Alschuler, 20 June 1919, FMCS, Box 42, 366; Testimony of Austin Williams, Hearings before Judge Samuel Alschuler, 20 June 1919, FMCS, Box 42, 449–54; Testimony of Walter Gorniak, Hearings before Judge Samuel Alschuler, 23 June 1919, FMCS, Box 42, 512–17.

23. Testimony of B. H. Rendell, "Arbitration of Wages and Hours of Labor in the Packing House Industry," 19–22 February 1918, Samuel Alschuler Papers, Box 1, Chicago History Museum, 1771.

24. CFL Minutes, 2 December 1917, 11.

25. Testimony of S. C. Calef, "Violation of Agreement by Employes [sic]," FMCS, Box 42, 9–13; Testimony of O. J. Wingert, "Violation of Agreement by Employes [sic]," FMCS, Box 42, 22–31; Testimony of Jacob H. Wurmle, "Violation of Agreement by Employes [sic]," FMCS, Box 42, 34–39.

26. Testimony of George Williams, FMCS, Box 42, 47.

27. Testimony of Louis Michora, FMCS, Box 42, 84.

28. Ibid., 84–85.

29. Testimony of Stanley Jinnicki, FMCS, Box 41, 59.

30. Grossman, *Land of Hope*, 220.

31. Ibid.

32. Resolution No. 55, *IFL Proceedings* (1917), 213; Report of Committee on Credentials, *IFL Proceedings* (1917), 233–34.

33. "Labor Launches Drive to Unionize Stockyards Men," *Chicago Daily Tribune* (10 September 1917), 13.

34. "Stock Yards Labor Council and the Colored Workers," editorial, *Chicago Whip* (14 February 1920), 8.

35. Spero and Harris, *Black Worker*, 95.

36. CFL Minutes, 20 January 1918, 13–14; see also Letter, Cyrus Miller to Samuel Gompers, 20 January 1918, John Fitzpatrick Papers, Box 6, Folder 45, Chicago History Museum; Report of Delegate to Convention of the American Federation of Labor, CFL Minutes, 7 July 1918, 32–35; Cohen, *Making a New Deal*, 45–46; Street, "Working in the Yards," 260; Grossman, *Land of Hope*, 219–20; Lewis, "Negro Worker," 26–33; Bigham, "Chicago Federation of Labor," 48–49.

37. Foster, *Steel Strike*, 211.

38. CCRR, *Negro in Chicago*, 428–29; Foner, "Organized Labor," 142.

39. "Chicago Commission on Race Relations Conference on Trade Unions and the Negro Worker," 16 August 1920, Fitzpatrick Papers, Box 25, Chicago History Museum.

40. Ibid.

41. Ibid.

42. Report of Delegate to Convention of the American Federation of Labor, CFL Minutes, 7 July 1918, 32–35.

43. CFL Minutes, 20 January 1918, 13–15; see also letter from Cyrus Miller to Samuel Gompers, 20 January 1918, Fitzpatrick Papers, Box 6, Folder 45, Chicago History Museum.

44. Resolution No. 3, CFL Minutes, 1 February 1920, 13–14.

45. CFL Minutes, 20 January 1918, 14.

46. Ibid., 15.

47. CFL Minutes, 5 January 1919, 13.

48. Ibid., 13–14; Grossman, *Land of Hope*, 219–20; Lewis, "Negro Worker," 26.

4. "BETWEEN TWO FIRES": WHITE AND BLACK WORKERS CONFRONT INTERRACIAL UNIONISM, 1916–1921

1. Arnesen, "Black Strikebreaker," 320; see also Coit, "Racial Violence," 65–68, 82–84.

2. Coit, 65–68, 82–84.

3. CCRR, *Negro in Chicago*, 71–78; Illinois State Council of Defense Committee on Labor, "Report to the Illinois State Council of Defense on the Race Riots at East St. Louis" (1917); Lumpkins, *American Pogrom*, 44–142; Rudwick, *Race Riot*, 27–57, 152–53; McLaughlin, *Power, Community, and Racial Killing*, 87–162; Barnes, *Never Been a Time*, 61, 123–68, 187–89.

4. "Labor Will Ask Laws to Check Negro Invasion," *Chicago Daily Tribune* (8 June 1917), 13.

5. "Insist Negroes Came Because Labor is Scarce," *Chicago Daily Tribune* (9 June 1917), 9; see also "Report of the Special Committee Authorized by Congress to Investigate the East St. Louis Riots," 15 July 1918, reprinted in *Proceedings of the 36th Annual Convention of the Illinois State Federation of Labor* (1918), 96.

6. "Report of the Special Committee Authorized by Congress to Investigate the East St. Louis Riots," 15 July 1918, reprinted in *Proceedings of the 36th Annual Convention of the Illinois State Federation of Labor* (1918), 222.

7. Ibid., 41; "Report of Committee on Officer's Reports, Proceedings of the 35th Annual Convention of the Illinois State Federation of Labor (1917), 222–23.

8. CCRR, *Negro in Chicago*, 394, 403–4; "Kavanaugh Lies Exposed," broadside from Joint Organization Committee, 11 August 1916, John Fitzpatrick Papers, Box 4, Folder 35, Chicago History Museum; Spero and Harris, *Black*

Worker, 128–32; Schneirov, *Labor and Urban Politics,* 188; Henri, *Black Migration,* 150; Robert Zieger, *American Workers, American Unions,* 2nd ed. (Baltimore: Johns Hopkins University Press, 1994), 83.

9. Barrett and Roediger, "Inbetween Peoples," 27.

10. "Southern Negro in the Meat Industry," *Butcher Workman* 2, no. 11 (November 1916), 5.

11. Testimony of Frank Custer, FMCS, Box 42, 292; see also "Exploiting Negroes," *Butcher Workman* 3, no. 7 (July 1917), 4; *Proceedings of the 35th Annual Convention of the Illinois State Federation of Labor, 1917,* 232; Schneirov, *Labor and Urban Politics,* 188; Henri, *Black Migration,* 150; Zieger, *For Jobs and Freedom,* 83; Spero and Harris, *Black Worker,* 128–32.

12. Tuttle, *Race Riot,* 106.

13. CCRR, *Negro in Chicago,* 413–14; CFL Minutes, 6 January 1918, 18–21.

14. CFL Minutes, 6 January 1918, 18–21.

15. Testimony of Frank Custer, FMCS, Box 41, 131–32.

16. "Giant Stockyards Union Celebration," *New Majority* 2, no. 2 (12 July 1919), 1; see also Grossman, *Land of Hope,* 244.

17. "Seek to Check Negro Arrivals from the South," *Chicago Daily Tribune* (16 March 1917), 13.

18. "Race Disintegration," unsigned letter to the editor, *Broad Ax* (26 July 1919), 4; see also Grossman, *Land of Hope,* 169; W. A. Evans, "How to Keep Well: The Negro in Industry," *Chicago Daily Tribune* (28 September 1921), 8; "Time to Act," *Chicago Defender* (14 October 1916), 2; "Overstepping the Bounds," *Chicago Defender* (4 August 1917), 12. See also Muhammad, *Condemnation of Blackness,* esp. 88–145; Daryl Michael Scott, *Contempt and Pity: Social Policy and the Image of the Damaged Black Psyche, 1880–1996* (Chapel Hill: University of North Carolina Press, 1997); Lee D. Baker, *From Savage to Negro: Anthropology and the Construction of Race, 1896–1954* (Berkeley: University of California Press, 1998).

19. A. L. Jackson, "Commission Delves into Old Problem," *Chicago Defender* (4 November 1922), 13; Tuttle, *Race Riot,* 106; see also Testimony of Manuel Meyerhoff, "Arbitration: Amalgamated Meat Cutters and Butcher Workmen of America, Volume 2," 8 September—13 October 1919, Samuel Alschuler Papers, Box 2, Chicago History Museum, 1789–1859.

20. "Overalls," *Chicago Defender* (30 October 1920), 8.

21. Tuttle, *Race Riot,* 147; Brody, *Butcher Workmen,* 85.

22. Brody, 85; see also Grossman, *Land of Hope,* 212–15; CCRR, *Negro in Chicago,* 424; Arnesen, *Black Protest,* 13.

23. Tuttle, *Race Riot,* 147.

24. "City Briefs," *Chicago Defender* (20 November 1920), 10.

25. CCRR, *Negro in Chicago*, 393–94.

26. CFL Minutes, 21 October 1917, 22; Coit, "Racial Violence,"77.

27. Street, "Working in the Yards," 10; Street, "Plant Loyalty," 663–64.

28. Andrew Holmes, "Labor Organizer Says Race Must Spurn Charity," *Chicago Whip* (14 February 1920), 1, 5.

29. CCRR, *Negro in Chicago*, 427; Street, "Working in the Yards," 10.

30. CFL Minutes, 21 October 1917, 22; Testimony of Frank Custer, FMCS, Box 42, 267–69; Testimony of C. M. Smith, FMCS, Box 42, 508–10; Testimony of Frank Smith, FMCS, Box 42, 545; Grossman, *Land of Hope*, 200, 228; Cohen, *Making a New Deal*, 45; Spero and Harris, *Black Worker*, 268; Street, "Working in the Yards," 295–96; Coit, "Racial Violence," 77.

31. Testimony of Frank Custer, FMCS, Box 42, 269.

32. Testimony of Frank Smith, FMCS, Box 42, 545; Testimony of Frank Custer, FMCS, Box 42, 267–69.

33. CFL Minutes, 21 October 1917, 22; Testimony of Frank Custer, FMCS, Box 42, 267–69; Testimony of C. M. Smith, FMCS, Box 42, 508–10; Testimony of Frank Smith, FMCS, Box 42, 545; Grossman, *Land of Hope*, 200, 228; Cohen, *Making a New Deal*, 45; Spero and Harris, *Black Worker*, 268; Street, "Working in the Yards," 295–96; Coit, "Racial Violence," 77.

34. Strickland, *Chicago Urban League*, 50.

35. Strickland, 49–50; "Co-Operation with Other Agencies," *Second Annual Report of the Chicago League on Urban Conditions among Negroes* (Chicago: Chicago Urban League, 1918), 6; "Improved Social Service for Negroes," *Second Annual Report of the Chicago League on Urban Conditions among Negroes*, 12.

36. Strickland, *Chicago Urban League*, 47–50.

37. Strickland, 47–50; Smith, *Racial Democracy*, 2–3.

38. Spero and Harris, *Black Worker*, 140.

39. "Plans," *Report of the Chicago Urban League* (1917), 12.

40. Spero and Harris, *Black Worker*, 139–44; Grossman, *Land of Hope*, 202–3, 236–40; Tuttle, *Race Riot*, 147–53; Coit, "Racial Violence," 77; Smith, *Racial Democracy*, 103. For more on the 1921 strike, see chapter 6.

41. Grossman, *Land of Hope*, 230.

42. Untitled editorial, *Chicago Defender* (27 May 1911), 4; Coit, "Racial Violence," 76; Grossman, *Land of Hope*, 216, 229–36; Grossman, "White Man's Union," 92; Barrett, *William Z. Foster*, 80; Brody, *Butcher Workmen*, 86.

43. Foster, *Steel Strike*, 210–11.

44. Foster, 211–12.

45. Andrew Holmes, "Labor Organizer Says Race Must Spurn Charity," *Chicago Whip* (14 February 1920), 1, 5.

46. Spero and Harris, *Black Worker*, 132.

47. CFL Minutes, 4 December 1921, 13; see also CFL Minutes, 20 January 1918, 9–10; Schneirov, *Labor and Urban Politics*, 188; Henri, *Black Migration*, 150; Zieger, *For Jobs and Freedom*, 83; Spero and Harris, *Black Worker*, 128–32.

48. Spero and Harris, 128–32. *Proceedings of the 35th Annual Convention of the Illinois State Federation of Labor*, 1917, 232; *Proceedings of the 37th Annual Convention of the Illinois State Federation of Labor*, 1919, 135.

49. "2,000 Southern Negroes Arrive in Last 2 Days," *Chicago Daily Tribune* (4 March 1917), 1.

50. "Southern Negro in the Meat Industry," *Chicago Daily Tribune* (November 1916); "Reasons Why Negro Is Leaving South," *Butcher Workman* 3, no. 7 (July 1917), 5; see also Resolution No. 1, CFL Minutes, 19 August 1917, 6–8; CFL Minutes, 20 January 1918, 9–10; "Railroads Bring Colored Men Here," *New Majority* 2, no. 5 (2 August 1919), 8; W. A. Evans, "How to Keep Well: The Negro in Industry," *Chicago Daily Tribune* (28 September 1921), 8. James R. Grossman has argued that the influence of labor agents and the "importation" of black workers have been overstated. Though he acknowledges efforts by northern companies such as Morris and Armour to recruit black workers, he argues that migrants "made careful decisions, based on a variety of sources" and "did not need labor agents to instill in them a desire to find a better life." See Grossman, *Land of Hope*, 69–74.

51. Testimony of Frank Custer, FMCS, Box 42, 260; see also Testimony of Robert Bedford, FMCS, Box 42, 182–88; Barrett, *Work and Community*, 224; Herbst, *Meat-Packing Industry*, 33–34.

52. Testimony of John E. O'Hern, Alschuler Papers, Box 1, CHM, 2399.

53. Both hair spinners and car storers negotiated a separate contract with the packers and were thus not subject to the Alschuler agreement, including its no-strike pledge. See Testimony of Robert Bedford, FMCS, Box 42, 182–88.

54. Testimony of Robert Bedford, FMCS, Box 42, 187–88.

55. Ibid., 187.

56. "Arbitration between Libby, McNeil & Libby and their Employes [*sic*] regarding the Discharge of Certain Employes [*sic*]," 14 August 1919, FMCS, Box 41, 2–3.

57. Testimony of Stanley Jinnicki, 14 August 1919, FMCS, Box 41, 42; see also Testimony of Thomas Robinson, 14 August 1919, FMCS, Box 41, 68–74; Grossman, *Land of Hope*, 212–13; Barrett, *Work and Community*, 215–16; Halpern, *Killing Floor*, 64; Tuttle, *Race Riot*, 153–56.

58. "Arbitration between Libby, McNeil & Libby and their Employes [sic] regarding the Discharge of Certain Employes [*sic*]," 14 August 1919, FMCS, Box 41, 8–9.

59. Testimony of Charles Jones, 14 August 1919, FMCS, Box 41, 101.

60. Ibid.

61. Letter, Samuel Alschuler to Stockyards Labor Council, 12 June 1919, John Fitzpatrick Papers, Box 8, Folder 60, Chicago History Museum.

62. Testimony of Joe Hodges, FMCS, Box 42, 476–77; see also Testimony of Thomas Robinson, 14 August 1919, FMCS, Box 41, 96.

63. Testimony of Frank Custer, FMCS, Box 42, 289.

64. Testimony of Robert Bedford, FMCS, Box 42, 164–65, 220–29; Testimony of Custer, FMCS, Box 42, 280–89; Grossman, *Land of Hope*, 212–13; Barrett, *Work and Community*, 215–16; Halpern, *Killing Floor*, 64; Tuttle, *Race Riot*, 153–56; see also Testimony of Austin Williams, FMCS, Box 42, 449–54.

65. Testimony of Frank Custer, FMCS, Box 42, 290.

66. Ibid., 291; see also Testimony of Robert Bedford, FMCS, Box 42, 149–50.

67. Testimony of Bedford, FMCS, Box 42, 150–54; Testimony of Custer, FMCS, Box 42, 281–82; Grossman, *Land of Hope*, 212–13; Barrett, *Work and Community*, 215–16; Halpern, *Killing Floor*, 64; Tuttle, *Race Riot*, 153–56.

68. Testimony of Walter Gorniak, 20 June 1919, FMCS, Box 42, 512–13; see also Testimony of Louis Michora, 20 June 1919, FMCS, Box 42, 91–92; Testimony of C. M. Smith, 20 June 1919, FMCS, Box 42, 502–5.

69. "Argo," *New Majority* 2, no. 5 (2 August 1919), 4; see also "Argo is a Shambles as Guards Kill Strikers," *New Majority* 2, no. 3 (19 July 1919), 3; "Argo Death Held Riot Result," *Chicago Daily News* (7 August 1919), 3; CCRR, *Negro in Chicago*, 14; Tuttle, *Race Riot*, 134–38.

70. CCRR, *Negro in Chicago*, 404.

71. CCRR, *Negro in Chicago*, 421; see also Barrett, *Work and Community*, 224; Street, "Plant Loyalty," 664–67; Street, "Working in the Yards," 327–28.

72. Untitled editorial, *Chicago Defender* (14 December 1912), 3; Arnesen, "Specter," 322–26.

73. "Our Men Made Checkers and Foremen," *Chicago Defender* (31 August 1918), 12.

74. Testimony of Austin Williams, 23 June 1919, FMCS, Box 42, 428–29.

75. Testimony of Austin Williams, 23 June 1919, FMCS, Box 42, 429–30.

76. Testimony of Custer, 20 June 1919, FMCS, Box 42, 293.

77. Robert E. Park, introduction to First Annual Report of the Chicago League on Urban Conditions Among Negroes (Chicago: Chicago Urban League, 1917), 4.

78. CCRR, *Negro in Chicago*, 422; see also Herbst, *Meat-Packing Industry*, 35–36; Brody, *Butcher Workmen*, 86; Grossman, *Land of Hope*, 226–29;

Barrett, *Work and Community*, 216–18; Lewis, "Negro Worker," 27; Street, "Working in the Yards," 294.

79. Lewis, "Negro Worker," 27.

80. Testimony of John E. O'Hern, "Arbitration of Wages and Hours of Labor in the Packing House Industry" c. 22–27 February 1918, Alschuler Papers, CHM, Box 1, 2393–9.

81. CCRR, *Negro in Chicago*, 423.

82. CCRR, *Negro in Chicago*, 423; CFL Minutes, 20 March 1921, 28–29; Herbst, *Meat-Packing Industry*, 35–36; Brody, *Butcher Workmen*, 86; Grossman, *Land of Hope*, 226–29; Barrett, *Work and Community*, 216–18; Lewis, "Negro Worker," 27; Street, "Working in the Yards," 294.

83. CCRR, *Negro in Chicago*, 423.

84. "Hoot Union Organizer," *Chicago Defender* (22 September 1917), 6.

85. CCRR, *Negro in Chicago*, 422–23.

86. "Jobless Colored Callers Fail to Find Mayor In," *Chicago Daily Tribune* (22 February 1921), 8.

87. "Breaking the 'Solid South,'" *Chicago Daily Tribune* (29 May 1921), 5.

88. "Mayor Asked by Negroes to Bar Ku Klux Here," *Chicago Daily Tribune* (18 August 1921), 15; CCRR, *Negro in Chicago*, 422–23; see also CCRR, *Negro in Chicago*, 122–29; Cohen, *Racketeer's Progress*, 217–18; Arnesen, *Black Protest*, 17; Grimshaw, "Three Cases," 109; Tuttle, *Race Riot*, 157–83; Adair and Allen, *Violence and Riots*, 36; Drake and Cayton, *Black Metropolis*, 64; Coit, "Racial Violence," 129–30.

89. See Reed, *Rise of Chicago's Black Metropolis*, 123.

90. CFL minutes, 20 March 1921, 28–29.

91. Testimony of Frank Smith, FMCS, Box 42, 545; see also "Hoot Union Organizer," *Chicago Defender* (22 September 1917), 6.

92. "Challenges Roscoe Simmons in Debate," *Chicago Defender* (10 April 1920), 18.

93. "Hon. Robert M. Sweitzer," *Chicago Defender* (29 March 1919), 1.

94. "The Disgrace of Chicago's Leaders," *Chicago Whip* (13 March 1920), 8; see also "Thousands of Colored Men," *Broad Ax* (4 January 1919), 1; "Hon. William Hale Thompson," *Broad Ax* (18 January 1919), 1; "Reasons Why the Negro Should Support the Municipal Ownership of Public Utilities," *Broad Ax* (22 February 1919), 1; CCRR, *Negro in Chicago*, 122–29; Cohen, *Racketeer's Progress*, 217–18; Arnesen, *Black Protest*, 17; Grimshaw, "Three Cases," 109; Tuttle, *Race Riot*, 157–83; Adair and Allen, *Violence and Riots*, 36; Drake and Cayton, *Black Metropolis*, 64; Coit, "Racial Violence," 129–30.

95. Strouthous, *Labor and Political Action*, 62.

96. Simonson, "Labor Party," n. 21; Strouthous, *Labor and Political Action*, 61–65; Horowitz, *Negro and White*, 30; Keiser, "John Fitzpatrick," 138; Gosnell, *Negro Politicians*, 15–19, 39–50; "Candidates of the Labor Party for Alderman," *New Majority* 1, no. 11 (15 March 1919), 18.

97. Cohen, *Racketeer's Progress*, 218; Horowitz, *Negro and White*, 15–17.

98. Untitled editorial, *Chicago Defender* (30 June 1917), 12.

99. "Mayor Thompson Opposes Segregation," *Chicago Defender* (7 September 1918), 10; Untitled editorial, *Chicago Defender* (30 June 1917), 12.

100. Gosnell, *Negro Politicians*, 27–28, 40–50; Merriam, *Chicago*, 96, 144–45; Strouthous, *Labor and Political Action*, 22; Horowitz, *Negro and White*, 15–17.

101. Grossman, "White Man's Union," 92.

5. "PATIENCE IS NO LONGER A VIRTUE": THE CFL AND THE CHICAGO RACE RIOT OF 1919

1. CCRR, *Negro in Chicago*, 1.

2. Tuttle, *Race Riot*, 66; U.S. Department of Labor, Division of Negro Economics, *The Negro at Work During the World War and During Reconstruction* (Washington, D.C.: U.S. Government Printing Office, 1921), 68–73; "Chicago Race Riots," *Broad Ax* (9 August 1919), 4; Henri, *Black Migration*, 51–52; Smith, *Racial Democracy*, 6; Merriam, *Chicago*, 11; Strickland, *Chicago Urban League*, 60.

3. "Home Sweet Home," *Chicago Defender* (30 August 1919), 20; CCRR, *Negro in Chicago*, 152–230; Drake and Cayton, *Black Metropolis*, 63–64; Philpott, *Slum and the Ghetto*, 157–61; Peter Hoffman, *The Race Riots: Biennial Report, 1918–1919, and Official Record of Inquests on the Victims of the Race Riots of July and August, 1919* (ca.1919–1920), 22–23.

4. Philpott, *Slum and the Ghetto*, 148–50; "Chicago's Race Riots," editorial, *Chicago Daily News* (29 July 1919), 8; "Chicago Race Riots," *Broad Ax* (9 August 1919), 4; Adair and Allen, *Violence and Riots*, 36; Drake and Cayton, *Black Metropolis*, 63–64; Tuttle, *Race Riot*, 74–107, 157–83; Strickland, *Chicago Urban League*, 60, 148–50.

5. CCRR, *Negro in Chicago*, 590. A number of these groups pushed for a variety of conservative causes. The Hyde Park Protective Association (later the Hyde Park Improvement Protective Club), was founded in 1890 with a protemperance, antivice mission; by the time of the Great Migration, the neighborhood's growing black population became its members' overriding concern. See Coit, "Racial Violence," 28–31; Philpott, *Slum and the Ghetto*, 154–56.

6. CCRR, *Negro in Chicago*, 591.

7. CCRR, *Negro in Chicago*, 592.

8. CCRR, *Negro in Chicago*, 592; see also Philpott, *Slum and the Ghetto*, 164–67. These efforts continued well after the riot. See "'They Shall Not Pass' Has Been Adopted as the Slogan of the Hyde Park Property Owners Association," *Broad Ax* (25 October 1919), 1.

9. Drake and Cayton, *Black Metropolis*, 60–61; see also "The National Race Crisis," editorial, *Chicago Daily News* (30 July 1919), 8.

10. Grimshaw, *"Three Cases,"* 109; Tuttle, *Race Riot*, 210–11; see also Schneider; "The 'Old Eight Regiment,'" *Broad Ax* (15 February 1919), 1, 4–5; "They Fought for the Flag," *Broad Ax* (9 August 1919), 8; "The People throughout the French Republic," *Broad Ax* (6 September 1919), 1.

11. Strickland, *Chicago Urban League*, 60; CCRR, *Negro in Chicago*, 591; Merriam, *Chicago*, 144–46; Tuttle, *Race Riot*, 184–207; Gosnell, *Negro Politicians*, 39–50.

12. Support for Thompson, and disregard for his administration's corruption, was not universal among the black community. At least two black newspapers based in the city, the *Chicago Whip* and the *Broad Ax*, were strenuous critics of Thompson; *Chicago Advocate* editor and American Unity Labor Union founder R. E. Parker held regular street-corner meetings on the South Side to publicize the bombing of black homes and decry Thompson's lack of action in response. See "Disgrace of Chicago's Leaders," *Chicago Whip* (13 March 1920), 8; "Thousands of Colored Men," *Broad Ax* (4 January 1919), 1; "Hon. William Hale Thompson," *Broad Ax* (18 January 1919), 1; "Breaking the 'Solid South,'" *Chicago Daily Tribune* (29 May 1921), 5.

13. "Confidential Bulletin of Radical Activities," 1 February to 7 February 1920, Bureau of Investigation Confidential Bulletins of Radical Activities, *U.S. Military Intelligence Reports: Surveillance of Radicals in the United States, 1917–1941*, 22; Robert K. Murray, *Red Scare: A Study in National Hysteria, 1919–1920* (Minneapolis: University of Minnesota Press, 1955), 178–80; Tuttle, *Race Riot*, 20–21; CCRR, *Negro in Chicago*, 587–89; Grimshaw, *"Three Cases,"*, 109.

14. William Howard Taft, "Causes of Race Riots," *Chicago Defender* (9 August 1919), 90.

15. CCRR, *Negro in Chicago*, 591.

16. CCRR, *Negro in Chicago*, 122–29; "Breaking the 'Solid South,'" *Chicago Daily Tribune* (29 May 1921), 5; Cohen, *Racketeer's Progress*, 217–18; Arnesen, *Black Protest*, 17; Grimshaw, *"Three Cases,"* 109; Tuttle, *Race Riot*, 157–83; Adair and Allen, *Violence and Riots*, 36; Drake and Cayton, *Black Metropolis*, 64; Philpott, *Slum and the Ghetto*, 168–69. The house bombings continued until 1923. See Coit, "Racial Violence," 129–30.

17. CFL Minutes, 5 January 1919, 13–14; Solomon, *Cry Was Unity*, 44–45.

18. CFL Minutes, 3 August 1919, 19–20; "Giant Stockyards Union Celebration," *New Majority* 2, no. 2 (12 July 1919), 1; John Riley, "Big Parade by Stockyards Workers Features Big Drive for Members," *Chicago Whip* (19 July 1919): 2, 7. "Black and White Workers Are Fighting the Same Battle Say Labor Chiefs," *Chicago Whip* (15 August 1919): 3; Grossman, *Land of Hope*, 208–9; Coit, "Racial Violence," 99–100. For a more complete description of the positive impacts of the parade, see chapter 2.

19. "Proclamation Concerning the Race Riots by the Chicago Federation of Labor," *New Majority* 2, no. 6 (9 August 1919), 1–2; "Black and White Workers Are Fighting the Same Battle Say Labor Chiefs," *Chicago Whip* (15 August 1919): 3; Grossman, *Land of Hope*, 208–9.

20. "Proclamation concerning the Race Riots by the Chicago Federation of Labor," *New Majority* 2, no. 6 (9 August 1919), 1; see also CFL Minutes, 3 August 1919, 19–20, 22–23; John Riley, "Serious Questions," *New Majority* 4, no. 1 (3 July 1920), 2; Coit, "Racial Violence," 99–100; Barrett, *William Z. Foster*, 98; Grossman, *Land of Hope*, 208–9.

21. "Proclamation concerning the Race Riots by the Chicago Federation of Labor, *New Majority* 2, no. 6 (9 August 1919), 1; see also "How Steel Gang Jobbed Negroes," *New Majority* 4, no. 1 (3 July 1920), 1–2; "Packers' Stool Pigeon Working for Race War," *New Majority* 5, no. 12 (19 March 1921), 3–4; CFL Minutes, 7 December 1919, 18–22; CFL Minutes, 20 March 1921, 28–29; Taft, "Causes of Race Riots," 90; Zieger, *For Jobs and Freedom*, 84.

22. Grossman, *Land of Hope*, 221; Foner, *Organized Labor*, 144–45.

23. Jablonsky, *Pride in the Jungle*, 96; Drake and Cayton, *Black Metropolis*, 64.

24. "Police Leave Stockyards; Strike Ends," *Chicago Daily Tribune* (10 August 1919), 1.

25. Grossman, *Land of Hope*, 221; Foner, *Organized Labor*, 144–45; see also CCRR, *Negro in Chicago*, 413–14.

26. "Angry at Guards, 10,000 Workers at Yards Strike," and "80,000 Packing Workers Demand 30 Per Cent Raise," *Chicago Daily Tribune* (19 July 1919), 2; "Police Leave Stockyards; Strike Ends," *Chicago Daily Tribune* (10 August 1919), 1; Grossman, *Land of Hope*, 221.

27. Testimony of Gus Grabe, FMCS, Box 42, 366; see also Testimony of Robert Bedford, FMCS, Box 42, 148–92.

28. For more on workplace disputes, see chapter 3.

29. Testimony of William Bremer, FMCS, Box 42, 194; see also Testimony of Frank Guzior, FMCS, Box 42, 304–6.

30. Testimony of William Bremer, FMCS, Box 42, 214–15; see also Testimony of William Ghee, FMCS, Box 42, 249–58; Testimony of Walter Gorniak, FMCS, Box 42, 512–17.

31. Testimony of Robert Bedford, FMCS, Box 42, 220–29; Testimony of Dennis Lane, FMCS, Box 42, 69. The man hit by the pipe was Charlie Jamieson; see testimony of Frank Custer, FMCS, Box 42, 280–81 and testimony of Austin Williams, FMCS, Box 42, 449–54.

32. Senechal, *Sociogenesis of a Race Riot*, 1, 196–97; CCRR, *Negro in Chicago*, 67–71; see also Blocker, *A Little More Freedom*.

33. Lumpkins, *American Pogrom*; Rudwick, *Race Riot*; McLaughlin, *Racial Killing*; Barnes, *Never Been a Time*. For a dispassionate primary source account, see Illinois State Council of Defense Committee on Labor, "Report to the Illinois State Council of Defense on the Race Riots at East St. Louis" (1917). For a recounting of the East St. Louis riot in relation to the Chicago riot, see CCRR, *Negro in Chicago*, 71–78. The East St. Louis riot and its roots in local labor struggles were topics of conversation in the state's unions; see *Proceedings of the 35th Annual Convention of the Illinois State Federation of Labor* (1917), 41–43, 222–23.

34. Lumpkins, *American Pogrom*, 1–10.

35. Sociologist Allen Grimshaw has referred to the Chicago conflict as the quintessential "Northern-style" race riot, characterized by "assaults upon the accommodative pattern related to secular spheres: housing, recreation, transportation and employment." See Grimshaw, "Three Cases," 107.

36. CCRR, *Negro in Chicago*, 1; see also CCRR., *Negro in Chicago*, 7–9, 17; Tuttle, *Race Riot*, 64–65, 231; Hoffman, *Race Riots*, 1, 20; Comment of Investigator Roy C. Woods, in Hoffman, *Race Riots*, 63; "Roster of Those Slain, White and Colored, in Race Riots in Chicago," *Chicago Daily News* (29 July 1919), 1; Schneider, *"We Return Fighting,"* 27.

37. "Report Two Killed, Fifty Hurt, in Race Riots," *Chicago Daily Tribune* (28 July 1919), 1; "300 Armed Negroes Gather; New Rioting Starts; Militia Next," *Chicago Daily News* (28 July 1919), 1; "Riot Sweeps Chicago," *Chicago Defender* (2 August 1919), 1; CCRR, *Negro in Chicago*, 4–5; Schneider, *"We Return Fighting,"* 27; Tuttle, *Race Riot*, 8.

38. Tuttle, 8; Jablonsky, *Pride in the Jungle*, 96; see also "Bloody Anarchy," *The Broad Ax* (2 August 1919), 1–2. The first officer on the scene, Patrolman Daniel Callahan, was the subject of considerable public outcry from the black community and was suspended from duty. The man alleged to have thrown the fatal rock, George Stauber, was eventually arrested. See Carl Sandburg, "Says Lax Conditions Caused Race Riots," *Chicago Daily News*

(28 July 1919), 1; "Alleged Starter of Race Riots in Court," *Chicago Daily News* (1 August 1919), 1; "The Colored Citizens Committee" and "Calls Copper Responsible for Rioting," *Broad Ax* (2 August 1919), 4.

39. CCRR, *Negro in Chicago*, 5; "Report Two Killed, Fifty Hurt, in Race Riots," *Chicago Daily Tribune* (28 July 1919), 1; "300 Armed Negroes Gather; New Rioting Starts; Militia Next," *Chicago Daily News* (28 July 1919), 1; "Bloody Anarchy," *Broad Ax* (2 August 1919), 1–2.

40. CCRR, *Negro in Chicago*, 6, 10–11; Hoffman, *Race Riots*, 45–49; "Lines and Employes [*sic*] Stand Firm; Claim Sympathy of Public," *Chicago Daily News* (29 July 1919), 2; "The Car Strike," *Chicago Daily News* (29 July 1919), 8; "Mahon is Expected in Chicago To-Day," *Chicago Daily News* (29 July 1919), 12; "Bloody Anarchy," *Broad Ax* (2 August 1919), 1–2; Williams and Williams, *Anatomy of Four Race Riots*, 83; Coit, "Racial Violence," 106–7.

41. "150 Negro Prisoners at County Jail Riot, Machine Gun Put In," *Chicago Daily News* (29 July 1919), 1; "War in a Great City's Streets," editorial, *Chicago Daily News* (31 July 1919), 8; "Ghastly Deeds of Race Rioters Told," *Chicago Defender* (2 August 1919), 1; "Bloody Anarchy," *Broad Ax* (2 August 1919), 1–2; Williams and Williams, *Four Race Riots*, 81–85; Foner, *Organized Labor*, 146; Coit, "Racial Violence," 121–22; see also "Troops Moving on Chicago as Negroes Shoot into Crowds," *Chicago Daily News* (29 July 1919), 2.

42. "Chicago Rioters Buy New Arms in Calumet Towns," *Chicago Daily Tribune* (30 July 1919), 4; "Negroes Seek Safety Haven at Milwaukee," *Chicago Daily Tribune* (31 July 1919), 2; "Expects Exodus of Negroes," *Chicago Daily News* (1 August 1919), 3; Williams and Williams, *Four Race Riots*, 83.

43. CCRR, *Negro in Chicago*, 6, 16–21; "Negro in Barricade Shoots Two Whites," *Chicago Daily News* (30 July 1919), 1; Coit, "Racial Violence," 138–39.

44. CCRR, *Negro in Chicago*, 16–21; "Troops Moving on Chicago as Negroes Shoot into Crowds," *Chicago Daily News* (29 July 1919), 2; "Ghastly Deeds of Race Rioters Told," *Chicago Defender* (2 August 1919), 1; Williams and Williams, *Four Race Riots*, 81–85; Foner, *Organized Labor*, 146; Coit, "Racial Violence," 136–37.

45. "For White Union Men to Read," *New Majority* 2, no. 8 (2 August 1919), 1.

46. CCRR, *Negro in Chicago*, 399.

47. Herbst, *Meat-Packing Industry*, 49; see also "Rush Food to Riot Zone," *Chicago Daily News* (1 August 1919); "Keep Up Relief Work in Riot and Fire Area," *Chicago Daily News* (5 August 1919), 4; "Food to Be Rushed to the Hungry in City's Riot Center," *Chicago Daily News* (31 July 1919), 1; "Paying

Off Colored Stockyards Workers in District Patrolled by Troops," *Chicago Daily News* (1 August 1919), 3; "Industries Gives [*sic*] Data on Workers," *Chicago Defender* (11 November 1922), 14; Spero and Harris, *Black Worker*, 276–78.

48. Barrett, *Work and Community*, 222; Barrett and Roediger, "Inbetween Peoples," 31–32; "Proclamation concerning the Race Riots by the Chicago Federation of Labor, *New Majority* 2, no. 6 (9 August 1919), 1–2; Arnesen, *Black Protest*, 13–15; Brody, *Butcher Workmen*, 87. This conclusion is disputed in some circles. Historian John Keiser has argued that "many white workers participated in the rioting in spite of the warning by [John] Fitzpatrick that the packers would be the only ones to profit." It is, of course, nearly impossible to ascertain the union affiliation of the mass of rioters, but the city's newspapers contain no real mention of any connection between Chicago's unions and the riot; given the local press's anti-union bent, it is likely they would have gleefully decried the CFL if an opportunity presented itself. The most likely explanation is that union workers participated in the riot, but not in significant numbers, and certainly not *because* of any connection with the CFL/SLC. See Keiser, 166–67; Fogel, *Meat Industry*, 34.

49. CCRR, *Negro in Chicago*, 38, 48–49; Cohen, *Making a New Deal*, 37; "Troops Moving on Chicago as Negroes Shoot into Crowds," *Chicago Daily News* (29 July 1919), 3; "Where Races Rioted Yesterday," *Chicago Daily Tribune* (30 July 1919), 2; Letter, John Fitzpatrick and Jack Johnstone to William B. Wilson, 23 August 1919, FMCS, Box 41; Barrett, *Work and Community*, 221–23.

50. See Drake and Cayton, *Black Metropolis*, 63; Barrett, *Work and Community*, 221–23. For more on gangs and the riot, see "Ragen's Colts Start Riot," *Chicago Defender* (28 June 1919), 1; "Ragen's Colts Deny Riot Responsibility," *Chicago Daily News* (2 August 1919), 3; "Clubs Accused in Riot Arson Plots," *Chicago Daily News* (14 August 1919); Williams and Williams, *Four Race Riots*, 75; CCRR, *Negro in Chicago*, 1, 11–17; Hoffman, *Race Riots*, 23; Tuttle, *Race Riot*, 32–33; Barrett, *Work and Community* 220–22; Schneider, *"We Return Fighting,"* 27; Coit, "Racial Violence," 108–10; Philpott, *Slum and the Ghetto*, 170–80. George Stauber, the man alleged to have thrown the rock that killed Eugene Williams, was reputed to be a member of Ragen's Colts. See "Alleged Starter of Race Riots in Court," *Chicago Daily News* (1 August 1919), 1; Keefe, *Guns and Roses*, 118.

51. Hoffman, *Race Riots*, 28–29, 42–43; CCRR, *Negro in Chicago*, 400; "Rioters in Attack on Soldiers; Mayor Bares Arson Plot," *Chicago Daily News* (31 July 1919); "Industries Gives [*sic*] Data on Workers," *Chicago Defender* (11 November 1922), 14.

52. "Strike Is On; Cars Stop! 20 Slain in Race Riots," *Chicago Daily Tribune* (29 July 1919), 1.

53. CCRR, *Negro in Chicago*, 7; "Bayonets Subdue White Mob," *Chicago Daily News* (30 July 1919), 1; "Shiny Bayonets and Rain Curb Rioters," *Chicago Daily News* (31 July 1919), 3; "Troops and Police Hold Mastery in Riot Area"—Lowden," *Chicago Daily Tribune* (1 August 1919), 2; "Mayor's Call for Troops to Stop Rioting," *Broad Ax* (2 August 1919), 5; see also "Situation Well in Hand, Says Lowden," *Chicago Daily News* (29 July 1919), 2; "Troops Moving on Chicago as Negroes Shoot into Crowds," *Chicago Daily News*; "Riots Wane, Lowden Will Rest on Farm," *Chicago Daily News* (1 August 1919), 4.

54. CCRR, *Negro in Chicago*, 7; "2,000 Homeless in Fire," *Chicago Daily News* (2 August 1919); "Echoes and Re-Echoes of the Reign of Anarchy," *Broad Ax* (9 August 1919), 1–2; Jablonsky, *Pride in the Jungle*, 96–97; Brody, *Butcher Workmen*, 87; Fogel, *Meat Industry*, 34.

55. "Argo," *New Majority* 2, no. 5 (2 August 1919), 2; see also "Argo Is a Shambles as Guards Kill Strikers," *New Majority* 2, no. 3 (19 July 1919), 3; "Argo Death Held Riot Result," *Chicago Daily News* (7 August 1919), 3; Graham Taylor, "An Epidemic of Strikes in Chicago," *Survey* (2 August 1919), 645; CCRR, *Negro in Chicago*, 14; Tuttle, *Race Riot*, 134–38.

56. Letter, John Fitzpatrick and Jack Johnstone to William B. Wilson, 23 August 1919, FMCS, Box 41; "Labor Blames Packers and Press for Riots," *Chicago Daily Tribune* (4 August 1919), 2; "Union Leaders Accuse Packers of Inciting Riot," August 1919, Fitzpatrick Papers, CHM, Box 8, Folder 61; "Proclamation concerning the Race Riots by the Chicago Federation of Labor," *New Majority* 2, no. 6 (9 August 1919), 1–2; see also CFL Minutes, 3 August 1919, 19–20; "Black and White Workers Are Fighting the Same Battle Say Labor Chiefs," *Chicago Whip* (15 August 1919), 3; Bart, *Working-Class Unity*, 11–12.

57. J. W. Johnstone, "Statement of the Stock Yards Labor Council," in *Chicago Race Riots*, ed. Harrison George (Chicago: The Great Western Publishing Company, 1919), 4.

58. Untitled Hearing, August 1919, FMCS, Box 41, 96.

59. "Chicago Race Riots," in *Chicago Race Riots*, ed. Harrison George (Chicago: The Great Western Publishing Company, 1919), 26.

60. Lewis, "Negro Worker," 31.

61. *Chicago Whip* (9 August 1919), 7.

62. CFL Minutes, 3 August 1919, 24–25.

63. "Negroes Not Leaving Chicago for South," *Chicago Daily News* (7 August 1919), 4; see also "To Colored Labor Seeking Homes," advertisement,

Broad Ax (16 August 1919), 8; Strickland, *Chicago Urban League*, 62–63; Lewis, "Negro Worker," 31.

64. "Jobs at Yards Open for Negroes Monday," *Chicago Daily News* (1 August 1919), 5; Herbst, *Meat-Packing Industry*, 47–48; Horowitz, *Negro and White*, 45–47. John Fitzpatrick later alleged that the packers "sent emissaries among their colored workers" to encourage them to come back to work, thus provoking more violence and maintaining a divide between white and black workers. See "Fitzpatrick Alleges Plan to Crush Union," *Chicago Daily News* (13 August 1919), 1.

65. Ibid.

66. "5,000 White Men Quit Yards; Negroes Back," *Chicago Daily News* (7 August 1919), 1.

67. "Proclamation concerning the Race Riots by the Chicago Federation of Labor, *New Majority* 2, no. 6 (9 August 1919), 2; see also Grossman, *Land of Hope*, 222–23; "Negroes Return to Yards Today Guarded by Host," *Chicago Daily Tribune* (7 August 1919), 17; Tuttle, *Race Riot*, 57–60.

68. "Jobs at Yards Open for Negroes Monday," *Chicago Daily News* (1 August 1919), 5.

69. "Bar Color Line in Yards," *Chicago Daily News* (2 August 1919), 1; "Grand Jury Asks Facts about White Rioters be Offered," *Chicago Daily News* (6 August 1919), 1.

70. "Bar Color Line in Yards," *Chicago Daily News* (2 August 1919), 1.

71. Ibid.; "Jobs at Yards Open for Negroes Monday," *Chicago Daily News* (1 August 1919), 5; "2,000 Are Homeless in Yards Fire," *Chicago Daily News* (2 August 1919); "Bar Color Line in Yards," *Chicago Daily News*; "Proclamation concerning the Race Riots by the Chicago Federation of Labor," *New Majority* 2, no. 6 (9 August 1919), 2; Herbst, *Meat-Packing Industry*, 47–48; "Yards Race Clashes Seen as Labor Mixup," *Chicago Daily News* (5 August 1919), 4; "Grand Jury Asks Facts about White Rioters Be Offered," *Chicago Daily News* (6 August 1919), 1; Horowitz, *Negro and White*, 45–47.

72. "Negroes Return to Yards Today Guarded by Host," *Chicago Daily Tribune* (7 August 1919), 17; "Union Plea Rejected, Police Stay in Yards," *Chicago Daily News* (9 August 1919), 1; "Armed Guards at the Stockyards," editorial, *Chicago Daily News*, 8; "Yards Men Back at Work; Guards Gone," *Chicago Daily News* (11 August 1919), 3; "Fitzpatrick Alleges Plan to Crush Union," *Chicago Daily News* (13 August 1919), 1; Herbst, *Meat-Packing Industry*, 47–48; Horowitz, *Negro and White*, 45–47; Barrett, *William Z. Foster*, 98.

73. "5,000 White Men Quit Yards; Negroes Back," *Chicago Daily News* (7 August 1919); Pacyga, *Polish Immigrants*, 217; Tuttle, *Race Riot*, 63.

74. "32,000 Threaten Strike at Yards: Unions Vote to Go Out if Guards Star," *Chicago Daily Tribune* (8 August 1919), 1; see also Testimony of Henry Smith, August 1919, FMCS, Box 41, 10–20; "Strikes End Gun Stunt of Packers," *New Majority* 2, no. 7 (16 August 1919), 1–2; Pacyga, *Polish Immigrants*, 240–42; Spero and Harris, *Black Worker*, 276–78.

75. "32,000 Threaten Strike . . ." *Chicago Daily Tribune* (8 August 1919), 1[emphasis added].

76. "5,000 White Men Quit Yards; Negroes Back," *Chicago Daily News* (7 August 1919), 1, 3.

77. "Union Plea Rejected, Police Stay in Yards," *Chicago Daily News* (9 August 1919), 1; Andrew Holmes, "Why Colored People Don't Organize," *Chicago Whip* (21 February 1920), 1, 6; Herbst, *Meat-Packing Industry*, 49; see also "Colored People throughout the Union," *Broad Ax* (16 August 1919), 1.

78. "Bar Color Line in Yards," *Chicago Daily News* (2 August 1919), 1.

79. Grossman, *Land of Hope*, 222–23.

80. "Negroes Join in Plea for More Guards at Work," *Chicago Daily Tribune* (1 August 1919), 3.

81. Robert Abbott, "Shall We Unionize?" *Chicago Defender* (23 August 1919); see also Abbott, "Shall We Unionize?" in George, *Chicago Race Riots*, 6–8.

82. "Grand Jury Asks Facts about White Rioters Be Offered," *Chicago Daily News* (6 August 1919), 1.

83. Resolution by Executive Board of Amalgamated Meat Cutters and Butcher Workmen Local Union 651, reprinted in *Chicago Whip* (9 August 1919), 7–8.

84. Brody, *Butcher Workmen*, 87–88; Grossman, *Land of Hope*, 223; Arnesen, *Black Protest*, 13–15; Fogel, *Meat Industry*, 41.

85. Carl Sandburg, "Yards Race Clashes Seen as Labor Mixup," *Chicago Daily News* (5 August 1919), 4.

86. "Union Plea Rejected, Police Stay in Yards," *Chicago Daily News* (9 August 1919), 1.

87. "Proclamation concerning the Race Riots by the Chicago Federation of Labor," *New Majority* 2, no. 6 (9 August 1919), 2; see also Untitled Hearing, August 1919, FMCS, Box 41, 20, 33–39; Letter, John Fitzpatrick and Jack Johnstone to William B. Wilson, 23 August 1919, FMCS, Box 41; CFL Minutes, 17 August 1919, 23–24; "Union Plea Rejected, Police Stay in Yards," *Chicago Daily News* (9 August 1919), 1; "Yards Men Back at Work; Guards Gone," *Chicago Daily News* (11 August 1919), 3; "Live Stock Booms as Workers Return," *Chicago Daily News*, 19; "Yards Strikers Hit by Loss of Seniority," *Chicago Daily News* (12 August 1919), 3; "Black and White

Workers Are Fighting the Same Battle Say Labor Chiefs," *Chicago Whip* (15 August 1919), 3.

88. Ibid.; Brody, *Butcher Workmen*, 87–88; Pacyga, *Polish Immigrants*, 218; Fogel, *Meat Industry*, 41.

89. "A Sickening Sight," *Chicago Whip* (9 August 1919), 10; "Second Ward Relief Committee Makes Report," *Chicago Defender* (20 September 1919), 14; Foner, *Organized Labor*, 146.

90. "Oscar De Priest Talks on Riot before Ministers," *Chicago Defender* (20 September 1919), 15.

91. M. A. Majors, "The Riot Commission," *Broad Ax* (30 August 1919), 2; see also "Negro No Shirker in War or Labor, Says Minster," *Broad Ax* (9 August 1919), 5.

92. "Negroes Call on Mayor, Lowden, to Stop Riots," *Chicago Daily Tribune* (31 July 1919), 3; CCRR, *Negro in Chicago*, 96.

93. Tuttle, "Views of a Negro during the 'Red Summer' of 1919," *Journal of Negro History* 51, no. 3 (July 1966): 209–18.

94. CCRR, *Negro in Chicago*, 131–32.

95. "Mayor Shifts Bomb Cases to Aldermen," *Chicago Defender* (14 May 1921), 1; "Start Searching for Bombers," *Chicago Defender* (21 May 1921), 1; "Chicagoans Raise Over $1,000 for Riot Victims," *Chicago Defender* (11 June 1921), 2.

96. CCRR, *Negro in Chicago*, 46, 59–60, 493, 592; Grant, *Negro with a Hat*, 206–10; Baldwin, *Chicago's New Negroes*, 237–39.

97. Christopher R. Reed, "Garveyism," Electronic Encyclopedia of Chicago (Chicago Historical Society, 2005); see also E. M. McDuffie, "Chicago, Garveyism, and the History of the Diasporic Midwest," *African and Black Diaspora* 8, no. 2 (2015): 129–45.

98. CCRR, *Negro in Chicago*, 59–64; Harry Haywood, *A Black Communist in the Freedom Struggle: The Life of Harry Haywood*, ed. Gwendolyn Midlo Hall (Minneapolis: University of Minnesota Press, 2011), 91–92; Christopher Robert Reed, *The Rise of Chicago's Black Metropolis, 1920–1929* (Urbana: University of Illinois Press, 2011), 180–82.

99. Tuttle, "Views of a Negro," 216.

100. "Negroes Urge Ending of Race Antagonism," *Chicago Daily News* (4 August 1919), 1; "Leaders Hold Meeting," *Chicago Defender* (9 August 1919), 9; see also "The Social Equality Bug Bear Seems to Strike Terror," *Broad Ax* (23 August 1919), 1.

101. Testimony of Alex Bernatowicz, FMCS, Box 41, 109. Testimony of Stanley Jinnicki, 14 August 1919, "Arbitration between Libby, McNeil & Libby and their Employes [*sic*] regarding the Discharge of Certain Employes

[*sic*]," FMCS, Box 41, 11. It should be noted that Hawkins denied saying those words, claiming "I don't use no profane language at all." See Testimony of Harry Hawkins, FMCS, Box 41, 160.

102. Testimony of Frank Custer, FMCS, Box 41, 129–30, 136–37; Testimony of Harry Hawkins, FMCS, Box 41, 161–66.

103. Testimony of Harry Hawkins, FMCS, Box 41, 161–66.

104. "A Sickening Sight," *Chicago Whip* (9 August 1919), 10; "Preparedness for the Coming Economic War," *Chicago Whip* (2 October 1920), 8.

105. Lewis, "Negro Worker," 30.

106. "Negroes Call on Mayor, Lowden, to Stop Riots," *Chicago Daily Tribune* (31 July 1919), 3; *Chicago Whip* (15 August 1919), 3; Strouthous, *U.S. Labor*, 63–64; Grossman, *Land of Hope*, 223.

107. Testimony of Stanley Jinnicki, FMCS, Box 41, 11; Testimony of Frank Custer, FMCS, Box 41, 129–30; Testimony of Harry Hawkins, FMCS, Box 41, 161–66.

108. Testimony of Frank Custer, FMCS, Box 41, 131–32.

109. "Arbitration between Libby, McNeil and Libby and Their Employes regarding the Discharge of Certain Employes [*sic*]," dated 14 August 1919, FMCS, Box 41, 155.

110. Testimony of Alex Bernatowicz, FMCS, Box 41, 111; Testimony of Harry Hawkins, FMCS, Box 41, 157–61.

111. Foner, *Organized Labor*, 147.

112. Lewis, "Negro Worker," 30.

6. "BORING FROM WITHIN": RACE AND THE DECLINE OF THE CFL, 1919–1922

1. "Labor Opens Fight against Radicals," *New York American*, 18 November 1920; Press release from John Fitzpatrick, 22 November 1920, John Fitzpatrick Papers, Box 9, Folder 67, Chicago History Museum.

2. Herbst, *Meat-Packing Industry*, 43; Street, "Working in the Yards," 275.

3. CFL Minutes: 18 April 1920, 15–17; 5 October 1919, 27; Minutes of Executive Board Meeting, 3; Report of Executive Board, 19 October 1919, 16–18, 2 November 1919, 7–8, 4 January 1920, 8; Report of Executive Board, 18 January 1920, 11–19, 18 January 1920, 19–25; Reports of Organizations, 15 February 1920, 11–12; Supplementary Report of Executive Board, 2 May 1920, 15–24. See also "Row between Labor Here and A. F. of L. Looms," *Chicago Daily Tribune* (16 November 1919), 10; Clark, "Labor and Capital," 182–86; Street, "Working in the Yards," 277–78; Brody, *Butcher Workmen*, 88–91; Herbst, *Meat-Packing Industry*, 43–45; Barrett, *William Z. Foster*, 98; Pacyga, *Polish Immigrants*, 243–46 Cohen, *Making a New Deal*, 46.

4. Letter, Frank Morrison to John Fitzpatrick, 20 September 1919, John Fitzpatrick Papers, Box 8, Folder 62, Chicago History Museum; see also Report of Stockyards Labor Council, CFL Minutes, 18 November 1917, 4; Report of Stockyards Labor Council, CFL Minutes, 16 December 1917, 45–46.

5. Ibid.

6. Ibid.

7. CFL Minutes, 18 April 1920, 15–17; CFL Minutes, 5 October 1919, 27; Minutes of Executive Board Meeting, 3; Report of Executive Board, 19 October 1919, 16–18; Report of Executive Board, 2 November 1919, 7–8; Report of Executive Board, 4 January 1920, 8; Report of Executive Board, 18 January 1920, 11–25; Reports of Organizations, 15 February 1920, 11–12; 18 April 1920, 15–17. See also "Stock Yards Council Offers Resignation," *New Majority* 3, no. 4 (24 January 1920), 6; "A Joint Meeting That Concerns the Race People," *Chicago Whip* (28 February 1920), 5; Clark, "Labor and Capital," 182–86; Street, "Working in the Yards," 277–78; Brody, *Butcher Workmen*, 88–91; Herbst, *Meat-Packing Industry*, 43–45; Barrett, *William Z. Foster*, 98; Pacyga, *Polish Immigrants*, 243–46 Cohen, *Making a New Deal*, 46.

8. CFL Minutes, 18 April 1920, 15–17; Supplementary Report of Executive Board, 2 May 1920, 15–21; 16 May 1920, 15–21. See also Brody, *Butcher Workmen*, 88–91; Clark, "Labor and Capital," 182–86; Street, "Working in the Yards," 277–78.

9. Resolution No. 1, Chicago Federation of Labor Minutes, 2 May 1920, 22–23.

10. CFL Minutes, 2 May 1920, 22–24; "Row between Labor Here and A. F. of L. Looms," *Chicago Daily Tribune* (16 November 1919), 10; "Stock Yards Council Offers Resignation," *New Majority* 3, no. 4 (24 January 1920), 6; "A Joint Meeting That Concerns the Race People," *Chicago Whip* (28 February 1920), 5.

11. "Yards Labor Leader Shot," *Chicago Daily Tribune* (18 May 1920), 1; "Kikulski, Labor Leader Shot by Sluggers, Dies," *Chicago Daily Tribune* (22 May 1920), 3; "Death Claims John Kikulski after Brutal Attack," *Butcher Workman* 6, no. 5 (May 1920), 1; "Thousands Mourn at Kikulski's Bier," *Butcher Workman* 6, no. 6 (June 1920), 1, 3; Clark, "Labor and Capital," 182–86; Street, "Working in the Yards," 277–78; Brody, *Butcher Workmen*, 88–91; Herbst, *Meat-Packing Industry*, 43–45; Barrett, *William Z. Foster*, 98; Pacyga, *Polish Immigrants*, 243–46 Cohen, *Making a New Deal*, 46.

12. Clark, "Labor and Capital," 182–86.

13. Brody, *Steelworkers in America*, 69–73; Murray, *Red Scare*, 137; McCartin, *Labor's Great War*, 40; also Greer, "Racism and U.S. Steel, 147–48;

see also Interchurch World Movement, *Steel Strike of 1919*, 135–37; Stone, "Origins of Job Structures," 113–73.

14. Interchurch World Movement, *Steel Strike of 1919*, 147, 154–55; Bigham, "Chicago Federation of Labor," 58; Dubofsky, *Industrialism*, 130–31; Brecher, *Strike!*, 133–44; Keiser, "John Fitzpatrick," 56–59.

15. Resolution No. 2, CFL Minutes, 7 April 1918, 5–7.

16. Report of Delegate to the Convention of the American Federation of Labor, Chicago Federation of Labor Minutes, 7 July 1918, 31–32; CFL Minutes, 19 May 1918, 2–3; CFL Minutes, 1 June 1919, 22–24; Report on Organizing the Steel Industry, CFL Minutes, 4 August 1918, 23; Report of Executive Board, CFL Minutes, 1 September 1918, 1–11; Foster, *Great Steel Strike*, 1, 17–19, 76–78; Olds, *Analysis of the Interchurch World*, 181–85; Interchurch World Movement, *Steel Strike of 1919*, 3; Barrett, *William Z. Foster*, 84–90; Brody, *Steelworkers*, 214–15; Brody, *Labor in Crisis*, 61–64; see also Letter, William Z. Foster to John Fitzpatrick, 12 June 1918, John Fitzpatrick Papers, Box 7, Folder 49, Chicago History Museum; Foster to Fitzpatrick, 22 June 1918, John Fitzpatrick Papers, Box 7, Folder 49, Chicago History Museum; Samuel Gompers to Fitzpatrick, 5 July 1918, John Fitzpatrick Papers, Box 7, Folder 50, Chicago History Museum; CFL Minutes, 18 August 1918, 7–8.

17. CFL Minutes, 1 June 1919, 24.

18. Foster, *Great Steel Strike*, 76–78; Interchurch World Movement, *Steel Strike of 1919*, 154–55; CFL Minutes, 15 December 1918, 27–29; CFL Minutes, 17 August 1919, 17–20; "Organizing the Steel Workers," *Butcher Workman* 5, no. 1 (January 1919), 5; Foster, "Manhood Rises in the Steel Industry," *New Majority* 1, no. 8 (22 February 1919), 3; "Labor Leaders Fight to Form Steel Unions," *Chicago Daily Tribune* (17 June 1919), 12; "Steel Men Vote for Demands; To See Firms First," *Chicago Daily Tribune* (21 August 1919), 3; "Twelve Demands of Steel Workers on Eve of Strike," *Chicago Daily Tribune* (19 September 1919), 2; *Proceedings of the 37th Annual Convention of the Illinois State Federation of Labor*, 1919, 160–73, 316–23; Brody, *Steelworkers*, 218–21; Brody, *Labor in Crisis*, 69–76; Barrett, *William Z. Foster*, 84–90; Dubofsky, *Industrialism*, 130; Bate, "Development of the Iron and Steel," 182–85; Murray, *Red Scare*, 141–42; Bigham, "Chicago Federation of Labor," 55–57; Taft, *A. F. of L.*, 385–91.

19. "Strikers Jeer Night Shift at Indiana Harbor," *Chicago Daily Tribune* (22 September 1919), 2.

20. Mackaman, "Foreign Element," 184, 194, 216–19; Brody, *Steelworkers in America*, 223–24.

21. Foster, *Great Steel Strike*, 78–80; CFL Minutes, 7 September 1919, 28–30; "Steel Men to Vote," *Chicago Daily Tribune* (10 August 1919), 1; Barrett, *William Z. Foster*, 89–90; Brecher, *Strike!*, 137.

22. "Steel Men Vote for Demands; To See Firms First," *Chicago Daily Tribune* (21 August 1919), 3; "Steel Strike Looms as Gary Denies Parley," *Chicago Daily Tribune* (27 August 1919), 3; "Gompers Goes to Capital for Steel Parley," *Chicago Daily Tribune* (28 August 1919), 1; "Wilson Urges Steel Strikes Be Postponed," *Chicago Daily Tribune* (11 September 1919), 1; "Must Strike, Steel Unions Tell Wilson," *Chicago Daily Tribune* (19 September 1919), 1; "284,000 Out All Over Nation, Says Union," *Chicago Daily News* (22 September 1919), 1–2; "Steel Industry Is Virtually Paralyzed in Chicago District," *Chicago Daily Tribune* (22 September 1919), 1; "75,000 Strike in Local Area; Million Loss," *Chicago Daily Tribune* (23 September 1919), 1; "Four Stabbed in Ohio Strike Riot," *Chicago Daily News* (24 September 1919), 1; "Steel Workers' Strike Affects Colored Men," *Chicago Whip* (27 September 1919), 10; "The Steel Strike," *Chicago Whip*, 12; Interchurch World Movement, *Steel Strike of 1919*, 154–55; Brecher, *Strike!*, 138; Keiser, "John Fitzpatrick," 47; Dubofsky, *Industrialism*, 130.

23. Brody, *Labor in Crisis*, 35–36.

24. Brody, *Steelworkers*, 123–24, 250–53; Foner, *Organized Labor*, 144.

25. Interchurch World Movement, *Steel Strike of 1919*, 15–16, 135–36; "Foreigners Go Back, Says Strike Picket," *Chicago Daily News* (25 September 1919), 3; Brody, *Steelworkers*, 135–37; Brody, *Labor in Crisis*, 43; Cohen, *Making a New Deal*, 39–43; Bate, "Iron and Steel," 129; Brecher, *Strike!*, 141–42. For a discussion of race in the AFL, see chapter 2.

26. Interchurch World Movement, *Steel Strike of 1919*, 154–55; see also Bigham, "Chicago Federation of Labor," 58; Dubofsky, Industrialism, 130–31; Brecher, *Strike!*, 133–44; Keiser, "John Fitzpatrick," 56–59.

27. CFL Minutes, 5 October 1919, 19; Interchurch World Movement, *Steel Strike of 1919*, 154–60; Brody, *Steelworkers in America*, 217; Brody, *Labor in Crisis*, 65–66; Bigham, "Chicago Federation of Labor," 58; Dubofsky, *Industrialism*, 130–31; Brecher, *Strike!*, 133–44; Keiser, "John Fitzpatrick," 56–59.

28. Brody, *Steelworkers in America*, 121; Spero and Harris, *Black Worker*, 256–58; see also Greer, "Racism and U.S. Steel," 52; Whatley, "African-American Strikebreaking."

29. Whatley, "Gary Looks upon Itself as Heart of Steel Fight," *Chicago Daily Tribune* (22 September 1919), 2.

30. "Steel Strikers Stick in Chicago District," *New Majority* 2, no, 14 (4

October 1919), 2; see also Dorothy Walton, "Scab Life Miserable in Chicago District," *New Majority* 2, no. 15 (11 October 1919), 2.

31. Interchurch World Movement, *Steel Strike of 1919*, 177–78; Brody, *Steelworkers in America*, 125–26, 224–25; Spero and Harris, *Black Worker*, 256–58; Greer, "Racism and U.S. Steel," 52; Norwood, *Strikebreaking and Intimidation*, 109–10; Betten and Mohl, "Evolution of Racism," 53–54; Dickerson, *Out of the Crucible*, 51; Barrett, *William Z. Foster*, 96; Bate, "Iron and Steel," *n.* 186; McCartin, *Labor's Great War*, 46.

32. Foster, *Great Steel Strike*, 209–11.

33. Mackaman, "Foreign Element," 186–89.

34. Foster, 211; see also Mackaman, "Foreign Element," 186–89; Interchurch World Movement, *Steel Strike of 1919*, 177–78; "How Steel Gang Jobbed Negroes," *New Majority* 4, no. 1 (3 July 1920), 1–2; Nelson, *Divided We Stand*, 167; Dickerson, *Out of the Crucible*, 92; Barrett, *William Z. Foster*, 96; Bate, "Iron and Steel," *n.* 186.

35. "Our Position in the Industrial World," *Chicago Defender* (October 4, 1919), 20; see also Brody, *Steelworkers in America*, 224–25; Brody, *Labor in Crisis*, 162–63.

36. "The Negro and the Union," *Chicago Whip* (11 October 1919), 12; see also Brody, *Steelworkers in America*, 224–25; Brody, *Labor in Crisis*, 162–63.

37. "Steel Strikers Stick in Chicago District," *New Majority* 2, no. 14 (4 October 1919), 2; see also Dorothy Walton, "Scab Life Miserable in Chicago District," *New Majority* 2, no. 15 (11 October 1919), 2.

38. "Gary Looks upon Itself as Heart of Steel Fight," *Chicago Daily Tribune* (22 September 1919), 2; Mackaman, "Foreign Element," 186–89.

39. Foster, *Great Steel Strike*, 209–11.

40. "Gary Looks upon Itself as Heart of Steel Fight," *Chicago Daily Tribune* (22 September 1919), 2; "Steel Strikers Stick in Chicago District," *New Majority* 2, no. 14 (4 October 1919), 2; see also Dorothy Walton, "Scab Life Miserable in Chicago District," *New Majority* 2, no. 15 (11 October 1919), 2; Foster, *Great Steel Strike*, 205–7; Dubofsky, *Industrialism*, 130–31; Dickerson, *Out of the Crucible*, 85–100; Spero and Harris, *Black Worker*, 262; Barrett, *William Z. Foster*, 95–96; Brody, *Steelworkers*, 224–25.

41. Foster, *Great Steel Strike*, 176, 207–8; Brody, *Steelworkers in America*, 254–55; Brecher, *Strike!*, 141–42; Feldman, 32–33; National Association for the Advancement of Colored People, "Open Letter to the American Federation of Labor, the Railway Brotherhoods, and Other Groups of Organized Labor," 3 July 1924, *Monthly Labor Review* 19, no. 3 (September 1924): 176–77; Betten and Mohl, "Evolution of Racism," 52; Bate, "Iron and Steel," 131–32; Barrett, *William Z. Foster*, 95–96; Foner, *Organized Labor*,

144; see also Dorothy Walton, "Scab Life Miserable in Chicago District," *New Majority* 2, no. 14 (11 October 1919), 2.

42. Interchurch World Movement, *Steel Strike of 1919*, 177–78; Foster, *Great Steel Strike*, 208; Spero and Harris, *Black Worker*, 262; Norwood, *Strikebreaking and Intimidation*, 109.

43. "Tribune Men Find Gary Plant Stricken Giant," *Chicago Daily Tribune* (24 September 1919), 3; Brody, *Steelworkers in America*, 184–86. Black AFL organizer John Riley responded directly to these strikebreakers in a scathing editorial, claiming they were "a few of the men who have not yet discovered how useful they can be to capital in trying to destroy conditions for people who labor" and reassuring readers that "this type of 'Tom' and 'Sam' is rapidly disappearing among the colored citizens of the United States." See Riley, "Reading between the Lines of the Chicago Tribune and Herald-Examiner on the Steel Strike," *Chicago Whip* (4 October 1919), 7.

44. "Gary New Mecca," *Chicago Defender* (24 January 1920), 13; see also "Says Gary Offers Best Opportunity," *Chicago Defender* (7 February 1920), 19.

45. Brody, *Steelworkers in America*, 184–86; Brody, *Labor in Crisis*, 46; Nelson, *Divided We Stand*, 164–67; Foner, *Organized Labor*, 132.

46. Interchurch World Movement, *Steel Strike of 1919*, 177–78.

47. "Booze and Dice to Lure Scabs," *New Majority* 2, no. 15 (11 October 1919), 13.

48. Dorothy Walton, "Scab Life Miserable in Chicago District," *New Majority* 2, no. 15 (11 October 1919), 2; "Steel Trust Spy Chiefs Try to Start Race Riot," *New Majority* 2, no 15 (11 October 1919), 6; Murray, *Red Scare*, 146–48; Bate, "Iron and Steel," 186; Brecher, *Strike!*, 14.

49. "Defy Strike; Open Mill; Coke Ovens, Slab Plant Start at Gary," *Chicago Daily Tribune* (25 September 1919), 1.

50. "Steel Strikers Meet and 'Dig In' for Fight to End," *Chicago Daily Tribune* (19 October 1919), 7.

51. "Strike Leaders Seek Ban on Use of Negro Labor," *Chicago Daily Tribune* (17 October 1919), 7.

52. Foster, Great Steel Strike, 169–70.

53. "Gary Riot Calls Troops," *Chicago Tribune* (5 October 1919), 1; see also "Steel Strike Situation," Chicago Daily Tribune (5 October 1919), 1; "Riot Calls Troops; Hospitals and Jail Filled as 5,000 Battle," *Chicago Daily Tribune* (5 October 1919), 1; "The Steel War," *Chicago Daily Tribune* (6 October 1919), 2.

54. Foster, *Great Steel Strike*, 169–70; see also "Steel Strike Situation," *Chicago Daily Tribune* (5 October 1919), 1; (5 October 1919), 1; "Riot Calls

Troops; Hospitals and Jail Filled as 5,000 Battle," *Chicago Daily Tribune* (5 October 1919), 1; "The Steel War," *Chicago Daily Tribune* (6 October 1919), 2; "Halt New Riots at Gary; Troops Stop Disorder; One Man is Shot," *Chicago Daily Tribune* (6 October 1919), 1; "Steel Strike Developments," *Chicago Daily Tribune* (6 October 1919), 1; Police Prevent Riot as Steel Picket is Shot," *Chicago Daily Tribune* (4 October 1919), 2; "U.S. Troops Armed With Cannon Stop Disorders in Gary," *Chicago Daily News* (7 October 1919), 1; CFL Minutes, 19 October 1919, 18–21; "Two Shot, Many Hurt in Steel Strike Riot," *Chicago Daily News* (9 October 1919), 1; Murray, *Red Scare*, 146–48; Brody, *Steelworkers in America*, 247, 252–53; Brody, *Labor in Crisis*, 134–36.

55. Interchurch World Movement, *Steel Strike of 1919*, 241; Testimony of Donald C. Van Buren, U.S. Senate Committee on Education and Labor, *Investigation of Strike in Steel Industries*, Hearings (Washington: Government Printing Office, 1919), 909; Testimony of Oscar Anderson, U.S. Senate Committee on Education and Labor, *Investigation of Strike in Steel Industries*, Hearings (Washington: Government Printing Office, 1919), 977.

56. Brody, *Steelworkers in America*, 246–53; Brody, *Labor in Crisis*, 129–39.

57. Foster, *Great Steel Strike*, 168–69; Interchurch World Movement, *Steel Strike of 1919*, 3; "1,500 Gary Strikers Return to Work," *Chicago Daily News* (2 October 1919), 1; "Union Council at Gary Admits Situation Bad," *Chicago Daily Tribune* (29 October 1919); "Mills at Gary Claim Victory, Strike Crushed." *Chicago Daily Tribune* (25 October 1919), 2; "Union Official in Gary Admits Strike Is Lost," *Chicago Daily Tribune* (28 October 1919), 4; "Gary Steel Mill to Run Day and Night," *Chicago Daily News* (29 October 1919), 3; "Call Off Steel Strike, Union Drive Goes On," *New Majority* 3, no. 3 (17 January 1920), 14; "Confidential Bulletin of Radical Activities," Bureau of Investigation Confidential Bulletins of Radical Activities, *Surveillance of Radicals* (1 January to 17 January 1920), 3; Brody, *Steelworkers*, 250–55; Keiser, "John Fitzpatrick," 48–50.

58. Press release from John Fitzpatrick, 22 November 1920, John Fitzpatrick Papers, Box 9, Folder 67, Chicago History Museum; Murray, *Red Scare*, 152; Brody, *Steelworkers in America*, 263–78; Barrett, "Revolution and Personal Crisis."

59. Foster, *Great Steel Strike*, 209–11; Interchurch World Movement, *Steel Strike of 1919*, 177–78; "How Steel Gang Jobbed Negroes," *New Majority* 4, no. 1 (3 July 1920), 1–2; Nelson, *Divided We Stand*, 167; Dickerson, *Out of the Crucible*, 92; Barrett, *William Z. Foster*, 96; Bate, "Iron and Steel," n. 186.

60. Foster, *The Great Steel Strike*, 209–11; Interchurch World Movement, *Steel Strike of 1919*, 177–78.

61. CFL Minutes, 3 August 1919, 22–23; CFL Minutes, 18 January 1920, 19–25; Reports of Organizations, CFL Minutes, 15 February 1920, 11–12; CFL Minutes, 21 November 1920, 14; Street, "Working in the Yards," 273–79.

62. CFL Minutes, 20 March 1921, 27–28; Grossman, *Land of Hope*, 225; Brody, *Butcher Workmen*, 101–5; Herbst, *Meat-Packing Industry*, 51–52.

63. CFL Minutes, 20 March 1921, 28–29; Open letter, R. E. Parker to packing companies, 9 March 1921, reprinted in *New Majority* 5, no. 12 (19 March 1921), 3; "Stock Yards Workers Vote to Uphold Rights," *New Majority* 5, no. 13 (26 March 1921), 3.

64. "Packers' Stool Pigeon Working for Race War," *New Majority* 5, no. 12 (19 March 1921), 3–4.

65. "Packers Again Inciting Race Hatred," *New Majority* 5, no. 12 (19 March 1921), 1. Oddly, Parker abruptly changed course once the stockyards strike of 1921–1922 began. He publicly refused to supply the packers with strikebreakers, urged black workers to walk off the job, and offered a personal pledge to John Fitzpatrick that AULU workers would not return to the yards until all AMCBW workers were reinstated. It is unclear what caused this abrupt about-face (or if it was legitimate), but as the strike was quickly crushed without his aid, it certainly appears he overestimated his centrality to the conflict. See "Yards Workers Talk Strike If Pay Is Slashed," *Chicago Daily Tribune* (8 March 1921), 6; "Packing Unions' Chiefs Gather to Fight Wage Cut," *Chicago Daily Tribune* (9 March 1921), 5; "Yards Strike Put to Vote of 100,000 Men," *Chicago Daily Tribune* (11 March 1921), 1; "Stock Yards Unions Start Strike Vote Today," *Chicago Daily Tribune* (13 March 1921), 1; "Halt Pay Cut, 25,000 Yards Workers Cry," *Chicago Daily Tribune* (14 March 1921), 1; "Packing Strike On Today; Both Sides Sanguine," *Chicago Daily Tribune* (5 December 1921), 3; "Both Sides Gird for Finish Fight in Yards Strike," *Chicago Daily Tribune* (11 December 1921), 5; Letter, R. E. Parker to John Fitzpatrick, 19 December 1921, John Fitzpatrick Papers, Box 11, Folder 77, Chicago History Museum.

66. "No More Scabbing for Negro Workers," *New Majority* 3, no. 26 (26 June 1920), 3.

67. "Halt Pay Cut, 25,000 Yards Workers Cry," *Chicago Daily Tribune* (14 March 1921), 1.

68. "Need of Colored Unity Appeals to Colored Workers," *Butcher Workman* 7, no 11 (November 1921), 12.

69. "Union Leaders See Further Pay Cut by Packers," *Chicago Daily Tribune* (28 September 1921), 5; "Negro Union Workers Federated in Chicago," *New Majority* 6, no. 23 (3 December 1921), 2; Lewis, "Negro Worker," 35; Herbst, *Meat-Packing Industry*, 54–57.

70. "Negro Unions Progress," *New Majority* 6, no. 25 (17 December 1921), 6; Herbst, *Meat-Packing Industry*, 54–57.

71. Lewis, "Negro Worker," 35.

72. "Life Is Dark and Weary Over Back of the Yards," *New Majority* 2, no. 21 (22 November 1919), 11; "Labor Situation," *Chicago Whip* (25 December 1920), 6; "Are You Out Of Work? Here's a Job," *Chicago Whip* (1 January 1921), 1; see also Letter, Chicago Federation of Labor to Members of Affiliated Unions of Chicago and Vicinity, reprinted in CFL Minutes, 16 January 1921, 7–8.

73. Resolution No. 2, CFL Minutes, 6 March 1921, 11–12; "Yards Workers Talk Strike If Pay Is Slashed," *Chicago Daily Tribune* (8 March 1921), 6; "Packing Unions' Chiefs Gather to Fight Wage Cut," *Chicago Daily Tribune* (9 March 1921), 5; "Yards Strike Put to Vote of 100,000 Men," *Chicago Daily Tribune* (11 March 1921), 1; "Packers Cut Wages; Revise Work Hours," *Chicago Whip* (12 March 1921), 1; "Wage Cutting," *Chicago Daily Tribune*, 8; "Beef Trust Jabs Labor," *New Majority* 5, no. 11 (12 March 1921), 1–2; "Stock Yards Unions Start Strike Vote Today," *Chicago Daily Tribune* (13 March 1921), 1; "Small Packers Close as Strike Ballot Nears," *Chicago Daily Tribune* (16 March 1921), 1; "Packers Try to Force Strike after Breaking Word to U.S.," *New Majority* 5, no. 12 (19 March 1921), 1–2; "Stock Yards Workers Vote to Uphold Rights," *New Majority* 5, no. 13 (26 March 1921), 3; Resolution No. 47, *Proceedings of the 39th Annual Convention of the Illinois State Federation of Labor*, 1921, 356–57; Herbst, *Meat-Packing Industry*, 52–58.

74. "Nationwide Strike Effective in All Packing Centers," *Butcher Workman* 7, no. 12 (December 1921), 1; "Police Prepare for Walkout of Packing Unions," *Chicago Daily Tribune* (4 December 1921), 10; "Big Stockyard Walkout is On," *New Majority* 6, no. 24 (10 December 1921), 1; "Yards Crippled by Huge Strike," *New Majority* 6, no. 25 (17 December 1921), 1; Clark, "Labor and Capital," 200; Barrett, *Work and Community*, 260–62.

75. "Strikers Renew Riots; Snipers Fire on Police," *Chicago Daily Tribune* (8 December 1921), A1; "On the Firing Line in the Stockyards Riots," *Chicago Daily Tribune* (8 December 1921), A3.

76. "Strikers Renew Riots; Snipers Fire on Police," *Chicago Daily Tribune* (8 December 1921), A1; "On the Firing Line in the Stockyards Riots," *Chicago Daily Tribune* (8 December 1921), A3; "Union Asks Yards Parley," *Chicago Daily Tribune* (8 December 1921), 1; CFL Minutes, 18 December 1921, 12–13; Slayton, *Back of the Yards*, 94–95; Jablonsky, *Pride in the Jungle*, 49–50; Pacyga, *Polish Immigrants*, 250; Street, "Plant Loyalty," 665.

77. "Union Asks Yards Parley," *Chicago Daily Tribune* (8 December 1921), 1; "Rioting Breaks Out in Yards; 9 Reported Hurt," *Chicago Daily Tribune*

(16 December 1921), 1; "Yards Strike is Still Going Big," *New Majority* 6, no. 26 (24 December 1921), 1–2; "Packers Create Small Pox Panic," *New Majority* 7, no. 3 (21 January 1922), 1; CFL Minutes, 15 January 1922, 15–16; Spero and Harris, *Black Worker*, 279–81; Hutton, "Negro Worker," 9; Grossman, *Land of Hope*, 224–25; Pacyga, *Polish Immigrants*, 252; Clark, "Labor and Capital," 202–4; Herbst, *Meat-Packing Industry*, 65–66; Street, "Working in the Yards," 296.

78. Herbst, *Meat-Packing Industry*, 59–60; Fogel, 34–35; Lewis, "Negro Worker," 37–39; Herbst, *Meat-Packing Industry*, 64–65; Zieger, 84–85; Smith, 102–3.

79. "'Y' Campaign On with Much Enthusiasm," *Chicago Whip* (29 October 1921), 4.

80. Fogel, 34–35; Lewis, "Negro Worker," 37–39; Herbst, *Meat-Packing Industry*, 64–65; Zieger, *For Jobs and Freedom*, 84–85; Smith, "Limitations of Racial Democracy," 102–3; Strickland, *Chicago Urban League*, 72–73.

81. "The Strike at the Yards," *Chicago Defender* (17 December 1921), 15.

82. Roscoe Simmons, "The Week," *Chicago Defender* (2 September 1922), 13.

83. "A Tactical Blunder," *Chicago Defender* (28 January 1922), 16.

84. "The Strike at the Yards," *Chicago Defender* (17 December 1921), 15; see also A. L. Jackson, "The Onlooker," ibid. (8 July 1922), 20; "'Walk-Out' Makes Jobs for Those Who Are Barred," ibid. (15 July 1922), 3; Strickland, *Chicago Urban League*, 72–73.

85. "Labor Leaders Confer with Defender Editor," *Chicago Defender* (12 November 1921), 3.

86. "The Week's Worst Editorial: 'Lowering the Wage Scale,'" *Chicago Whip* (26 March 1921), 8.

87. Jablonsky, *Pride in the Jungle*, 49–50; Clark, "Labor and Capital," 204; Halpern, "Iron Fist," 164; Barrett, *Work and Community*, 263; Keiser, "John Fitzpatrick," 50; Grossman, *Land of Hope*, 209; Slayton, *Back of the Yards*, 94–95; "Stockyards Strike Off," *New Majority* 7, no. 6 (11 February 1922), 3; "Packers Give 8-Hours Day the Gate," *New Majority* 7, no. 22 (3 June 1922), 3; CFL Minutes, 15 January 1922, 3–4; see also Report of President John Walker, *Proceedings of the 40th Annual Convention of the Illinois State Federation of Labor*, 1922, 51.

88. Street, "Working in the Yards," 325; Cohen, *Making a New Deal*, 43; Barrett, *William Z. Foster*, 98–99; Hutton, "Negro Worker," 9.

89. Grossman, *Land of Hope*, 225; Street, "Plant Loyalty," 660–64; Street, "Working in the Yards," 298–307; Cohen, *Making a New Deal*, 205; Halpern, "Iron Fist," 164–68.

90. McKillen, *Chicago Labor*, 128–29, 190–91.

91. McKillen, *Chicago Labor*, 136–39, 160; "Resolution Endorsing Industrial Co-Operation or Labor's American Plan," c. June–July 1921, John Fitzpatrick Papers, Box 10, Folder 73, Chicago History Museum; "Platform of State Farmer Labor Party," *New Majority* 6, no. 17 (22 October 1921), 7; Letter, Frank J. Esper to National Committee of Farmer-Labor Part of the United States, c. November 1920, John Fitzpatrick Papers, Box 9, Folder 67, Chicago History Museum; CFL Minutes, 6 April 1919, 13–16; CFL Minutes, 20 March 1921, 12–27; CFL Minutes, 4 July 1920, 13–14; "Mr. Gompers Rages at Labor Party of U.S.," *New Majority* 3, no. 9 (28 February 1920), 2; Fine, *Labor and Farmer*, 385–90; Strouthous, *Labor and Political Action*, 48–50; Simonson, "Labor Party," 89–90; Keiser, "John Fitzpatrick," 140; Shapiro, "Hand and Brain," 71–74, 182–84; Bigham, "Chicago Federation of Labor," 140–45; Cohen, *Making a New Deal*, 49–51; McCartin, *Labor's Great War*, 197–98.

92. "Going to Labor Party Convention," *Chicago Defender* (29 May 1920), 2; see also "Honored by Labor Party," *Chicago Defender* (21 February 1920), 1; "Challenges Roscoe Simmons in Debate," *Chicago Defender* (10 April 1920), 18; Report of Labor Party, CFL Minutes, 15 February 1920, 11; Cohen, *Making a New Deal*, 50–51. For an elaboration on black Chicagoans and the city's Republican machine, see chapter 4.

93. McKillen, *Chicago Labor*, 156.

94. McKillen, *Chicago Labor*, 142–48, 201–4; Weinstein, *Decline of Socialism*, 274–89.

95. Barrett, "Racial and Ethnic Fragmentation," 296.

96. Grossman, *Land of Hope*, 225–27; see also Dubofsky, "Abortive Reform," 214–15; Murray, *Red Scare*, 106–17; Keiser, "John Fitzpatrick," v–vi; Cohen, *Making a New Deal*, 12–13.

CONCLUSION: THE PAST, PRESENT, AND FUTURE OF INTERRACIAL UNIONISM

1. Barrett, *Work and Community*, 242–48; Street, "Swift Difference," 20–23; Halpern, "Iron Fist," 171–74; Cohen, *Making a New Deal*, 160–61.

2. Cohen, *Making a New Deal*, 160–61.

3. Halpern, *Killing Floor*, 77–80; Cohen, *Making a New Deal*, 165–67.

4. Halpern, *Killing Floor*, 85–88; Cohen, *Making a New Deal*, 205.

5. Cohen, *Making a New Deal*, 159–211.

6. Halpern, *Killing Floor*, 78.

7. Brody, *Butcher Workmen*, 153; Halpern, *Killing Floor*, 112–14.

8. Halpern, *Killing Floor*, 99–101, 105–12.

9. Halpern, *Killing Floor*, 155–58.

10. Brody, *Butcher Workmen*, 177.

11. Cohen, *Making a New Deal*, 333; see also Halpern, *Killing Floor*, 97.

12. Halpern, *Killing Floor*, 158–60.

13. Sitkoff, *A New Deal for Blacks*, 187.

14. Brody, *Butcher Workmen*, 168, 176–77.

15. Sitkoff, *New Deal for Blacks*, 183–84.

16. Halpern, *Killing Floor*, 169.

17. Faue, *Rethinking*, 5, 202–9.

BIBLIOGRAPHY

ARCHIVAL SOURCES

Chicago History Museum, Chicago, IL
   Chicago Federation of Labor Minutes
   John Fitzpatrick Papers
   Mary McDowell Settlement Records
   Proceedings, Hotel and Restaurant Employes' International Alliance
     and Bartenders' International League of America
   Samuel P. Alschuler Papers
National Archives, College Park, MD
   Records of the Federal Mediation and Conciliation Service, Record
     Group 280: Dispute Case Files

NEWSPAPERS AND PERIODICALS

American Federationist
Broad Ax
Butcher Workman
Chicago Daily News
Chicago Daily Tribune
Chicago Defender
Chicago Eagle
Chicago Socialist
Chicago Whip
Mixer and Server
Monthly Labor Review
New Majority
New York American
New York Times
Socialist
Survey
World's Work

PUBLISHED PRIMARY SOURCES

Bigham, Truman Cicero. "The Chicago Federation of Labor." MA thesis, University of Chicago, 1925.

Chicago Commission on Race Relations. *The Negro in Chicago: A Study of Race Relations and a Race Riot.* Chicago: University of Chicago Press, 1922.

Chicago Urban League. *Report of the Chicago League on Urban Conditions among Negroes.* Chicago: Chicago Urban League, 1917, 1918.

Clark, Edna Louise. "History of the Controversy between Labor and Capital in the Slaughtering and Meat Packing Industries of Chicago." MA thesis, University of Chicago, 1922.

Commission on Industrial Relations. *Final Report of the U.S. Commission on Industrial Relations.* Washington, D.C.: Government Printing Office, 1916.

Commons, John R. *Trade Unionism and Labor Problems.* Boston: Ginn and Company, 1905.

Department of Labor. Division of Negro Economics. *The Negro at Work during the World War and during Reconstruction.* Washington, D.C.: Government Printing Office, 1921.

Federal Trade Commission. *Report on the Meat-Packing Industry.* Parts 1, 3, 5. Washington, D.C.: Government Printing Office, 1919.

Foster, William Z. *The Great Steel Strike and Its Lessons.* New York: B. W. Huebsch, 1920.

George, Harrison. *Chicago Race Riots.* Chicago: The Great Western Publishing Company, 1919.

Haywood, Harry. *A Black Communist in the Freedom Struggle: The Life of Harry Haywood.* Edited by Gwendolyn Midlo Hall. Minneapolis: University of Minnesota Press, 2011.

Hoffman, Peter M. *The Race Riots: Biennial Report, 1918–1919, and Official Record of Inquests on the Victims of the Race Riots of July and August, 1919.* Ca. 1919–20.

Illinois State Council of Defense Committee on Labor. "Report to the Illinois State Council of Defense on the Race Riots at East St. Louis." 1917.

Interchurch World Movement of America. *Report on the Steel Strike of 1919.* New York: Harcourt, Brace, and Howe, 1920.

Merriam, Charles Edward. *Chicago: A More Intimate View of American Politics.* New York: Macmillan, 1929.

Olds, Marshall. *Analysis of the Interchurch World Movement Report on the Steel Strike.* New York: B. W. Huebsch, 1920.

Proceedings of the Annual Convention of the Illinois Federation of Labor, 1914–1922.

Proceedings of the Convention of the American Federation of Labor, 1894–1925.

Sandburg, Carl. *The Chicago Race Riots: July, 1919.* New York: Harcourt, Brace, and Howe, 1919.

Scott, Emmet J. "Letters of Negro Migrants of 1916–1918." *Journal of Negro History* 4, no. 3 (July 1919): 290–340.

Thompson, Carl William. "Labor in the Packing Industry." *Journal of Political Economy* 15 (February 1907): 88–108.

U.S. Military Intelligence Reports: Surveillance of Radicals in the United States. 1917–1921. Edited by Randolph Boehm. Microfilm.

Walsh, Frank P. *Over the Top at the Yards: Arguments of Frank P. Walsh in the Stockyards Arbitration Hearing and the Award of U.S. Administrator Samuel P. Alschuler.* Chicago: Chicago Labor News Press, 1907.

Watkins, Gordon S. *Labor Problems and Labor Administration in the United States during the World War.* Urbana: University of Illinois Press, 1919.

BOOKS

Adair, Charles H., and Rodney F. Allen, eds. *Violence and Riots in Urban America.* Worthington, OH: Charles A. Jones Publishing Company, 1969.

Arnesen, Eric. *Black Protest and the Great Migration: A Brief History with Documents.* Boston: Bedford/St. Martin's, 2003.

———. *Brotherhoods of Color: Black Railroad Workers and the Struggle for Equality.* Cambridge: Harvard University Press, 2001.

Baker, Lee D. *From Savage to Negro: Anthropology and the Construction of Race, 1896–1954.* Berkeley: University of California Press, 1998.

Baldwin, Davarian L. *Chicago's New Negroes: Modernity, the Great Migration, and Black Urban Life.* Chapel Hill: University of North Carolina Press, 2007.

Barnes, Harper. *Never Been a Time: The 1917 Race Riot That Sparked the Civil Rights Movement.* New York: Walker and Company, 2008.

Barrett, James R. *William Z. Foster and the Tragedy of American Radicalism.* Urbana: University of Illinois, 1999.

———. *Work and Community in the Jungle: Chicago's Packinghouse Workers, 1894–1922.* Urbana: University of Illinois Press, 1987.

Bart, Phil. *Working-Class Unity: The Role of Communists in the Chicago Federation of Labor, 1919–1923.* New York: New Outlook Publishers, 1975.

Bates, Beth Tompkins. *Pullman Porters and the Rise of Protest Politics in Black America, 1925–1945.* Chapel Hill: University of North Carolina Press, 2001.

Blocker, Jack S. *A Little More Freedom: African Americans Enter the Urban Midwest, 1860–1930*. Columbus: Ohio State University Press, 2008.

Bracey, John H., August Meier, and Elliott Rudwick, eds. *Black Workers and Organized Labor*. Belmont: Wadsworth Publishing, 1971.

Brecher, Jeremy. *Strike!* Cambridge: South End Press Classics, 1997.

Brody, David. *The Butcher Workmen: A Study of Unionization*. Cambridge: Harvard University Press, 1964.

———. *Labor in Crisis: The Steel Strike of 1919*. Philadelphia: J. P. Lippincott Company, 1965.

———. *Steelworkers in America: The Nonunion Era*. Urbana: University of Illinois Press, 1960.

Cohen, Andrew Wender. *The Racketeer's Progress: Chicago and the Struggle for the Modern American Economy, 1900–1940*. New York: Cambridge University Press, 2004.

Cohen, Lizabeth. *Making a New Deal: Industrial Workers in Chicago, 1919–1939*. New York: Oxford University Press, 1990.

Conner, Valerie Jean. *The National War Labor Board: Stability, Social Justice, and the Voluntary State in World War I*. Chapel Hill: University of North Carolina Press, 1983.

Dickerson, Dennis C. *Out of the Crucible: Black Steelworkers in Western Pennsylvania, 1875–1950*. Albany: State University of New York Press, 1986.

Dubofsky, Melvyn. "Abortive Reform: The Wilson Administration and Organized Labor, 1913–1920." In *Work, Community, and Power: The Experience of Labor in Europe and America, 1900–1925*, edited by James E. Cronin and Carmen Sirianni, 197–220. Philadelphia: Temple University Press, 1983.

———. *Industrialism and the American Worker, 1865–1920*. 3rd ed. Wheeling: Harlan Davidson, 1996.

Drake, St. Clair, and Horace Cayton. *Black Metropolis*. Chicago: University of Chicago Press, 1945.

Faue, Elizabeth. *Rethinking the American Labor Movement*. New York: Routledge, 2017.

Feldman, Herman. *Racial Factors in American Industry*. New York: Harper, 1931.

Fine, Nathan. *Labor and Farmer Parties in the United States, 1828–1928*. New York: Rand School of Social Science, 1928.

Fink, Leon. *In Search of the Working Class: Essays in American Labor History and Political Culture*. Urbana: University of Illinois Press, 1994.

Fitch, Robert. *Solidarity for Sale: How Corruption Destroyed the Labor Movement and Undermined America's Promise*. New York: Public Affairs, 2006.

Fogel, Walter A. *The Negro in the Meat Industry.* Philadelphia: University of Pennsylvania Press, 1970.

Foner, Philip S. *Organized Labor and the Black Worker, 1919–1973.* New York: Praeger, 1974.

Gosnell, Harold F. *Negro Politicians: The Rise of Negro Politics in Chicago.* Chicago: University of Chicago Press, 1935.

Grant, Colin. *Negro with a Hat: The Rise and Fall of Marcus Garvey.* New York: Oxford University Press, 2008.

Griffler, Keith P. *What Price Alliance? Black Radicals Confront White Labor, 1918–1938.* New York: Garland, 1995.

Grimshaw, Allen D. "Three Cases of Racial Violence in the United States." In *A Social History of Racial Violence*, edited by Allen D. Grimshaw, 105–15. New Brunswick: Transaction Publishers, 2009.

Grossman, James R. *Land of Hope: Chicago, Black Southerners, and the Great Migration.* Chicago: University of Chicago Press, 1989.

Guglielmo, Thomas. *White on Arrival: Italians, Race, Color, and Power in Chicago, 1890–1945.* New York: Oxford University Press, 2004.

Gutman, Herbert G. *Work, Culture, and Society in Industrializing America: Essays in American Working-Class and Social History.* New York: Alfred A. Knopf, 1976.

Halpern, Rick. *Down on the Killing Floor: Black and White Workers in Chicago's Packinghouses, 1904–54.* Urbana: University of Illinois Press, 1997.

Halpern, Rick, and Roger Horowitz. *Meatpackers: An Oral History of Black Packinghouse Workers and Their Struggle for Racial and Economic Equality.* New York: Twayne Publishers, 1996.

Henri, Florette. *Black Migration: Movement North, 1900–1920.* Garden City: Anchor Press, 1975.

Herbst, Alma. *The Negro in the Slaughtering and Meat-Packing Industry in Chicago.* Boston: Houghton Mifflin, 1932.

Hinshaw, John. *Steel and Steelworkers: Race and Class Struggles in Twentieth-Century Pittsburgh.* Albany: State University of New York Press, 2002.

Horowitz, Roger. *"Negro and White, Unite and Fight!": A Social History of Industrial Unionism in Meatpacking, 1930–90.* Urbana: University of Illinois Press, 1997.

Jablonsky, Thomas J. *Pride in the Jungle: Community and Everyday Life in Back of the Yards Chicago.* Baltimore: Johns Hopkins University Press, 1993.

Jacobson, Matthew Frye. *Whiteness of a Different Color: European Immigrants and the Alchemy of Race.* Cambridge: Harvard University Press, 1999.

Josephson, Matthew. *Union House, Union Bar: The History of the Hotel and Restaurant Employees and Bartenders International Union, AFL-CIO.* New York: Random House, 1956.

Katzman, David M., and William M. Tuttle Jr. *Plain Folk: The Life Stories of Undistinguished Americans.* Urbana: University of Illinois Press, 1982.

Keefe, Rose. *Guns and Roses: The Untold Story of Dean O'Banion, Chicago's Big Shot before Al Capone.* Nashville: Cumberland House Publishing, 2003.

Laurie, Bruce. *Artisans into Workers: Labor in Nineteenth Century America.* Urbana: University of Illinois Press, 1997.

Letwin, Daniel. *The Challenge of Interracial Unionism: Alabama Coal Miners, 1878–1921.* Chapel Hill: University of North Carolina Press, 1998.

Lumpkins, Clarence L. *American Pogrom: The East St. Louis Race Riot and Black Politics.* Athens: Ohio University Press, 2008.

McCartin, Joseph. *Labor's Great War: The Struggle for Industrial Democracy and the Origins of Modern American Labor Relations, 1912–1921.* Chapel Hill: University of North Carolina Press, 1997.

McKillen, Elizabeth. *Chicago Labor and the Quest for a Democratic Diplomacy, 1914–1924.* Ithaca: Cornell University Press, 1995.

McLaughlin, Malcolm. *Power, Community, and Racial Killing in East St. Louis.* New York: Palgrave Macmillan, 2005.

Michaeli, Ethan. *The Defender: How the Legendary Black Newspaper Changed America.* New York: Houghton Mifflin Harcourt, 2016.

Montgomery, David. *The Fall of the House of Labor: The Workplace, the State, and American Labor Activism, 1865–1925.* New York: Cambridge University Press, 1989.

Muhammad, Khalil Gibran. *The Condemnation of Blackness: Race, Crime, and the Making of Modern Urban America.* Cambridge: Harvard University Press, 2010.

Murray, Robert K. *Red Scare: A Study in National Hysteria, 1919–1920.* Minneapolis: University of Minnesota Press, 1955.

Needleman, Ruth. *Black Freedom Fighters in Steel: The Struggle for Democratic Unionism.* Ithaca, NY: Cornell-ILR Press, 2003.

Nelson, Bruce. *Divided We Stand: American Workers and the Struggle for Black Equality.* Princeton: Princeton University Press, 2001.

Northrup, Herbert R. *Organized Labor and the Negro.* New York: Harper, 1944.

Norwood, Stephen H. *Strikebreaking and Intimidation: Mercenaries and Masculinity in Twentieth Century America.* Chapel Hill: University of North Carolina Press, 2002.

Pacyga, Dominic. *Polish Immigrants and Industrial Chicago: Workers on the South Side, 1880–1922.* Chicago: University of Chicago Press, 2003.

Philpott, Thomas Lee. *The Slum and the Ghetto: Neighborhood Deterioration and Middle-Class Reform, Chicago 1880–1930.* New York: Oxford University Press, 1978.

Reed, Christopher Robert. *The Rise of Chicago's Black Metropolis, 1920–1929.* Urbana: University of Illinois Press, 2011.

Roediger, David R. *The Wages of Whiteness: Race and the Making of the American Working Class.* London: Verso, 1991.

———. *Working toward Whiteness: How America's Immigrants Became White.* New York: Basic Books, 2005.

Rudwick, Elliott. *Race Riot at East St. Louis, July 2, 1917.* Cleveland: Meridian Books, 1969.

Schneider, Mark Robert. *"We Return Fighting": The Civil Rights Movement in the Jazz Age.* Boston: Northeastern University Press, 2002.

Schneirov, Richard. *Labor and Urban Politics: Class Conflict and the Origins of Modern Liberalism in Chicago, 1864–97.* Urbana: University of Illinois Press, 1998.

Scott, Estelle Hill. *Occupational Changes among Negroes in Chicago.* Chicago: Works Progress Administration, 1939.

Scott, Michael. *Contempt and Pity: Social Policy and the Image of the Damaged Black Psyche, 1880–1996.* Chapel Hill: University of North Carolina Press, 1997.

Senechal, Roberta Howe. *The Sociogenesis of a Race Riot: Springfield, Illinois, in 1908.* Urbana: University of Illinois Press, 1990.

Sitkoff, Harvard. *A New Deal for Blacks.* New York: Oxford University Press, 1978.

Slayton, Robert A. *Back of the Yards: The Making of a Local Democracy.* Chicago: University of Chicago Press, 1986.

Solomon, Mark. *The Cry Was Unity: Communists and African-Americans, 1917–1936.* Jackson: University Press of Mississippi, 1998.

Spero, Sterling D., and Abram L. Harris. *The Black Worker: A Study of the Negro and the Labor Movement.* New York: Columbia University Press, 1931.

Strickland, Arvarh E. *History of the Chicago Urban League.* Urbana: University of Illinois Press, 1966.

Strouthous, Andrew. *U.S. Labor and Political Action, 1918–1924: A Comparison of Independent Political Action in New York, Chicago, Seattle.* New York: St. Martin's Press, 2000.

Taft, Philip. *The A. F. of L. in the Time of Gompers.* New York: Octagon Books, 1970.

Taillon, Paul Michel. *Good, Reliable, White Men: Railroad Brotherhoods, 1877–1917.* Urbana: University of Illinois Press, 2009.

Tuttle Jr., William M. *Race Riot: Chicago in the Red Summer of 1919.* Urbana: University of Illinois Press, 1970.

Voss, Kim. *The Making of American Exceptionalism: The Knights of Labor and Class Formation in the Nineteenth Century.* Ithaca: Cornell University Press, 1993.

Weinstein, James. *The Decline of Socialism in America, 1912–1925.* New York: Monthly Review Press, 1967.

Williams, Lee E., and Lee E. Williams II. *Anatomy of Four Race Riots: Racial Conflict in Knoxville, Elaine (Arkansas), Tulsa and Chicago, 1919–1921.* Oxford: University Press of Mississippi, 1972.

Witwer, David. *Corruption and Reform in the Teamsters Union.* Urbana: University of Illinois Press, 2003.

Zieger, Robert H. *American Workers, American Unions.* 2nd ed. Baltimore: Johns Hopkins University Press, 1994.

———. *For Jobs and Freedom: Race and Labor in America Since 1865.* Lexington: University Press of Kentucky, 2007.

ARTICLES

Arnesen, Eric. "Like Banquo's Ghost, It Will Not Down": The Race Question and the American Railroad Brotherhoods, 1880–1920." *American Historical Review* 99, no. 5 (December 1994): 1601–33.

———. "Specter of the Black Strikebreaker: Race, Employment, and Labor Activism in the Industrial Era." *Labor History* 44, no. 3 (2003): 319–35.

Barrett, James R. "Racial and Ethnic Fragmentation: Toward a Reinterpretation of a Local Labor Movement." In *African American Urban Experience: Perspectives from the Colonial Period to the Present,* edited by Joe W. Trotter, Earl Lewis, and Tera W. Hunter. New York: Palgrave Macmillan, 2004: 287–309.

———. "Revolution and Personal Crisis: William Z. Foster, Personal Narrative, and the Subjective in the History of American Communism." *Labor History* 43, no. 4 (November 2002): 465–82.

Barrett, James R., and David Roediger. "Inbetween Peoples: Race, Nationality and the 'New Immigrant' Working Class." *Journal of American Ethnic History* 16, no. 3 (Spring 1997): 3–44.

Betten, Neil, and Raymond Mohl. "The Evolution of Racism in an Industrial City, 1906–1940: A Case Study of Gary, Indiana." *Journal of Negro History* 59, no. 1 (January 1974): 51–64.

Brody, David. "The Old Labor History and the New: In Search of an American Working Class." *Labor History* 20, no. 1 (1979): 111–26.

———. "Reconciling the Old Labor History and the New," *Pacific Historical Review* 62, no. 1 (February 1993): 1–18.

Greer, Edward. "Racism and U.S. Steel, 1906–1974." *Radical America* 10 (September–October 1976): 45–68.

Grossman, James R. "The White Man's Union: The Great Migration and the Resonance of Race and Class in Chicago, 1916–1922." In *The Great Migration in Historical Perspective: New Dimensions of Race, Class, and Gender*, edited by Joe William Trotter. Bloomington: Indiana University Press, 1991.

Halpern, Rick. "The Iron Fist and the Velvet Glove: Welfare Capitalism in Chicago's Packinghouses, 1921–1933." *Journal of American Studies* 26, no. 2 (August 1992): 159–83.

Hill, Herbert. "The Problem of Race in American Labor History." *Reviews in American History* 24, no. 2 (June 1996): 189–208.

Kazin, Michael. "The Limits of Union-Centered History: Responses to Howard Kimeldorf." *Labor History* 32, no. 1 (1991), 104–27.

Kimeldorf, Howard. "Bringing Unions Back In (Or Why We Need a New Old Labor History)." *Labor History* 32, no. 1 (1991), 91–103.

Mandel, Bernard. "Samuel Gompers and Negro Workers, 1866–1914." *Journal of Negro History* 40, no. 1 (January 1955): 34–60.

McCartin, Joseph A. "Industrial Unionism as Liberator or Leash? The Limits of 'Rank and Filism' in American Labor Historiography." *Journal of Social History* 31, no. 3 (Spring 1998): 701–10.

McDuffie, E. M. "Chicago, Garveyism, and the History of the Diasporic Midwest." *African and Black Diaspora* 8, no. 2 (2015): 129–45.

Montgomery, David. "Strikes in Nineteenth Century America." *Social Science History* 4, no. 1 (Winter 1980): 81–104.

Painter, Nell Irvin. "The New Labor History and the Historical Moment." *International Journal of Politics, Culture, and Society* 2 (Spring 1989): 367–70.

Reed, Christopher R. "Garveyism," *Electronic Encyclopedia of Chicago* (Chicago Historical Society, 2005). http://www.encyclopedia.chicagohistory.org/pages/502.html.

Roediger, David R. "Race and the Working-Class Past in the United States: Multiple Identities and the Future of Labor History." *International Review of Social History* 38 (1993, Supplement 1): 127–43.

Stone, Katherine. "The Origins of Job Structure in the Steel Industries." *Review of Radical Political Economics* 6, no. 2 (July 1974): 113–73.

Street, Paul Louis. "The Logic and Limits of 'Plant Loyalty': Black Workers, White Labor, and Corporate Racial Paternalism in Chicago's Stockyards, 1916–1940." *Journal of Social History* 29, no. 3 (Spring 1996): 659–81.

———. "The Swift Difference: Workers, Managers, Militants, and Welfare Capitalism in Chicago's Stockyards, 1917–1942." In *Unionizing the Jungles: Labor and Community in the Twentieth Century Meatpacking Industry,* edited by Shelton Stromquist and Marvin Bergman. Iowa City: University of Iowa Press, 1997.

Tuttle, William M. "Views of a Negro during the 'Red Summer' of 1919." *Journal of Negro History* 51, no. 3 (July 1966): 209–18.

Whatley, Warren C. "African-American Strikebreaking from the Civil War to the New Deal." *Social Science History* 17, no. 14 (Winter 1993): 525–58.

Witwer, David. "Race Relations in the Early Teamsters Union." *Labor History* 43, no. 4 (November 2002): 505–32.

DISSERTATIONS AND THESES

Bate, Phyllis. "The Development of the Iron and Steel Industry of the Chicago Area, 1900–1920." PhD diss., University of Chicago, 1948.

Coit, Jonathan S. "The Discourse of Racial Violence: Chicago, 1914–1923." PhD diss., University of Illinois, 2004.

Dolnick, David. "The Role of Labor in Chicago Politics since 1919." MA thesis, University of Chicago, 1939.

Horowitz, Roger. "The Failure of Independent Political Action: The Cook County Labor Party, 1919–1920." BA essay, 1982. Chicago History Museum.

Hutton, Oscar D. "The Negro Worker and the Labor Unions in Chicago." MA thesis, University of Chicago, 1939.

Keiser, John Howard. "John Fitzpatrick and Progressive Unionism, 1915–1925." PhD diss., Northwestern University, 1965.

Lewis, Catherine Elizabeth. "Trade Union Policies in Regard to the Negro Worker in the Slaughtering and Meatpacking Industry of Chicago." MA thesis, University of Chicago, 1945.

Mackaman, Thomas. "The Foreign Element: New Immigrants and American Industry." PhD diss., University of Illinois, 1998.

Meyers, Howard Barton. "The Policing of Labor Disputes in Chicago: A Case Study." PhD diss., University of Chicago, 1929.

Scipes, Steven R. "Trade Union Development and Racial Oppression in Chicago's Steel and Meatpacking Industries, 1933–1955." PhD diss., University of Illinois at Chicago, 1998.

Sell, Harry Bird. "The A.F. of L. and the Labor Party Movement of 1918–1920." PhD diss., University of Chicago, 1922.

Shapiro, Stanley. "Hand and Brain: The Farmer-Labor Party of 1920." PhD diss., University of California-Berkeley, 1967.

Simonson, David Ficke. "The Labor Party of Cook County, Illinois, 1918–1919." MA thesis, University of Chicago, 1959.

Smith, Preston Howard. "The Limitations of Racial Democracy: The Politics of the Chicago Urban League, 1916–1940." PhD diss., University of Massachusetts, 1990.

Street, Paul Louis. "Working in the Yards: A History of Class Relations in Chicago's Meatpacking Industry, 1886–1960." PhD diss., State University of New York–Binghamton, 1993.

Young, Paul Clinton. "Race, Class, and Radicalism in Chicago, 1914–1936." PhD diss., University of Iowa, 2001.

INDEX

Page numbers in italics indicate illustrations.

CFL's role, 120, 122, 123–24, *125*;
employers' uses of, 126, 217n64;
impact summarized, 112, 124,
126, 129–30, 138–39, 141–42; map
of, *121*; and stockyard reopening,
126–32; violence patterns, 118–20,
121, 122–23
race riots (1908–17), 88–89, 118,
213n33
racial conflicts. *See specific topics,*
e.g., nonunion labor; scab race
accusations; workplace attitudes,
conflict factors
Ragen's Colts, 122, 215n50
Raglan, E., 23
recruitment tactics, employers',
97–98, 116, 152–53, 207n50
red scare tactics, 151, 155
Reed, G. W., 57
Republican Party, 109–10, 166
Ricketts, Ben, 12, 15
Riley, John, 68, 96, 109, 143, 225n43
Robinson, James, 33–34

Sandburg, Carl, 131
scab race accusations: employers'
use of, 98; expectations of interracial organizing, 90–91; from
living conditions, 91–92; during
steel industry strike, 149–50, 154;
during stockyards strikes, 20, 22,
25, 89, 161, 164; during teamsters
strike, 26–27, 35, 89; white workers'
statements, 100, 107
school strike, 30
Sears Roebuck, 55
segregated neighborhoods, 113–14
sharecropping, 42–43
Shea, Cornelius P., 26, 27, 35
Simmons, Roscoe, 163
simpleton/capitalist dupe idea, 89–90,
116, 124, 137, 225n43
Sims's testimony, to commission,
83–85

SLC. *See* Stockyards Labor Council
(SLC)
Slowacki Hall, significance, 76
smallpox, 18–19
Spero, Sterling, 95
Springfield riot (1917), 118
Stauber, George, 213n38, 215n50
steel industry: immigrant worker
dispute, 41; organizing campaign,
146–48; strikes, 141, 148–56; work-
ing conditions, 145–46
Steelworkers Organizing Committee
(SWOC), 171
Steward, Eugene, 152
Stockyards Community Clearing
House, 95–96
Stockyards Labor Council (SLC):
CIO compared, 170–72; establishment of, 53; internecine conflict
with AMCBW, 140–45; membership patterns, 71–72, 197n75; and
1919 race riot, 120, 215n48. *See also*
specific topics, e.g., Alschuler, Samuel
P.; Chicago Federation of Labor;
Fitzpatrick, John; Labor Party;
wildcat strikes
stockyards strike (1904), 10–11,
17–25, 36–37, 181n40, 183n54,
184n63
stockyards strike (1921–22), 141,
156–64, 227n65
Stowers, T. A., 26
Street, Paul, 76
strikebreakers: from community
organizations, 96, 97, 162–63; and
East St. Louis riot, 88–89; meatpacking industry, 18–25, 141, 160–62,
183n54, 184n63; opportunity arguments, 102–3, 110, 153–54, 162–64;
racial specter of, 88–89; steel
industry, 151–56, 225n43; teamsters,
25–36. *See also* nonunion labor
student strike, 30
Sweitzer, Robert, 68

David Bates is an assistant professor of history at Concordia University Chicago. His writing has appeared in the *Illinois Reading Council Journal*, the *Wisconsin State Reading Association Journal*, the *Journal of Interdisciplinary History*, and the *Encyclopedia of American Reform Movements*.

Jealousy

"Why would you be jealous when you have free will to strive for anything you want?"

— Brian Michael Good

Judgement

"Avoid judgment of ethnic, racial, sexual orientation, gender identity, and religious differences in society."

— Brian Michael Good

"No one is all good nor is one person all bad."

— Brian Michael Good

"The color of my skin at birth was white. It is several layers deep. If I shine an ultraviolet lamp on my skin which emits pure UV (no visible light), it shows that my skin is actually multicolored. I chose to wear my skin multicolored."

— Brian Michael Good

"At some point in your life, you may wonder if your soul is hanging by a thread. This thread is the conduit in which your belief system flows defining your human spirit and binding to the fabric of your soul. Religious, Philosophical, and Ideological fibers are spun into a single strand giving strength to your beliefs. It is this thread's strength that allows you to be broad-minded and even-handed. Be aware that you may be surrendering your soul in your judgment or treatment of others."

— Brian Michael Good

"We may be judged on what we could have done when you had a moral obligation to help someone in need. You have free will. It is your choice."

— Brian Michael Good

"Do not judge your lot in life and do not over judge yourself. Do not feel sorry for yourself. Stop whining. Do not self-pity. Life can always be worse than it is. Nothing is the end of the world. There is always a way to fix it."

— Brian Michael Good

"Millions of years ago the entire human species might have been hermaphrodites, having both testicular and ovarian tissue which is present in one percent of all mammals including humans. If humans are still born with both reproductive tissues then this might explain that our species might have been biologically gay or transgender from the very beginning.

Using knowledge, reason, and logic may help to understand what we do not understand. We may have always been gay or transgender as a species but only in the past 6,000 years, religious dogma has taught us it was taboo to be homosexual. Be careful who you judge, only We-she-me-he – God – The Creator – Universe knows the truth."

— Brian Michael Good

Kindness

"Have kindness, compassion, and empathy towards others and the natural environment."

— Brian Michael Good

"Help someone in need with kindness including yourself."

— Brian Michael Good

Knowledge

"Humans have become more logical, facts build our knowledge and belief system. A logical person gathers facts and does not rely on faith alone."

— Brian Michael Good

"We are gravitating towards building a knowledge belief system that is constructed mainly on materials based on facts.

— Brian Michael Good

"Survival often requires not only knowledge and wisdom but the willingness to adapt to new challenges."

— Brian Michael Good

"There is enough wealth in our world to teach and share knowledge so each town or village can provide their own food, shelter, clothing and other commodities and services that are essential for survival."

— Brian Michael Good

"If you decide to walk the path of life in complete control of your free will you must resist mind control by adopting a knowledge or faith belief system that is aided with logic and facts."

— Brian Michael Good

"Think about a car not having ample petro/gas to start the engine, as the body not getting the proper nutrition, preventing the driver from arriving at their desired destination, an engaged mind likewise cannot develop the knowledge base of life skills that will be needed to achieve upward mobility."

— Brian Michael Good

"You learn more from your mistakes and failures than from any degree of success. Success can only be grasped for a moment before it becomes a distant oasis not to be found again unless you thirst for the knowledge found in the well fed by your mistakes and failures."

— Brian Michael Good

Loyalty

"Trust, faithfulness, and loyalty should define your relationships."

— Brian Michael Good

"Integrity, Honor, Trust, Loyalty, Respect, Reputation. These values should be nurtured as a mother cares for an infant. Without the proper attention, all of these values can be lost from one careless decision."

— Brian Michael Good

Love

"I love you with all the love I have gathered in my lifetime."

— Brian Michael Good

"I have no doubt there is a Creator and that the Creator loves and cares about all of us. When we were given the gift of free will, our greatest gift after life itself, we were expected to solve our own problems. When you look to the Creator for guidance, do it knowing that it is your responsibility to find a solution."

— Brian Michael Good

"If you want to control your lover then do not even think of controlling them. When you do not try to control your partner in a relationship, then you are in control and your partner will always be at your side as your best friend. You will receive far more love and respect than a person who wants control in a relationship."

— Brian Michael Good

"Find a man/woman/partner that will appreciate everything about you and won't try to change you or control your free will."

— Brian Michael Good

"I know the tide that has not come to shore in over several years will greet me like a tidal wave of open embrace."

— Brian Michael Good

"You should be wise who you love and invest your emotions. If you love your soulmate you will seldom get hurt, if at all."

— Brian Michael Good

Passion

"Every day starts fresh when you have a good night sleep, a passion to pursue and a positive attitude. A choice."

— Brian Michael Good

"Every endeavor in life is not about the odds of success but about your belief, your passion, and your indomitable will."

— Brian Michael Good

"You need to take the necessary steps to put your life on the right course to develop your passion."

— Brian Michael Good

"You are in the center of your happiness when you pursue your passion."

— Brian Michael Good

"Meeting your destiny doesn't happen without a plan, a plan doesn't happen without a purpose, a purpose doesn't happen without finding your passion, a passion isn't discovered without the pursuit of activities that you enjoy."

— Brian Michael Good

BRIAN MICHAEL GOOD

"Find a purpose for your life and you will do extraordinary things.

You are in center of your happiness when you pursue your passion.

When you pursue your passion, you are the master of your environment.

"When you are the master of your environment you often meet your destiny."

— Brian Michael Good

117

Peace

"I am a feminist in the exact definition of the word, I believe in social, political, and all rights to be equal to both women and men. I believe in the equalism movement for all humans, absence of required roles, labels, or behaviors that gender may require. That being said, we need more emphasis that men and women are equal and it should not be a battle of the sexes. Equalism is not a gender issue concerning men or women; it is about treating every human with respect and equality.

The only path to world peace is through women's equality to men. The only way women will be considered equal to men is when the world realizes that women are better than men. Only then will mankind accept that women are their equal. When women are equal to men, women will run the world like they run their families. Do you even think women would allow what's happening in the Middle East, the Ukraine or allow nuclear warheads to be in existence on our planet? Women would not allow the threat of one person having access to the button that would cause Game Over/Armageddon and kill their children or grandchildren.

There is no such thing as limited nuclear war. If one nuclear bomb is successful, then all of them will be eventually launched. Free will comes with a price.... God will not save you. The human race (women) must save themselves."

"What are you waiting for? The clock's ticking...

Oh... It's a nuclear clock."

— Brian Michael Good

Present

"Acceptance – Let go of the past to get ahead in the present."

— Brian Michael Good

"You can effect change in the present. In the Now!"

— Brian Michael Good

"Live life in the present, in the now and it will happen."

— Brian Michael Good

"All we can really do or control is living in the moment."

— Brian Michael Good

"Dwelling on negatives affects our rhythm and holds us back from the present."

— Brian Michael Good

"Live in the present, where it is the best place to live."

— Brian Michael Good

"Tomorrow becomes Today when Today becomes Tomorrow."

— Brian Michael Good

"You can change the future only by implementing change in the present."

— Brian Michael Good

"If you can feel pain living in the past, forgiving others will help you move into the present."

— Brian Michael Good

"The wisdom in our future is discovered in the present. You cannot go forward unless you let go of the past."

— Brian Michael Good

"Yes, you can replace old memories with new ones and start over in the present. I find that the best place to live is in the now."

— Brian Michael Good

"Acceptance helps you to skip forward and live in the present."

— Brian Michael Good

"What you choose today, you live with tomorrow."

— Brian Michael Good

"Living in the present and being a survivor will be always how I stay in the eye of my hurricane; safe from the storm around me."

— Brian Michael Good

"It has been said that in a lifetime we live many lives. If you don't like your life begin your next life within your present life by implementing change in the present."

— Brian Michael Good

"The present, this moment is all we truly own and are guaranteed. Why not enjoy it."

— Brian Michael Good

Problems

"Do not dwell on problems in which you cannot effect any change."

— Brian Michael Good

"If you have a problem then do everything you can to correct or rectify this problem. You can't change the negatives of the past. Dwelling on negatives affects our rhythm and holds us back in the present. The future may be viewed and anticipated but it is not laid out precisely like a blueprint. You can effect change in the present. We have free will to choose to steer off course or amend it. We have choices."

— Brian Michael Good

"Mind over matter. If it matters; you will put your mind to it. The mind is capable of solving any problem that matters."

— Brian Michael Good

Reputation

"We are defined by the decisions we make and the actions we take. Before you respond to any situation, put your brain into gear before you put your mouth or any reaction into motion."

— Brian Michael Good

"What you say does make a difference. Think of this motto before you react or respond to any situation: The 3 R's…

Readiness. Right, Reaction."

— Brian Michael Good

"Your values have much to do with accomplishing your goals and fulfilling your potential."

— Brian Michael Good

"Integrity, Honor, Trust, Loyalty, Respect, Reputation. These values should be nurtured as a mother cares for an infant. Without the proper attention, all of these values can be lost from one careless decision."

— Brian Michael Good

Respect

"Often respect is like seeing your reflection while looking at the surface of still water."

— Brian Michael Good

"Respect, like your reflection, must be projected first (good manners) in order to see the same reflection of respect returned."

— Brian Michael Good

"Women do eighty percent of the buying and handle the family finances in many households. Yet, the most widely used US dollar bill, the twenty dollar bill is not good enough, nor does the ten dollar bill show enough "Respect" to the women of the United States of America."

— Brian Michael Good

Revenge

"Don't trouble trouble or trouble will trouble you."

— Brian Michael Good

"Forgiving is not forgetting; it's actually remembering by not becoming an abuser; yet, using your free will not to hit back with anger or revenge. It's an opportunity for a new beginning, a second chance, a learning experience by not allowing anyone to hurt or abuse you again."

— Brian Michael Good

Scars

"I used to blame others for every hurt and the scars, from the years of abuse (emotionally, physically, and mentally) during my childhood and teenage years, but now, having forgiven them (my abusers) for everything I realize the abuse was self-inflicted. It was my acceptance of their mistreatment. I blame myself for not being able to heal from the hurt and the scars."

— Brian Michael Good

"You cannot go forward unless you let go of the past/scar."

— Brian Michael Good

"You are chained by your decision to accept the fear, scars, and pain that you allowed others to bestow on you. It was your acceptance of their mistreatment that stops you from being able to heal from all the attacks. You have the key once you discover that the fear, scars, and pain were self-inflected. Just unlock your chains. A choice."

— Brian Michael Good

"The thorn in your arm that could have been self-inflicted by you will do you no harm if you know the right facts. That every road has its own thorn that can hold you back from the way you react. That it has always been your decision to accept the hurt and the scars that stops you from not being able to heal from all the attacks. Now that you know that how you react is what makes this to be a fact; it's never too late to take this road with thorns called life to where you want to be at."

— Brian Michael Good

"A scar often reminds us of the past. Sometimes a scar is an invisible wound that was not mended and never healed. When you accept that people do not scar or give you pain; you'll realize that your open wound was self-inflicted. It is your acceptance of their mistreatment that stops the open wound from being healed that prevents you from moving past the hurt that only you view as a scar no matter how fresh or old the wound."

— Brian Michael Good

Soul "your very essence"

"The soul of any vessel are the sailors who navigate the ship."

— Brian Michael Good

"At some point in your life, you may wonder if your soul is hanging by a thread. This thread is the conduit in which your belief system flows defining your human spirit and binding to the fabric of your soul. Religious, Philosophical, and Ideological fibers are spun into a single strand giving strength to your beliefs. It is this thread's strength that allows you to be broad-minded and even-handed. Be aware that you may be surrendering your soul in your judgment or treatment of others."

— Brian Michael Good

"Each individual should focus on their own personal spiritual life, aware that they may be surrendering their soul in the judgment or treatment of others."

— Brian Michael Good

"If you are prepared to enter the afterlife, the day you die should be a bigger celebration than the day you are born."

— Brian Michael Good

"We should not commercially hunt, allow testing, or separate any mammal from their family or social unit. Many mammals have similar emotional characteristics as humans. Who is to say they do not have souls, when many people believe that, their cat or dog will go to heaven. Just because we believe that human beings are the highest part of Creator's (God's) creation, does not make it so.

We have yet to explore the universe where there are estimated to be billions of Earth like planets. We might discover truths that would be inconceivable within our present day reality. Just because we have always hunted does not make it right to instill fear in the mammal we hunt.

Except for providing food for your family, thou shall not kill might pertain to many mammals of the animal kingdom."

— Brian Michael Good

"Beauty on this earthly plane is often short lived... A beautiful heart and soul will last an eternity."

— Brian Michael Good

Strength

"Challenges, hardships and obstacles are what life is all about and if you face them with a positive attitude; you will find that it takes half the effort to overcome them. You will find that the sum of your challenges, hardships, and obstacles will define your human spirit and years later as you reflect on your experiences you will realize they have become your strength."

— Brian Michael Good

Stress

"A proactive approach can result in a better opportunity for control and fulfillment; whereas the reactive mode can result in stress, which can make any problem even more difficult to solve and may lead to failure."

— Brian Michael Good

Success

"Every endeavor in life is not about the odds of success but about your belief, your passion, and your indomitable will."

— Brian Michael Good

"No one can defeat you. You can only defeat yourself. That is a choice."

— Brian Michael Good

"No success is ever met without a series of failures."

— Brian Michael Good

Tolerance

"Have tolerance and respect towards others and their culture."

— Brian Michael Good

"A person should weigh all twelve of the universal values to live by equally, following one value and not another is as if you follow none of them. The true lesson gained from having good values comes from valuing the rights of others, not just your own."

— Brian Michael Good

Trust

"Trust and loyalty should define your relationships."

— Brian Michael Good

"Integrity, Honor, Trust, Loyalty, Respect, Reputation. These values should be nurtured as a mother cares for an infant. Without the proper attention, all of these values can be lost from one careless decision."

— Brian Michael Good

"Mind control decays your ability to pursue and discover the truth. Mind control can use fear to control you. Do not let them control your free will with fear. Remove mind control and you will remove fear. Hit the reset button in your brain and live your life with less fear. Follow the truth but follow no one blindly."

— Brian Michael Good

"Be careful of anyone that states everything in a particular book or religion is one hundred percent the truth. There are over four thousand religions in our world and over thirty-four thousand Christian denominations. Only Weshemehe knows all the truth. Respect everyone's free will to search for the truth. Own your human gift of free will by exercising it; read, discover, assimilate, and question anything you want."

— Brian Michael Good

"I will not belong to a place of worship that says I have to believe one hundred percent in their dogma or their unique religious perspective. I refuse to give up my free will to pursue what I believe to be the truth."

— Brian Michael Good

Truth

"No one should resolutely affect your pursuit of the truth."

— Brian Michael Good

"History and religion are often written with a controlled message, a form of mind control."

— Brian Michael Good

"You will decipher the truth about how to find happiness and meet your destiny. If you haven't developed a passion, concept, or goal for your life and an action plan on the best way to achieve it, you will never know whether you could have made it to a place you once thought was impossible."

— Brian Michael Good

"If a quote does not fit the person's profile on social media or it sounds very familiar, look up the quote and tweet the quote correctly, honoring the author who took the time to write the quote that impacted your life."

— Brian Michael Good

Universal Values to Live By

Have tolerance and respect towards others and their culture.

No one should resolutely affect your pursuit of the truth.

Avoid judgment of ethnic, racial, sexual orientation, gender identity, and religious differences in society.

Do not attempt to control anyone's free will.

Avoid gossip, bullying, rumors, hearsay, hazing, harassment, shaming, shunning, and slurs.

Forgiving others sets us free.

Do not steal anything in any way.

Integrity and honor should be part of every fabric of your beliefs.

Do not kill emotionally, mentally, physically or spiritually.

Trust, faithfulness, and loyalty should define your relationships.

Value the passion you have for your life's work more than you value material gain.

Have kindness, compassion, and empathy towards others and the natural environment.

The number of people with no religion will continue to grow. You do not have to be religious to have good morals. "Universal Values to Live By" is meant to be a guide, a map for when we choose to use our free will and detour from the path we were taught to walk earlier in our lives. Free will is our greatest gift after life itself, that being said, free will must be exercised wisely, as much as humanly possible...

A person should weigh all twelve values equally, following one value and not another is as if you follow none of them. The true lesson gained from having good values comes from valuing the rights of others, not just your own.

When you meet another person or when two or more are gathered you will have the opportunity to create the gift of acceptance, the epitome of what humanity should be! The higher you raise yourself in the better treatment of others, the better view you will have of the future.

Humans have become more logical, facts build our knowledge and belief system. A logical person gathers facts and does not rely on faith alone. No one should resolutely affect your pursuit of the truth. We are gravitating towards building a belief system that is constructed mainly on materials based on facts. Without collaboration we could never make the strides of progress. No human is an island if they want to be successful.

Wealth

"I did not realize how much I had before my hurricanes occurred but each time after I weathered the storm. I wanted to live. There is always a possibility of a storm on the horizon. I hope that you too will find wisdom in these pearls that have washed ashore as a result of my hurricanes and count yourself a survivor."

— Brian Michael Good

"You do not get extra credit when you bequeath your wealth in your will because you cannot take money with you when you die."

— Brian Michael Good

"Authority, control, and wealth come with great responsibility. The Creator expects major shareholders, management and business owners to pay honest wages for an honest day's work. Greed does not give you any reward in the afterlife. You have already taken more than your fair share."

— Brian Michael Good

"There is enough wealth in our world to teach and share knowledge so each town or village can provide their own food, shelter, clothing and other commodities and services that are essential for survival."

— Brian Michael Good

"Luxuries are not a necessity and someday we will realize that the money spent on luxuries could have greatly influenced most of the world's problems."

— Brian Michael Good

"A person who chooses luxuries as prudently as they should choose their friendships will have a greater opportunity to be rewarded in the afterlife. Everything is a choice, enjoy life on Earth without a care in the world, or help others in need in the world."

— Brian Michael Good

"Now will be your defining moment. Will you look at giving away all your wealth as an empty glass, a glass half-full, or a glass half-empty? If you do this at the age of twenty-one, most likely your family paid for a great education which gave you the opportunity to make influential contacts. The other ninety-nine percent of your peers will never have the chance to make these connections. I hope that you will realize your glass is full without any money."

— Brian Michael Good

Wisdom

"Today, I will try to stay in the eye of my hurricane where I am safe from the storm around me. I will try to deal with my hurricanes and struggles in life with no blame or excuses. But my hurricanes keep coming. I gain strength with each pearl of wisdom that washes ashore."

— Brian Michael Good

"A book is food for thought… By reading a well written book you will reap pearls of wisdom and have a lifetime of meals."

— Brian Michael Good

"Life's most valuable pearls of wisdom that are nourishment for the body, mind and soul are often found in quotes."

— Brian Michael Good

"A spiritual or personal growth self-help book can help you change your perspective allowing you to infuse new activities into your life."

— Brian Michael Good

"My hurricanes keep coming. I gain strength with each pearl of wisdom that washes ashore."

— Brian Michael Good

"We use the term human being very loosely in our society. I feel when we call someone a human being it should be a great compliment. A human is what you are but a human being is who you can become."

— Brian Michael Good

"Judaism, Hinduism, Christianity states that God is omnipresent; it might be referenced in Islam, Quran 2:115. If God is present everywhere (in all places at all times), then God is part of every atom in the universe. If the universe is God. Therefore, God does not have a gender.

If God does not have a gender, I choose to use the word Weshemehe (We-she-me-he), my own English name for God, who represents all genders. More importantly, it means more than just the male gender as the word God denotes to many of us. Weshemehe means we are all part of the universe and part of Weshemehe."

— Brian Michael Good

"I am in the eye of my hurricane where I am safe from the storm around me. I will try to deal with my hurricanes and struggles in life with no blame or excuses. Nevertheless, my hurricanes keep coming. I gain strength with each pearl of wisdom that washes ashore. We-she-me-he (the Creator) of second chances I am safe, for the moment at least."

— Brian Michael Good

Social Media Links

Brian Michael Good: Author | Writer | Entrepreneur

Meet the Author: www.BrianMichaelGood.com

Twitter: www.twitter.com/1PearlofWisdom

Facebook: www.facebook.com/profile.php?id=100000235296330

LinkedIn: www.linkedin.com/profile/view?id=386147212

Best to Live Foundation, a 501(c)(3) not-for-profit

Website: www.BestToLive.org

Twitter: www.twitter.com/Best2Live

Facebook: www.facebook.com/Best2Live

Spiritual & Personal Growth Self-Help Books

Facebook: https://www.facebook.com/pages/Spiritual-Personal-Growth-Self-Help-Books/357581144409444

Tattoo You AfterCare: Tattoo, Piercing, and Organically Made Skincare Products

Website: www.TatsYou.com/Tattoo-You

Twitter: www.twitter.com/TatUAftercare

Facebook: www.facebook.com/pages/Tattoo-You-AfterCare/307399982774862

Pinterest: www.pinterest.com/TatUAfterCare

Instagram: www.instagram.com/TatUAfterCare

Vine: www.vine.co/u/1205160774373654528

NutriCare Plus: Best Organic and Natural Skincare Products

Website: www.NutriCarePlus.com

NutriCare Plus Shop: http://www.NCPCares.com/Shop.html

Twitter: www.twitter.com/NCPCARES

Facebook: www.facebook.com/NutriCarePlus

Pinterest: www.pinterest.com/NutriCarePlus

Instagram: www.instagram.com/NutriCarePlus

Vine: www.vine.co/u/1202132242860838912

Thank You

No person is an island if they want to succeed. I would like to thank the following people who helped me through my journey of writing:

- Helga Holscher who I met in 2008 and who reviewed my journal in early 2009 gave me much needed encouragement.

- Stacie Morgan, even though she was working on her novel in the research stage, reviewed my writings and gave me suggestions that helped me to begin to pull together some initial ideas that proved helpful in the creation of the book's vision in 2010.

- Bryan Hunt, a great talent, who I would like to recognize for his strong work ethic. Bryan has a college degree in Animation. He helped me over several years with my passion for organic and natural skincare by creating the numerous labels, brochures and advertising I needed created. His expertise certainly helped keep my hope alive.

- I would like to thank Laurie Callihan, Dara Rochlin, Christine Rice, and Charlene Truxler who assisted me in the editing and formatting process during various stages of "Never Surrender Your Soul", "RESET: Control, Alt, Delete", "Quotes Of Wisdom To Live By.

- In addition, I would like to thank Shelter, Inc. Cambridge, Massachusetts, HomeStart, Inc., Cambridge, Massachusetts, and the Waterfront Rescue Mission, Pensacola, Florida for providing a roof over my head when I was a person of need.

Book Offer

Never Surrender Your Soul – your very essence

Here is the link to visit the book page:

www.authl.it/B00RKW5U2O?d

If you wish for personal – spiritual growth and fulfillment in your life and less fear, it is possible! Never Surrender Your Soul unlike other self-help books is written specifically to help you to find the encouragement, strength, and spiritual growth that you will need to change your perspective with less mind control so you can live a hopeful life that creates a path with less fear.

"RESET: Control, Alt, Delete"

Here is the link to visit the book page:

www.authl.it/B00ZUYLHMQ?d

Learn how to rise from the ashes of defeat. Get self help, Embrace positive thinking, Live a happier life, and Find your destiny.

RESET: Control, Alt, Delete, unlike other self-help books, is written specifically to help you to find the encouragement, strength, and personal growth that you will need to change your perspective with positive thinking so you can live a hopeful life that creates a path allowing you to find your destiny.

No one can defeat you; you can only defeat yourself. No one can truly save you. You must save yourself. The question is what are you willing to do to change your life? There is hope and a way out! Help yourself by reading Never Surrender Your Soul, RESET: Control, Alt, Delete, and Quotes of Wisdom to Live By find answers and change your life for the better.

Take action by getting yourself a copy of one of Brian's 3 books. You will be so happy you did!

Join our email list

www.BrianMichaelGood.com/contact-me

Write a Review

----

http://www.amazon.com/dp/B00ZYX4FW2

It will have an impact and you can make a difference.

BRIAN MICHAEL GOOD